iPod

11th Edition

the missing manual®

The book that should have been in the box

J.D. Biersdorfer
with David Pogue

O'REILLY®

Beijing | Cambridge | Farnham | Köln | Sebastopol | Tokyo

iPod: The Missing Manual, Eleventh Edition

BY J.D. Biersdorfer with David Pogue

Copyright © 2013 J.D. Biersdorfer. All rights reserved.
Printed in Canada.

Published by O'Reilly Media, Inc., 1005 Gravenstein Highway North, Sebastopol, CA 95472.

O'Reilly books may be purchased for educational, business, or sales promotional use. Online editions are also available for most titles (*safari.oreilly.com*). For more information, contact our corporate/institutional sales department at 800.998.9938 or corporate@oreilly.com.

Senior Editor: Brian Sawyer
Editor: Peter McKie
Production Editor: Kristen Borg
Illustrations: Lesley Keegan, Rob Romano, Rebecca Demarest, Katherine Ippoliti, and J.D. Biersdorfer

Copyeditor: Marcia Simmons
Indexer: Julie Hawks
Cover Designers: Randy Comer, Karen Montgomery, and Suzy Wiviott
Interior Designer: Monica Kamsvaag, Ron Bilodeau, & J.D. Biersdorfer

December 2011:   Tenth Edition
December 2012:   Eleventh Edition.

ISBN: 978-1-449-31619-8
[TI]

Contents

CHAPTER 4

Get Organized With the iPod Touch 53

CHAPTER 5

Surf the Web and Manage Email On the Touch 87

CHAPTER 6

Add More Apps to the Touch 121

CHAPTER 7

Tour the iPod Nano 129

The Missing Credits

About the Authors

J.D. Biersdorfer (author) is the author of several O'Reilly books, including the first 10 editions of this book; *iPad: The Missing Manual*; *Best iPhone Apps, Second Edition*; and *Netbooks: The Missing Manual*. She's been writing the weekly computer Q&A column for *The New York Times* since 1998 and has covered everything from 17th-century Indian art to female hackers for the newspaper. She's also written articles

for the *AIGA Journal of Graphic Design*, *Budget Travel*, *The New York Times Book Review*, and *Rolling Stone*. J.D. can be heard each week on the Pop Tech Jam audio podcast at *www.poptechjam.com*. She has a degree in Theatre & Drama from Indiana University. You can reach her at *jd.biersdorfer@gmail.com*.

David Pogue (co-author) writes a weekly technology column for *The New York Times* and a monthly column for *Scientific American*. He's an Emmy-winning correspondent for *CBS News Sunday Morning*, the host of *NOVA scienceNOW* on PBS, and the creator of the Missing Manual series. He's the author or coauthor of 55 books, including 28 in this series; six in the *For Dummies* line (including *Macs*,

Magic, *Opera*, and *Classical Music*); two novels (one, *Abby Carnelia's One and Only Magical Power*, for middle-schoolers); and *The World According to Twitter*. In his other life, David is a former Broadway show conductor, a piano player, and a magician. He lives in Connecticut with his three awesome children.

Links to his columns and weekly videos await at *www.davidpogue.com*. He welcomes feedback about his books by email at *david@pogueman.com*.

About the Creative Team

Peter McKie (editor) lives in New York City, where he archives historic images of his summer community. He has a master's degree in journalism from Boston University. Email: *pmckie@oreilly.com*.

Kristen Borg (production editor) is busily planning her summer wedding. Now living in Boston, she hails from Arizona and considers New England winters a fair trade for no longer finding scorpions in her hairdryer. Email: *kristen@oreilly.com*.

Julie Hawks (indexer) is an indexer for the Missing Manual series. She is currently pursuing a master's degree in Religious Studies while discovering the joys of warm winters in the Carolinas. Email: *juliehawks@gmail.com*.

Marcia Simmons (proofreader) is a writer and editor who lives in Petaluma, California. She's the author of *DIY Cocktails: A Simple Guide to Creating Your Own Signature Drinks*. Her personal blog can be found at *marciaisms.com*.

Acknowledgements

I would like to thank David Pogue for suggesting this book to me way back in 2002, and for being a terrific editor through the mad scramble of the first two editions. Also thanks to editors Peter Meyers and Peter McKie for guiding me through the past ten updates. Thanks to Kristen Borg, Lesley Keegan, Ron Bilodeau, Katherine Ippoliti, Monica Kamsvaag, Rob Romano, Rebecca Demarest, Sara Peyton, Betsy Waliszewski, Laurie Petrycki, and all the folks at O'Reilly for all their help. Thanks to Apple for courteously providing the iPod images and to the assorted iPod accessory companies who made their photos available.

I'd also to thank all my friends and family (especially and most importantly, Betsy Book) for putting up with me every year when Apple announces new iPods and I disappear into my computer for several weeks, muttering incoherently and cranking up the show tunes and bluegrass playlists to a hearty volume.

The Missing Manual Series

Missing Manuals are witty, superbly written guides to computer products that don't come with printed manuals (which is just about all of them). Each book features a handcrafted index and cross-references to specific pages (not just chapters). Recent and upcoming titles include:

Access 2013: The Missing Manual by Matthew MacDonald

CSS: The Missing Manual, Third Edition, by David Sawyer McFarland

Creating a Website: The Missing Manual, Third Edition, by Matthew MacDonald

Dreamweaver CS6: The Missing Manual by David Sawyer McFarland

Excel 2010: The Missing Manual by Matthew MacDonald

Flash CS6: The Missing Manual by Chris Grover

Galaxy S II: The Missing Manual by Preston Gralla

Galaxy Tab: The Missing Manual by Preston Gralla

Google+: The Missing Manual by Kevin Purdy

HTML5: The Missing Manual by Matthew MacDonald

iMovie '11 & iDVD: The Missing Manual by David Pogue and Aaron Miller

iPhone: The Missing Manual, Sixth Edition by David Pogue

iPhoto '11: The Missing Manual by David Pogue and Lesa Snider

JavaScript & jQuery: The Missing Manual, Second Edition by David Sawyer McFarland

Kindle Fire: The Missing Manual by Peter Meyers

Mac OS X Lion: The Missing Manual by David Pogue

Mac OS X Snow Leopard: The Missing Manual by David Pogue

Microsoft Project 2013: The Missing Manual by Bonnie Biafore

NOOK Tablet: The Missing Manual by Preston Gralla

Office 2013: The Missing Manual by Nancy Connor, Chris Grover, and Matthew MacDonald

Office 2011 for Macintosh: The Missing Manual by Chris Grover

Personal Investing: The Missing Manual by Bonnie Biafore

Photoshop CS6: The Missing Manual by Lesa Snider

Photoshop Elements 11: The Missing Manual by Barbara Brundage

PHP & MySQL: The Missing Manual, Second Edition, by Brett McLaughlin

Switching to the Mac: The Missing Manual, Mountain Lion Edition by David Pogue

Windows 7: The Missing Manual by David Pogue

WordPress: The Missing Manual by Matthew MacDonald

For a full list of all Missing Manuals in print, go to *www.missingmanuals.com/ library.html.*

Introduction

WHEN THE IPOD FIRST arrived in 2001, it was known primarily as a music player. But during the iPod's first few years, Apple quietly slipped new features into the device to make the player more versatile—a rudimentary game here, an address book copied over from your computer there, and so on. Those may have seemed like insignificant add-ons, but here's the thing: Apple *hasn't stopped* adding new features to its iPod line—11 years later, the company's still at it.

Take the iPod Touch, the top-of-the-line model that plays music, videos, photo slideshows, and runs more than 700,000 programs from the App Store. In 2012, Apple added a much-improved 5-megapixel camera and flash to the Touch, along with a faster processor and the biggest screen (4 inches!) of any iPod ever. Its iOS 6 software brings a slew of new features, too, including the Siri virtual assistant and easy posting to Facebook and Twitter.

The iPod Nano, Apple's sporty player, has grown from its small square shape of the past few years to a versatile media machine that handles music and photos—and, once again, movies—on its 2.5-inch screen. The iPod Classic and Shuffle, while not significantly updated, are still proud members of the iPod family. The Classic offers the highest storage capacity of all the 'Pods, while the Shuffle is the lightest iPod ever—but still able to tote 2 gigabytes of your favorite music, podcasts, and audiobooks.

This book covers all iPod models, as well as the iTunes software that lets you fill up your player with media. No matter which iPod you have, you'll learn all its new features here—or discover ones that were there all along.

How to Use This Book

THE TINY PAMPHLET THAT Apple includes with each iPod is enough to get your player up and running, charged, and ready to download music.

But if you want to know more about how your iPod works, all the great things it can do, and where to find its secret features, that pamphlet is skimpy in the extreme. And the iTunes help files that you have to read on your computer aren't much better: You can't mark your place, there aren't any pictures or jokes, and, let's face it, help files are a little dull. This book gives you more iPod info than that wee brochure, is available in both ebook and treeware editions, *and* it has lots of nice color pictures.

ABOUT→THESE→ARROWS

Throughout this book, and throughout the Missing Manual series, you'll find sentences like this: "Go to File→Library→Organize Library." That's shorthand for a longer series of instructions that goes something like this: "Go to the menu bar in iTunes, click the File menu, select the Library submenu, and then slide over to the Organize Library entry." Our shorthand system avoids lots of long, drawn-out instructions and helps keep the book snappy.

THE VERY BASICS

To use this book, and indeed to use a computer at all, you need to know a few basics. This book assumes that you're familiar with these terms and concepts:

Clicking. To *click* means to point the arrow cursor at something on your screen and then to press and release the left clicker button on your mouse (or laptop trackpad). To *right-click* means the same thing, but you press the right mouse button instead (or the top-right corner of a Mac mouse). Often, right-clicking calls up a menu of commands you select from.

To *double-click* means to click twice in rapid succession without moving the cursor. To *drag* means to move the cursor *while* pressing the button.

When you're told to *Ctrl-click* something on a PC, or ⌘-*click* something on a Mac, you click while pressing the Ctrl or ⌘ key.

Menus. The *menus* are the words at the top of your screen or window: File, Edit, and so on. Click one to make a list of commands appear, as though they're written on a window shade you just pulled down.

Keyboard shortcuts. Jumping up to menus in iTunes takes time. That's why you'll find keyboard workarounds that perform the same functions sprinkled throughout the book—Windows shortcuts first, followed by Mac shortcuts in parentheses, like this: "To quickly summon the Preferences box, press Ctrl+comma (⌘-comma)."

If you've mastered this much information, you have all the technical background you need to enjoy *iPod: The Missing Manual*.

ABOUT THE MISSING CD

As you read this book, you'll find references to websites that offer additional resources. To save yourself some typing, you'll find a clickable list of those sites on this book's Missing CD page at *www.missingmanuals.com/cds/ipodtmm11/*.

The Missing CD page also includes corrections and updates to this book. Click the View Errata link to see them. You can submit your own corrections by clicking "Submit your own errata" on the same page. To keep this book as accurate as possible, each time we print more copies, we'll make any confirmed corrections.

While you're online, you can register this book at *www.oreilly.com/register*. Registering means we can send you updates about the book, and you'll be eligible for special offers like discounts on future editions of the iPod Missing Manual.

SAFARI® BOOKS ONLINE

Safari® Books Online is an on-demand digital library that lets you search over 7,500 technology books and videos.

With a subscription, you can read any page and watch any video from our library online. Read books on your smartphone and mobile devices. Access new titles before they're available for print, get exclusive access to manuscripts in development, post feedback for the authors. Copy and paste code samples, organize your favorites, download chapters, bookmark key sections, create notes, print out pages, and benefit from tons of other time-saving features.

O'Reilly Media has uploaded this book to the Safari Books Online service. To have full digital access to this book and others on similar topics from O'Reilly and other publishers, sign up for free at *http://my.safaribooksonline.com*.

You'll learn to:

- Find the features of each iPod model

- Install iTunes

- Connect your iPod to your computer

- Charge up a stationary or on-the-go iPod

- Preserve battery life

iPod 101

IF YOU'RE LIKE MOST people, you want to jump right in and get your spiffy new iPod up and running. Apple thoughtfully includes a tiny folding pamphlet of starter info with every iPod it sells. And while it's nicely designed, you may find that it doesn't go far enough; you want more help than a few line drawings and some haiku-like instructions can give you.

This book—and especially this chapter—is designed for you.

You won't get bogged down in a gray ocean of print here. You'll learn how to get your iPod whistling sweet tunes in your ear in no time and find out how to control your particular iPod model. If you want more on in-depth 'Podding or getting the most out of iTunes, you can find that in chapters farther down the road, one (or more) sections devoted to each and every iPod model.

But for now, let's get rolling with your new iPod. Ready?

Meet the iPod Touch

SINCE ITS ARRIVAL IN 2007, the iPod Touch has become the most popular member of the iPod family. It's also the most versatile; it runs thousands of programs called apps, makes and takes FaceTime video calls, keeps you on schedule, surfs the Web, handles your email, takes text and audio notes, and serves up plenty of fun as a handheld game console. Oh, it also plays music, videos, slideshows, and podcasts, and it displays ebooks on a gorgeous screen whenever you feel like reading. Yes, the Touch is the Swiss Army knife of iPods.

The Touch gets its moniker from its responsive *touchscreen*, the smooth glass surface that lets you navigate through your music, videos, and photos with nothing more than a tap or drag of your finger.

While the Touch may have inherited its sensitive screen from the iPhone, it gets its playback stability from the flash memory that holds all your media. No matter how hard you run or rock out, you'll probably never hear your music skip a beat. Nor is it likely you'll run out of juice: The Touch gives you about 40 hours of audio playback, or 8 hours of video viewing, on a single battery charge.

Speaking of video, the Touch sports the same eye-catching 4-inch Retina display the iPhone does, giving it an impressive 1136 x 640 pixel resolution. To see the display in its finest form, flip the Touch sideways when you look at photos, movies, and TV shows. You don't have to be content just *watching* videos, either—the Touch lets you shoot and edit high-definition movies as well, and you can upload them directly to YouTube. Need a still camera? The Touch has one of those, too—a 5-megapixel model that includes autofocus, face detection, and the ability to shoot panoramic photos. It even comes with a plastic wrist strap like a point-and-shooter. Chapter 3 has more on using the camera.

You can buy the Touch in two memory configurations: a 32-gigabyte (GB) model that holds 7,000 songs or 40 hours of video and a 64-gig model that stores a relatively whopping 14,000 songs and 80 hours of video. Unlike the rather monochromatic iPod Touches of years past, the 2012 Touch comes in pink, yellow, blue, silver, and black—as well as a special red model, some of the proceeds of which go to charity.

As an entertainment device, the Touch is tops, but its ability to reach out and touch the Internet is what makes it an iPod you can do business with (if you can tear yourself away from all the fun stuff, that is). Thanks to its built-in WiFi chip and a mobile version of Apple's Safari browser, you can surf the Web whenever you're in range of a wireless network. And where there's Internet, there's email, stock-market updates, weather forecasts, YouTube videos, and online maps. You use your fingertips to point your way around the Web—or to fire up the Touch's on-screen keyboard for a little good, old-fashioned text entry.

With iOS 6, the latest version of Apple's system software for the Touch, you also get Reminders (a to-do list app), Messages (so you can send text messages and photos to other iOS 5 and iOS 6 users), and Newsstand (a place to park your eMagazines). Chapter 4 has more on these new, built-in apps. And if they leave you wanting, you can customize your Touch with purchases from the iTunes App Store, where more than 700,000 portable programs await you.

One more thing: if you've ever been out and about with your iPod and wished you could buy music or video on the fly, you can. With the Touch and a wireless network connection, this little Internet iPod can step right up to the iTunes Store and shop away.

NOTE The Touch and the iPhone may look like kissing cousins, but they have some distinct differences. For one thing, the Touch isn't a mobile phone, like the iPhone is. While this means that Touch owners get to skip The Wireless Carrier Experience, it also means there's no ubiquitous cellphone network to tap into when you run out of WiFi hotspots. (The good news: no phone bill, either.) In addition, the Touch's built-in camera—5 megapixels of photo resolution—isn't as good as the iPhone 5's 8-megapixel gem. On the plus side, without the extra hardware inside, the Touch is much more svelte.

Meet the iPod Nano

WITH THE 2012 MODEL, Apple's iPod Nano continues the tradition of changing its look every year or two. Gone is the Triscuit-sized metal square with the tiny touch screen and clip on the back for wearing around the gym. Apple has completely overhauled the Nano yet again and made it into a whole new player.

So, what's new about the Nano? While it keeps the touchscreen technology found on the 2010 and 2011 models, it adds a Home button to the front of the player for first time. It also has a Bluetooth radio tucked inside that lets you stream music to compatible Bluetooth speakers over the air or connect with fitness equipment like a wireless heart-rate monitor.

Standing just a hair more than 3 inches tall and 1.56 inches wide, the 2012 Nano is bigger than earlier models, but it does more. It still uses multitouch screen for tapping, flicking, and swiping your way to music, podcasts, audiobooks, and photos. But unlike the past few generations, Apple has returned video-playback powers to the Nano, which means you can watch movies and TV shows from the iTunes Store wherever you happen to be. The bright color screen shows all your media off in 240 x 432 pixel resolution on a 2.5-inch display.

Designed with runners and other fitness enthusiasts in mind, the Nano has a built-in pedometer that tracks your steps and helps you chart your workouts. You don't even need special gym shoes and an electronic sensor to have this iPod compile your workout data—it does all that on its own now.

This Nano also includes Apple's VoiceOver feature, which recites menus and song titles into your headphones when you're too busy running to look at the screen. And since it stores all your music on a nice, stable flash-memory chip, you don't have to worry about your music skipping, even if you are.

When you get tired of recorded music, switch to the Nano's integrated FM radio. Unlike standard receivers, the Nano can pause live shows for a few minutes should someone start talking at you in the middle of a song.

The Nano comes in a 16-gigabyte model, and you can choose from eight anodized aluminum colors (pink, red, blue, green, yellow, purple, silver, and graphite gray). With a full battery charge, you'll get up to 30 hours of audio playback. That should get you through even the most intense cardio routine.

Meet the iPod Shuffle

THE SMALLEST MEMBER OF Team iPod doesn't have a screen—but it doesn't need one, because it's designed for fuss-free music on the go. You don't have to worry about losing your Shuffle because it clips right onto your lapel or pocket— it's like jewelry you can rock out with.

Take your pick of eight standard Shuffle colors: blue, orange, green, purple, pink, red, black, and silver. It comes with a 2-gigabyte memory chip that holds hundreds of songs, audio podcasts, and audiobooks. And even though it's called the Shuffle, you don't *have* to shuffle your music; you can play your tracks in order with the nudge of a button. Chapter 9 explains the Shuffle in detail.

The Shuffle may not have a screen, but it does include VoiceOver technology. Just press the VoiceOver button to make your Shuffle announce the name and artist of the song currently playing. Speaking of playing, you get about 15 hours of music between battery charges.

If you just want a lightweight workout player for the gym, a starter iPod for your kid, or just a little music in your pocket, the Shuffle is a great choice for an entry-level iPod. It may not be the fanciest, most versatile player of the bunch, but if you want pure, uncomplicated audio, the Shuffle is one little iPod that delivers a lot of sonic boom for your buck.

Meet the iPod Classic

WITH ITS SOLID, RECTANGULAR shape and horizontal screen, the faithful iPod Classic still retains the look of the original, boxy white-and-chrome iPod that started it all back in 2001.

A decade later, Apple has transformed that humble little 5-gigabyte music player with its black-and-white screen into a gorgeous full-color portable media system that can play movies, TV shows, and video games—and it still fits comfortably in the palm of your hand.

Although Apple hasn't added any new features to the Classic in the past few years, it's still a beloved model, especially for media lovers who want to carry around all (or most) of their music collections with them. That's because the Classic has more than double the storage of even the highest-capacity new-gen iPods—and tons more storage than the Classic's original 5 gigs. You can stuff 160 GB of music, photos, videos, and more onto the Classic. That's 40,000 songs or 200 hours of video. And you don't have to stock up on the Duracells, either, because the Classic has a rechargeable battery that can play audio for 36 hours or video for 6 hours.

The Classic comes in either silver or black. Unlike earlier iPods that sported hard glossy plastic on the front, Apple's latest version comes outfitted in a full metal jacket—anodized aluminum on the front and shiny stainless steel on the back.

Along with the click wheel—think of it as the Classic's mouse—the 2.5-inch color screen is the player's other main component. Capable of displaying more than 65,000 colors at a resolution of 320 x 240 pixels (translation: high-quality), the Classic is a great place to store and show off your latest vacation photos. In fact, you can keep up to 25,000 pictures on your 'Pod. The screen also makes it a delight to catch up on that episode of *The Big Bang Theory* you missed or play a few rounds of solitaire while you listen to your favorite music.

The Classic comes with a USB cable so you can connect it to your Windows PC or Mac, along with those iconic see-what-I've-got white earphones. Want more stuff? Check out the Classic accessories in Chapter 16.

Install iTunes

BEFORE YOU CAN HAVE hours of iPod fun, you need to install iTunes, Apple's media manager and content-to-iPod broker, on your computer. Apple's QuickTime program, a video helper for iTunes, comes along with the download. (Technically, you don't need iTunes to manage the Touch, but it *is* a great place to store your big video files.) To get iTunes:

1. **Fire up your computer's web browser and point it to** *www. itunes.com/downloads*.

2. **Click the Download Now button**. (Turn off the "Email me…" and "Keep me up to date…" checkboxes to spare yourself future marketing missives.) Wait for the file to download to your computer.

3. **When the file lands on your hard drive, double-click the** *iTunes-Setup.exe* **file**. If you use a Mac, double-click the *iTunes.dmg* file, and then open the *iTunes.mpkg* file to start the installation. If your Mac is younger than 8 years old, you probably already have iTunes installed. Go to ◉→Software Update and tell your Mac to see if there's a newer version of the program, just in case.

Download iTunes

🏁 iTunes for Windows XP, Vista, Windows 7, or Windows 8

☐ Email me New On iTunes and special iTunes offers.

☐ Keep me up to date with Apple news, software updates, and the latest information on products and services.

Apple Customer Privacy Policy

Email Address

Download Now ➊

Windows System Requirements
- PC with a 1GHz Intel or AMD processor and 512MB of RAM
- Windows XP Service Pack 2 or later, 32-bit editions of Windows Vista, Windows 7, or Windows 8
- 64-bit editions of Windows Vista, Windows 7, or Windows 8 require the iTunes 64-bit installer
- 400MB of available disk space
- Broadband Internet connection to use the iTunes Store

Macintosh Requirements
Get iTunes for Macintosh

4. **Follow the screens until the software installer says it's done**.

You may need to restart your computer after you install iTunes. Once you do, you're ready to connect your new iPod to your computer.

NOTE The hardware and operating-system requirements needed to run iTunes are listed below the Download Now button. If you have an older computer, it's worth a glance just to make sure your rig can handle the program. Likewise, newer systems may not be iTunes-compatible at first.

The iPod-Computer Connection

UNLESS YOU HAVE AN iPod Touch and can activate and load up your new media player over a WiFi network, you need to introduce that new purchase of yours to your computer, with its brand-new copy of iTunes. To do that, you need to get the USB cable that came with your iPod (it's the white cord in the box that's *not* the pearly Apple-white earbuds).

The iPod's cable has a traditional flat USB connector on one end—the same kind used by computer mice, printers, external hard drives, and scores of other hardware devices you can attach to your PC or Mac. The other end of the cable varies, depending on which iPod you have.

Your choices are:

❶ **Lightning Connector.** If you have a brand new iPod Touch or iPod Nano (the models introduced in October 2012), your iPod uses this new, petite connector. It's smaller so your iPod can be smaller, too. Compatible accessories are still rolling out, though, so they're not as plentiful as equipment that fits Apple's older connector.

❷ **Dock Connector.** This wide, flat 30-pin connector was a mainstay on most of the iPod line from Spring 2003 to Fall 2012—plenty of time for manufacturers to make a lot of speaker docks, AV cables, and other gear. Of the current iPod line, only the iPod Classic and the 4th-generation iPod Touch (which Apple has not quite retired from the sales floor) use the Dock Connector.

❸ **Shuffle Connector.** If you have the smallest iPod, you get this short adapter that plugs into the Shuffle's headphone port for charging and syncing the player. It's easy to misplace, so keep it in a safe place

Once you link iPod to computer, the iPod icon appears on the left side of the iTunes window, under Devices. It's ready for you to fill up with music, videos, photos, and other entertainment-to-go. Chapter 10 has more on doing that.

Disconnecting the iPod

When it comes to portable devices, what gets connected usually needs to get disconnected. Because computers get cranky and flash stern warning messages about "device removal" when you yank the USB cable out of your iPod or computer, resist the impulse to do so without checking your 'Pod first. If you see menus or the battery icon on the screen, you can safely unplug your player. (Shuffle owners who have no screen—see the steps below.)

If your iPod is set to automatically fill itself up with music and other content from your iTunes library, you can unplug the iPod anytime after it finishes syncing. Likewise, the iPod Touch doesn't make you click anything in iTunes to release it from the computer—as long as iTunes has finished its syncing chores.

But if you see a screen like the one on the right, you need to *manually* eject the iPod from your computer to safely undock it from the mother ship.

iTunes gives you two easy ways to do that:

1. If your iPod is already selected in the main iTunes window, click the Eject button next to its name in the top-left corner. If not...

2. Click the Eject icon on the right side of the main iTunes window.

With either method, the iPod announces onscreen that it's disengaging, displaying an "OK to Disconnect" progress bar as it breaks its connection with the computer. Once all the gray screens go away and you see the regular menus again, you can safely liberate your iPod.

Charge Your iPod

RIGHT OUT OF THE box, your iPod probably has enough juice to run for a while without having to charge it up. Eventually, though, you'll need to go in for an electronic fill-up. All you need to do is plug the iPod into your computer using the USB cable (the iPod charges itself by drawing power from the USB connector). Just make sure you have your computer turned on and that it isn't asleep.

It takes only a few hours to fully charge your iPod, and even less time to do what Apple calls a *fast charge*, which quickly powers up the battery to 80 percent of its capacity. That should be plenty of gas in your iPod's tank for a quick spin.

Here's how much time each iPod needs for both a fast and a full charge:

	FAST CHARGE	FULL CHARGE
iPod Touch	2 hours	4 hours
iPod Nano	1.5 hours	3 hours
iPod Shuffle	2 hours	3 hours
iPod Classic	2 hours	4 hours

Using the computer to charge your iPod is fine if you're home and your computer is on to share its power with your iPod, but what if you're traveling and don't want to drag your laptop with you just to charge your iPod? Or you don't want to leave your iPod plugged into the family computer all the time? In times like these, iPod accessory makers will gladly come to your rescue. Before you buy, make sure you get gear that fits your iPod's charging port. Remember, the new iPod Touch and Nano use the newer Lightning connector, while the iPod Classic and the fourth-generation iPod Touch (the latter still hanging around the Apple Store) use the older, bigger Dock Connector.

You generally have your choice of:

- **A car charger that connects to the standard 12-volt power outlet in most cars.** Several companies make auto chargers for the iPod for around $20. You can find them at Apple Stores (including *www.apple.com/ipodstore*); retail stores like Best Buy that sell iPod gear; and specialty iPod-accessory web shops like Griffin Technology (*www.griffintechnology.com*).

- **A USB power adapter.** Many iPod accessory shops sell wall chargers as well as car chargers, and some give you one of each in a set. Apple also makes its own matching white cube to go with your USB cable. These power blocks typically have a jack on one side that accepts your iPod's USB cable (and connected iPod) and a set of silver prongs on the other side that plugs into a regular electrical outlet. Chapter 16 has more on finding power for your iPod, and you can get Apple's AC adapter for around $29 in iPod-friendly stores or at *www.apple.com/ipodstore*.

Griffin Technology's $25 PowerJolt SE car charger with a Lightning connector for the new iPod Touch and Nano

- **A charging dock.** Those same accessory shops also sell iPod cradles that plug into the wall and give your iPod a place to perch at night. Some iPod-enabled speakers also charge the iPod as it sits there playing your music.

Adjust the iPod's Settings for Better Battery Life

If you find your iPod's battery running down too quickly, adjusting certain settings may help. For example, decreasing the amount of time the Classic's screen backlight stays on or reducing screen brightness on the Touch can reduce the juice you need. The Touch and Nano both have a Bluetooth wireless radio that draw power when not in use, so leave it off when you're not streaming.

For some Apple-approved tips for prolonging your iPod's battery life, flip a few hundred pages ahead, to page 309. Chapter 2 also has information about the Touch's settings menu, Chapter 7 explains how to adjust the Nano's settings, and Chapter 8 is all about the Classic, including its settings.

You'll learn to:

- Set up and activate your Touch

- Learn to control your iPod by touchscreen

- Load the Touch with music, videos, and other content

- Adjust the Touch's settings

Tour the iPod Touch

THAT SHINY NEW IPOD Touch is more than just a media player, it's a palm-size computer in its own right. Think of it as the iPad Micro. But as with any new computer, you need to take a few moments to get to know it before you can get the most out of it.

This chapter starts with the basics, like turning the Touch on or off, setting it up to use email and buy apps, and plugging it in to sync content from your other computer—you know, the one with the big hard drive and all the music, videos, and photos you may want to take with you on your iPod.

In 2001, the original iPod used a scroll wheel and buttons to get around its music library, a method the iPod Classic continues. But the iPod Touch brings a whole new level of control to your fingertips. In fact, your fingertips *do* control the way you use this very special 'Pod. This chapter shows you all the moves you need to surf the Web, look at pictures, find your music, and make this little touchscreen device work for you.

To get started on your guided tour of the iPod Touch, turn the page.

iPod Touch Ports and Switches

THE IPOD TOUCH KEEPS most of its controls behind its sensitive screen, but it does have a few physical buttons and jacks on the outside. Here's a tour of the Touch from top to bottom:

❶ **Sleep/Wake**. Press the thin button on top of the Touch to put it to sleep and save some battery power. If you've got a song playing, no problem: A sleeping Touch still plays music—it's just the display that goes dark.

❷ **Volume**. These two buttons reside on the left side of the Touch (bottom left). Press the top one to increase the sound on either the tiny external speaker or an attached pair of headphones; the bottom button lowers the volume. As you press the physical volume buttons, the Touch's screen gives you an on-screen graphic to show how loud or soft the sound is getting (bottom right).

Home. Forget clicking your heels together three times to get home—just push the indented button below the Touch's screen and you'll always return Home. The iPod's Home screen is where your tappable icons for music, photos, Safari web browsing, and more hang out. If you ever wander deep into the iPod and don't know how to get out, push the Home button to escape. You can also push Home to wake the Touch from sleep.

Lightning Connector. This tiny jack is the port you use to plug in the iPod's USB cable for charge-ups and media transfers from iTunes. This connector replaces the old 30-pin Dock Connector on previous iPods, so if you're shopping for speakers and other audio accessories, make sure you get gear that fits your iPod's jack. The Touch's own tiny external speaker sits to the port's right, with the headphone port on the left.

Headphones. Plug the included EarPod headphones into the small, round jack on the bottom edge of the Touch. Non-Apple headphones with the standard 3.5mm stereo plug work, too.

Set Up and Activate Your Touch

EVER SINCE APPLE DEBUTED its iOS 5 software in 2011, the Touch could jump onto the Internet over the airwaves with its WiFi chip, making it the easiest iPod to set up. Touch owners no longer have to get to a computer and unwind a USB cable to get their iPods ready for action—they can do all that wirelessly. This, of course, means you need a WiFi network nearby. (If you don't have one, flip ahead to page 18 to learn how to set up the Touch via dependable USB cable.)

Here's how you set up your player as a brand-new iPod Touch right out of the box—providing that the tablet retained its charge on the trip from China; if power is running low, see page 10 for charge-up instructions.

1. Press the Touch's Home button. You see a gray screen with the word "iPod" in the middle of it and a right-pointing arrow underneath it. Put your finger on the arrow and slide it to the right.

2. Tap your preferred language for iPod screens and menus. English is the default for U.S. users, but tap the arrow for more than 30 other linguistic choices from around the world.

3. Pick your country or region. The United States is the default choice, but if you're not there, tap Show More.

4. Choose your WiFi network. If you're at home, find your personal network on the list and tap it to select it. Type in your network's password. If you're in range of a public network, you can connect to it, but be leery of typing in any personal information, like a credit-card number, to set up an Apple ID.

5. Wait for Apple's servers to activate your iPod over the WiFi connection. Once the iPod connects to the 'Net, activation takes just a few minutes.

6. Decide whether you want to turn on Location Services. Location Services pinpoints the position of your Touch on a map, using a database of WiFi hotspots to guide it. It's great for finding restaurants close to you, but not so much for your privacy. If you leave Location Services off, you can always turn it on later by tapping Home→Settings→Location Services→On.

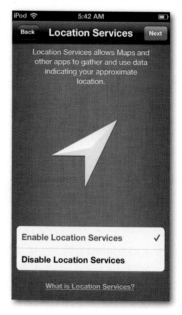

7. Decide if you want to set up this Touch as a new, empty iPod, or restore your previous content (music, photos, apps, and so on) using iCloud or iTunes backup files from an old iPod (page 116).

8. Sign in with or create an Apple ID. Your Apple ID (page 240) is the online user name and password you use to buy and download apps, music, books, videos, podcasts, and more from the iTunes and App Stores. If you already have an Apple ID, sign in with it here. If not, tap "Create a new Apple ID" to go to the next screen, where you can base your new ID on an existing email address or set up a spiffy new—and free—iCloud mail account (see below). If you don't want to deal with this Apple ID stuff now, tap the Skip This Step link at the bottom of the screen.

9. Set up iCloud. On this screen, you can turn on Apple's free iCloud service, where you can back up all your apps, contacts, calendars, and more to Apple's online servers. You can also restore the Touch from an iCloud backup. You get a free *@icloud. com* email account with your account, but you can also set up existing Mail accounts on the Touch later, as page 110 explains; Chapter 5 has more on iCloud.

10. Turn on the Siri personal assistant (or not). This voice-activated helper program—described on page 70—can grab movie listings, sports scores, restaurant suggestions, and more out of the air when you push the iPod's Home button and ask clearly. Siri does need to upload info like your contacts and location information to Apple to do her work, so if you have privacy issues, leave Siri off and do the research yourself.

11. Decide if you want to anonymously send diagnostic data to Apple to help the company improve its services.

12. Register the iPod Touch with Apple. If you need service on the player later, from an Apple store or authorized repair shop, your iPod is on record.

Now, start using your Touch! You don't see these setup screens again, unless you need to replace the software on an ailing iPod (page 306). You get the option during the setup steps to restore a backup of the iPod's settings and account data from an iCloud or iTunes backup file, so you're not totally back on Square One. The iPod setup process has come a long way, baby.

Set Up and Sync Your Touch With iTunes

IF YOU SKIPPED THE PC-free iPod Touch setup because you didn't have a WiFi network around (or because all your stuff is on your computer), you can set up the player using iTunes instead. Just connect your iPod to the computer with the USB cable. When you do, iTunes pops up and walks you through the setup, which includes naming your gadget and choosing sync options.

If you already use iTunes to manage media on an iPhone or iPad, odds are you already have a healthy media library on your computer. And if you've had an iPod before, iTunes offers to put the content from your old player onto your new one. Depending on the size of your new iPod's drive, you may be able to fit all your stuff on it—or not, if you have more than 32 or 64 GB of digital treasures on your computer. If you have less than that and want to take it all with you, choose the "Set Up as New iPod" option shown below and then click Continue. On the main iTunes screen, click the iPod button in the horizontal row. On the next screen, click the type of content you want to autosync, like Music. Turn on the Sync Music checkbox, click the Apply button, and then hit the Sync button..

iTunes Wi-Fi Sync

Now, just because you chose to set up your iPod with iTunes instead of doing it wirelessly doesn't mean you *always* have to dig up your USB cable when you want to put new stuff on your Touch. That's because you can now sync your 'Pod wirelessly. The iPod and the computer you're syncing with just need to be on the same WiFi network, and iTunes has to be open at the time of the sync.

To set up Wi-Fi Sync, connect the Touch to your computer. Click the iPod icon at the top of the iTunes window, and then click the Summary tab on the next screen. Scroll to the Options area and turn on the checkbox next to "Sync this iPod over Wi-Fi" as shown below. Click the Apply button, and then click Sync to change the setting and allow syncing over the network airwaves.

An icon for your Touch now stays visible in the iTunes window, where you can manually add stuff to the player (as page 204 explains). The Touch wirelessly syncs itself once a day when it's plugged into power. It's slower than a USB sync, but often more convenient, and you can still sync by USB when you want.

Ready to sync over that new album? Click the Sync button in the iTunes window—or, on the iPod Touch, tap Home→Settings→General→iTunes Wi-Fi Sync→Sync Now.

Turn the Touch On and Off

WHILE ITS NICE, BRIGHT interactive touchscreen gets most of the attention, the Touch does have a few physical controls—a quartet of buttons along its edges and front. Two of these buttons let you turn the Touch on. One is the narrow little Sleep/Wake button on the Touch's top-right edge (circled). The other is the Home button on the front of the Touch (described on the next page).

The Sleep/Wake button serves a second purpose, too—it puts the Touch in Sleep mode. Give it a gentle press and the Touch goes down for a nap in standby mode.

To wake a sleeping Touch, press the Sleep/Wake button once more or press the Home button.

If you want to turn your Touch off completely, the Sleep/Wake button acts as an On/Off button, too—just press and hold it down for a few seconds. The screen fades to black, and the no-nonsense "slide to power off" red arrow appears. Drag the arrow to the right to power down your 'Pod.

When it's time to play, press the Sleep/Wake button to turn the Touch back on.

The Home Button and Home Screen

EVEN WITH ITS SIMPLE design, the Touch has one very promi-
nent physical button, smack-dab on the player's glass front: the
Home button. You'll press this one a lot, because it's the portal to
all the stuff stored on your Touch.

Most people associate the word *Home* with peace and stability, and this button
lives up to that notion. No matter where you are in the Touch—16 levels up in a
game, deep into the new Mumford & Sons album, or out on the Internet, pressing the Home button always brings you back to the main Touch screen. You
don't even have to click your heels three times.

When you turn on your brand-new Touch, the
Home screen will probably look something like
this, with its included apps in their standard
order. The Touch divides the icons into two
groups: One is the four-by-five grid in the main
part of the screen, and the other is the single
row of four icons along the bottom. (Older versions of the Touch have a shorter screen with
only five rows of icons.) You can have up to 11
flickable pages of icons on the Touch's Home
"screen," but no matter which page you flick to,
the four icons stay anchored to the bottom of
the screen.

Want to rearrange the icons—including that
bottom row of four—so you can put your most-
used apps up front? Press down on an icon until
it wiggles, and then drag it to a new location.
When you're done rearranging, press the Home button to make the icons sit still
again. Once you fill up the first Home screen with icons, swipe your finger to
the left to go to the next screen of icons. Swipe your finger the other way to go
back to that first screen. (If you find all this finger dragging, well, a drag, you can
rearrange your icons more easily in iTunes; see page 125.)

The Home button can do other tricks, too, like letting you switch quickly from
one app to another (page 127) and forcing misbehaving apps to quit. If an app
is stuck on-screen, hold down the Sleep/Wake button until the red "power off"
slider appears (opposite page). Let go of Sleep/Wake and hold down the Home
button until the app closes—and you're back Home. To take a quick pic from the
Lock Screen, press the Home button twice to get a 📷 icon that takes you right
into the Touch's Camera app.

Finger Moves for the iPod Touch

UNTIL THE TOUCH ARRIVED on the scene, iPods were controlled by a click wheel or control ring on the front of the player. The Nano has a limited version of the touch-sensitive screen, and the Shuffle and the Classic still use the circular control. But with a Touch, you don't need a steering wheel to get around your iPod—you just tap the on-screen icons and menus to navigate.

You'll use some moves more often than others as you navigate the Touch:

- **Tap.** Lightly touch a song title, app icon, or picture thumbnail with your fingertip. The Touch isn't a crusty old calculator, so you don't have to push down hard; a gentle tap on the glass starts a song, launches an app, or pops a picture into view.

- **Drag.** This time, keep your fingertip pressed down on the screen. As you slide it around the Touch glass, you scroll to different parts of a web page, photo, or other item that goes beyond the screen's boundaries. You also use the drag move to nudge on-screen volume sliders up and down. It's the same concept as holding down the button on a computer mouse and dragging. A *two-finger drag* scrolls a web window within a web window (which is, fortunately, not too common on mobile sites).

- **Slide.** A slide is like a drag, but you need it only a couple of times on the Touch. The first is on the "slide to unlock" screen you see when you wake the iPod from a nap (see below). The second is when you want to power down the Touch completely; press the Sleep/Wake button until the "slide to power off" slider appears.

> **NOTE** The iPod Touch relies on the human touch—skin-on-glass contact—to work. If you have really long fingernails, a Band-Aid on the tip of your finger, or happen to be wearing gloves at the time, you're going to have problems working the Touch. You can't use a pencil eraser or pen tip, either.

You can, however, find special styluses that work with the Touch screen. These cost anywhere from $10 to $30, and include the Hand stylus (*handstylus.com*) and models from Pogo (*tenonedesign.com/stylus.php*). Apple has a couple of options on its accessibility page for its iOS devices at *http://tinyurl.com/appleaccessibility*.

- **Flick.** This move lets you speed-scroll up and down through long lists of songs, or side to side through overstuffed photo albums. To flick properly, quickly whip your finger along the length or width of the screen. (Make it a light movement—this isn't a slide or a drag here.) The faster you flick, the faster the screens fly by. For example, use the flick when you're in Cover Flow mode (page 36)—tap the Home screen's Music icon and hold the Touch horizontally. All your album covers appear on-screen, and you can flick through them until you find the one you want to hear.

- **Finger spread and pinch.** Can't see what you want because it's too small on the screen? To make it bigger, put your thumb and index finger together, place them on that area of the screen, and then spread your fingers apart. To go the opposite way and zoom out so things shrink back down, put those same fingers on the screen, separated this time, and then pinch them together. Twisting your fingers as you pinch can rotate a 3D map, too.

- **Double-tap.** This two-steppin' tap comes into play in a couple of situations. First, it serves as a shortcut to automatically zoom in on a photo or a section of a web page. You can also double-tap to zoom in on a section of an Apple map (Chapter 4).

Second, if you're watching a movie or TV show, tap the screen twice to toggle back and forth between screen aspect ratios—the full-screen view (top), where the edges of the frame get cropped off, or the letterboxed view (bottom), which movie lovers favor because it's what the director intended a scene to look like. Movies tend to get letterboxed on the top and bottom of the screen, while pre-HD TV shows, as shown here, get side bars to preserve the older 4:3 screen ratio.

- **Two-finger tap.** Two fingers, one tap. That's what you do to zoom *out* of an Apple map view (remember, you use *one* finger and *two* taps to zoom in—Apple just wants to keep you on your fingers...er, toes).

Sync Content to the iPod Touch

AS EXPLAINED BACK ON page 18, there's an easy way to fill up your new Touch with music, videos, photos, and other stuff from your computer: connect it to iTunes during the setup process, select the 'Pod in the iTunes window, and then click the various tabs at the top of the next screen for the types of content you want to sync. Click Sync Music on the Music tab, for example, and all your tunes transfer to the iPod; repeat for each tab of content you want.

While autosyncing means never having to worry that you left that new album behind, some people like more control over what goes on their iPods. If you're one of those more discriminating folks, you need to load songs onto it manually. Until you do, the Touch just sits there, empty and forlorn in your iTunes window, waiting for you to give it something to play with. Here are your options:

Manual Method #1: Selective Syncing

1. Click the iPod icon in the row of buttons at the top of the iTunes window. This opens up a world of syncing preferences.

2. Click the Music tab, and then turn on the Sync Music checkbox.

3. Click the button next to "Selected playlists, artists, and genres," and tick off the items you want to copy to your iPod. (No playlists yet? See Chapter 12.)

4. Click along the top row of tabs (Photos, Apps, Books, and so on) for other types of content. On each screen, select the items from the iTunes library you'd like to sync. Then click the Apply button at the bottom of the iTunes window to make it so.

While any podcasts you downloaded to your computer from the iTunes Podcast Directory (page 244) appear in the computer's iTunes library, they don't sync over to the Music app on the Touch on iOS 6 or later. Instead, podcasts appear in Apple's optional Podcasts app, which you can download free in the App Store. The same goes for any iTunes U educational material or ebooks from Apple's iBookstore—those files are filed in the optional iTunes U and iBooks apps, which are also free in the App Store. Chapter 3 has more on grabbing and using these apps.

Manual Method #2: Drag 'n' Drop

1. This one's for those into detailed picking and choosing: Click the Summary tab and turn on "Manually manage music and videos." Now you can click the songs, albums, or playlists you want on your iPod. Drag them to the right side of the window to the magically appearing Touch icon, as shown below.

Manual Method #3: Check the Box

1. Every item in your iTunes library has a checkmark next to its name when you first import it. Clear the checkmark next to whatever you *don't* want on your Touch. (If you have a big library, hold down the Ctrl [⌘] key while clicking any title; that performs the nifty trick of removing *all* the checkmarks. Then go back and check only the stuff you *do* want.)

2. Click the iPod icon in the horizontal row of buttons on the main iTunes screen, and then click the Summary tab.

3. At the bottom of the Summary screen, turn on the checkbox next to "Sync only checked songs and videos," and then click the Sync button.

What's in the Settings Menu

THE TOUCH IS A powerful little media machine, and you fine-tune the way it works in the Settings menu. Here's what you find by tapping the Settings icon on the Home screen:

- **Airplane Mode.** When the flight attendant tells you to turn off all Internet devices, tap Airplane Mode to On—that turns *off* your WiFi, the airborne data streams the pilot is worried about.

- **WiFi.** Turn the iPod's WiFi antenna on or off here—or see what wireless network you're currently connected to.

- **Bluetooth.** Flip this setting on to link up wireless keyboards and headsets.

- **Do Not Disturb.** The Touch has a Quiet Time setting, as page 79 explains.

- **Notifications.** Many apps can alert you to news and updates (like football scores) with "push" notifications that automatically pop up on-screen. Turn the alerts on or off here.

- **General.** Here you'll find the Touch's About menu (listing the iPod's serial number, software version, and number of songs, videos, apps, and more), plus network info. You control wireless settings, like those for iTunes Wi-Fi Sync and over-the-air software updates, from here as well. You can also restrict Spotlight searches to certain file types, set up a passcode for your Touch, and adjust the date and time. The Keyboard settings let you turn off (or on) the iPod's spell-checker and auto-correction features. In the International area, you can choose the iPod's display language or switch to a foreign-language keyboard. The Accessibility options include VoiceOver settings, spoken-word alerts, and high-contrast screen text. You can also reset all the settings you've fiddled with—and even erase all the iPod's content.

- **Sounds.** The Touch can make all sorts of external noises, from ringtones for FaceTime calls to keyboard clicks. Set your sounds (and volumes) here.

- **Brightness & Wallpaper.** If you don't like the Touch's Auto-Brightness sensor adjusting your screen, override it and make your own adjustments here. You can also change the background image on the Touch screen.

- **Privacy.** Tap here to get to the GPS-like iPod's Location Services settings and see apps that have permission to see your data, like contacts and photos.

- **iCloud.** Tap here to set preferences for syncing your personal data—contacts, calendars, mail, notes, reminders, bookmarks—as well as your Photo Stream (page 286) and data to Apple's free online storage locker.

- **Mail, Contacts, Calendars.** Tap here to set up an email account right on the Touch. You can adjust all other mail-related preferences here, too (like how often the Touch looks for new mail), and delete unwanted accounts. Scroll farther down to dictate the look of Contacts and Calendars, and the way each app alerts you. Chapter 4 has more on syncing contacts and calendars.

- **Notes.** Tap here to pick one of three fonts for your little yellow iPod notes.

- **Reminders.** Choose the calendar with which you sync your iPod's to-do list.

- **Messages.** Set up your account to use Apple's free iMessage service for iOS 5 and later devices here. Page 73 has more on Messages.

- **FaceTime.** Turn the FaceTime feature on here, and set up the email account you want to use with it so FaceTime callers can find you.

- **Maps.** Choose miles or kilometers here, as well as map label size.

- **Safari.** Specify the Safari web browser's default search engine (Google, Yahoo, or Bing), and whether you want the Autofill feature to fill in website user names and passwords on your behalf. The security settings are here, too: Turn on warnings for potentially fraudulent websites, block annoying pop-up ads and cookies, or clear your browser cache—which erases all the accumulated page parts left behind from your web surfing. Chapter 5 has more on this fun stuff.

- **iTunes & App Stores.** Sign in or out of the Apple ID you use to buy iTunes stuff here. You can also turn on Automatic Downloads (page 254).

- **Music.** You can set the iPod to shuffle with a shake (or not), turn the Equalizer and Sound Check features off or on (Chapter 5), set limits for maximum volume, and choose to display lyrics and podcast titles here.

- **Video.** Instruct the Touch to play videos from where you left off and turn closed captioning on or off. You can log into Home Sharing here, too.

- **Photos & Camera.** The settings for iCloud Photo Streams (Chapter 15) are here, as well as those for your Touch slideshows—including the time each slide stays onscreen, the transition between shots, and whether the Touch repeats the show or shuffles the slides.

- **Twitter.** If you use the popular microblogging service, log into your account here to tweet photos, links, and more from the Touch.

- **Facebook.** Log into your Facebook account here for the quick 'n' easy sharing of Safari links, photos, and more.

- **Individual application settings.** Depending on the apps you have installed, you'll also see settings for programs like iBooks, Podcasts, and third-party apps.

You'll learn to:

- Play music, audiobooks, and podcasts

- Shoot and edit videos and photos

- Play games and compete through Game Center

- Read papers and magazines

- Get fit with the Nike + iPod Touch exercise program

CHAPTER 3

Entertain Yourself With the iPod Touch

FROM ITS HUMBLE BEGINNINGS as a boxy little music player in 2001, the iPod has always been about entertainment. Back then, that meant music and maybe an audiobook or two.

Today, the Touch has significantly expanded the iPod's repertoire, and this chapter shows you the ways. Sure, the Touch still plays music and audiobooks, but it also serves up movies, TV shows, and video podcasts. And your iPod doesn't just *play* videos—it shoots them, too, so you're never without a camcorder with your Touch on hand. The same camera that shoots videos can snap good-quality still photos as well, and you can enhance and crop the images right on your 'Pod.

The Touch is also a handheld videogame console, an ebook reader, a podcast player, and a personal trainer. You'll learn how to get rolling with all of these features in this chapter, which is all about *play*. (If you're looking for *work*, skip ahead to Chapter 4 to learn about the Touch's business-like apps, like Contacts and Calendars.)

The Touch is still an iPod, so to jump into your music—a task the device still excels at after all these years—turn the page.

What's in the Music Menu

SINCE YOU HAVE AN iPod, you probably want to play some music, right? To do that, tap the Music icon; you'll see your audio collection sorted into all kinds of helpful categories, like songs, artists, and albums. Click a category to reveal its list of tunes, musicians, or albums. Flick your finger up and down the screen to scroll through a list. In categories that include songs, tap a song's title to hear the tune. For other categories, like Artists or Albums, click a name or title to see all the songs in that category, and then tap a song to play it.

Icons on the bottom row of the Touch's screen take you to the first four music categories, which vary depending on whether you synced up Genius Mixes (Chapter 12) from iTunes. Here's what the categories look like:

- **Genius.** If you *did* sync Genius Mixes, tap this button to play them.

- **Playlists.** If you didn't go for a Genius Mix sync session (or haven't gotten to it yet), Playlists shows up as the first icon. In case you haven't heard of a *playlist*, it's a collection of songs you think sound good together A playlist for your gym routine could contain high-energy dance tracks, for example. (Chapter 12 shows you how to create playlists.)

- **Artists.** To sort your music by band or performer, tap Artists. Even if your collection has just one measly track from an obscure bar band, the band's name will show up proudly next to Elvis Presley and The Beatles. Tap the band's or artist's name to see the available tracks, and then tap a song to start playing it.

- **Songs.** Tap here to see a complete list of the songs on your iPod, nicely arranged in alphabetical order. If you don't feel like flicking forever to get down to "Zing! Went the Strings of My Heart," tap the vertical index bar to jump to a specific letter—and all the songs that start with it.

NOTE If you didn't sync Genius Mixes to your Touch, the fourth category (the one before the More button) is Albums. There's more on More—and Albums—on the next page.

The last icon in the row is aptly named More. Tap it to see *more* ways to sort your audio collection, including these categories:

- **Albums.** Far from its roots on discs of black vinyl, the notion of "album" still thrives on music players everywhere, whether you have a complete set of tracks or not. Tap here to see all your music grouped according to the name of the album it appears on.

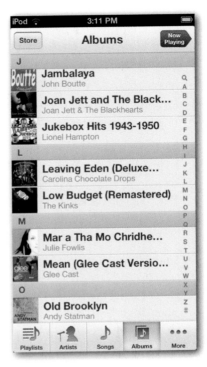

- **Audiobooks.** Tap here to see the narrated books you bought and downloaded from the iTunes Store or Audible.com (Chapter 13). Tracks you ripped from audiobook CDs don't show up here automatically; you have to edit the file type first (see page 198).

- **Compilations.** Soundtracks, tribute records, and any other album with tracks from multiple artists are usually considered a *compilation*. If iTunes doesn't automatically tag these albums as compilations, you can do it yourself by heading to page 200.

- **Composers.** All your music, listed by songwriter, resides here.

- **Genres.** If you're in a jazz, country, pop, or other music-specific mood, tap Genres to see all the music in a particular category.

- **Shared.** If you're hooked into iTunes Home Sharing (page 190), you can stream music over your home network from the iTunes libraries of computers on the same network and logged in with the same Apple ID.

As you tap around your collection, your Touch is ready if you want to add tunes right there: A Store button in the top-left corner of most screens awaits your impulses. (Looking for Podcasts and iTunes U content? See page 36.)

TIP Don't like the way Apple orders things, and want to put your lists where *you* want them? Tap More and, on the next screen, tap the Edit button in the top-left corner. On the black Configure screen, drag the ghostly white list icons down into the bottom row in the order you prefer them. Once you get your favorite icons within easy reach, tap Done.

Explore the Now Playing Screen

THE TOUCH SHOWS OFF photos and videos quite nicely, and it even makes your music look good. Cover Flow (page 36) is one way it does that, but even if you're just listening to an album, you get a big, lovely album cover on the Now Playing screen.

In addition to cover art, the Now Playing screen has icons and information along its top edge to help you manage your music. Here's what everything means, starting from left to right:

- **Back arrow (←).** Just like the Back button on a web browser, tap here to go back to the screen you were on before you landed here. This could be back to the playlist the current song is from, the album containing the track, or the artist's track list.

- **Song information.** The top-center of the Now Playing screen displays the name of the current song, the artist performing it, and the album it's on.

- **Track listing (☰).** The information in the middle of the screen tells you the current song's name. Tap this icon to see all the tracks you have from that album. You can also double-tap the album cover to spin it around and reveal the track list.

TIP Ever wanted a computer like the ones on *Star Trek*, where you could speak a music playback command and have the machine obey? On the fifth-generation iPod Touch (October 2012), Siri (page 70) handles that for you. Summon her and tell her what you want.

On Touch models from 2010 or 2011 (or older models with Apple's headset/microphone combo), you can get things done with the Voice Control feature. Hold down the Home button until the Voice Control screen appears and beeps, and then speak your commands into the Touch.

Sample commands include "Play artist Beyoncé" or "Play album "Let It Be." Say "Shuffle" to shuffle tunes or "Genius" to hear similar tracks. "Play" and "Pause" work as spoken commands, and you can even ask "What's playing?" To turn off Voice Control, say "Stop" or "Cancel." If English isn't your native tongue, you can change the language that Voice Control responds to by choosing Settings→General→International→Voice Control→[Language].

When you tap ▤ on the Now Playing screen to see an album's song list in high-contrast white-on-black, a blue triangle identifies the track currently playing. If you're tired of that tune, tap a different title.

Once you have songs listed on the Now Playing screen, you can rate them. As the song plays, swipe the row of dots along the top of the screen to convert the dots to stars. You can rate songs from 1 to 5 stars, and the ratings you add to your songs here get synced back to iTunes when you connect Touch to computer. Chapter 11 has more on star ratings.

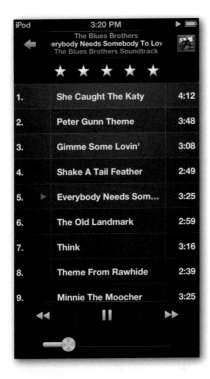

Once you tire of looking at track names and rating songs, you can return to the full-screen album art view by tapping the tiny album cover in the top-right corner.

The Now Playing screen looks the coolest when you have big, bright, colorful album covers for your songs. If you purchased your music from the iTunes Store or another online music emporium, the album art should have come with the song. If you ripped the tracks yourself and didn't add any album art, you probably see a boring old gray music note. If that doesn't thrill you, flip to page 201 for art lessons.

Control Music on the Now Playing Screen

THE NOW PLAYING SCREEN is more than just a pretty face for your music. It lets you manage current-song playback from this screen, too. Here's what the various icons mean, starting with that strip along the bottom of the screen:

- **Play/Pause (▶/II) button.** The Now Playing screen usually means something is playing; you pause the song by tapping **II**, and restart it by tapping ▶.

- **Previous, Next (◀◀, ▶▶).** To hear a currently playing song from the beginning, tap I◀◀. If you're already at the beginning of a song, tap ◀◀ to go to the previous track. Conversely, if you want to skip a long fade-out and blow on through to the end of a song, tap ▶▶. Tapping the same key at the end of a song takes you to the next track.

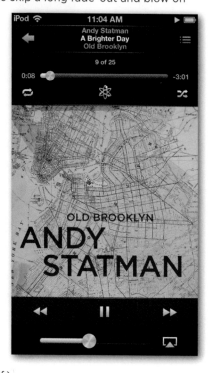

Miss the days of fast-forwarding or rewinding cassette tapes to hear the quality parts of a song? Press and hold ◀◀ or ▶▶ to simulate the process. The longer you keep the button pressed, the faster the song leaps by.

- **Volume.** Sure, your Touch has physical volume buttons on its outer edge, but sometimes you don't feel like readjusting your grip on the player to scootch the volume up a notch. With the volume slider at the bottom of the screen, you can boost or reduce the sound by dragging the big white dot with the tip of your finger. (If you *do* use the physical volume buttons while looking at the Now Playing screen, you see the on-screen slider move magically by itself.)

If you connect an Apple TV or an AirPort Express to your TV, home-entertainment sound system, stereo, or set of powered speakers (page 292), you also see the AirPlay icon (⊡) on the playback control bar. Tap it and choose a set of speakers from the drop-down list.

But wait, there's more to the Now Playing screen! Look closely, right above the top edge of the album cover—this collection of four controls lets you fine-tune your music playback down to the second or change the order of an album or playlist on the fly. Here's what each does:

- **Loop.** Certain songs are so good that you want to play them over and over and over again. To make that happen, tap the Loop button (⟳) button twice until it looks like ⟳. If you want to put the album itself on repeat, tap the Loop button only once, so that it turns a nice shade of orange (⟳).

- **Scrubber bar.** This slider at the top of the screen shows you the total length of the current song, how much time has elapsed, and how much is left to go. Drag the white dot (formally known as the "playhead") to a different time to skip to that part of the song. The "2 of 19" (or whatever) number above the scrubber bar tells you where this track falls in the album or playlist.

- **Genius playlist.** Tap the ✳ icon to make a Genius playlist based on the current song. Chapter 12 has details.

- **Shuffle.** If you like to mix things up, the Touch can shuffle the tracks in the current album or playlist. Just tap the ✄ button. When it turns orange, the Touch plays songs in random order. Tap ✄ again to turn off shuffle and return to the standard playback order.

Playing Audiobooks

If you're listening to an audiobook, you might see three other icons. They include:

- **Repeat the last 15 seconds.** Tap the first 15-in-a-circular-arrow icon to jump back a quarter of a minute in the book's narration to repeat a line you missed.

- **Skip the next 15 seconds.** Tap the second 15-in-a-circular-arrow icon to jump ahead in 15-second leaps.

- **Playback speed.** Tap until you see ⟨2X⟩ to hear the audio in double time, or tap ⟨½X⟩ to hear it slowed to half-speed. Tap the default ⟨1X⟩ icon to hear the narrator at normal speed. Whenever you switch from ⟨1X⟩ narration, the icon turns orange to remind you that you adjusted the audio.

Cover Flow in Motion

THE TOUCH CAMERA IS great, but if you like moving pictures—or pictures that *really* move—check out Cover Flow. Designed to show off your music collection to maximum effect, Cover Flow is basically a parade of album artwork that also lets you start playing music right away.

To use Cover Flow, tap the Music icon on the Home screen to get into your audio library. Instead of tapping through lists with the Touch in portrait mode, rotate it to landscape (horizontal) view. The text-based lists go away, replaced by full-color album covers. Flick your finger across the screen to see them whiz by.

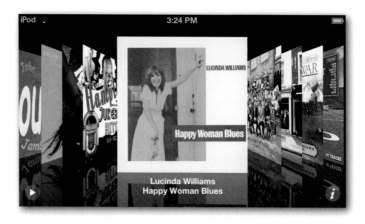

An album cover doesn't tell you what songs are on the disk, so tap it to see its track listing. You can also tap ❶ in the lower-right corner to spin the cover around and see the song list. To hear a song play, tap its title. To pause the song, tap ❙❙ in the lower-left corner; press ▶ to start it up again.

To flip back to the album art, tap the track listing (▤) or ❶ button again. Once you exhaust the sheer visual excitement of Cover Flow (or you have to do something else for a while), turn the iPod back to portrait mode (upright) to return to your lists and screen icons. Cover Flow may not do much for some people, but it sure is pretty to watch.

Use the Podcasts and iTunes U Apps

In 2012, Apple overhauled its Music app by spinning off two of its components, Podcasts and iTunes U, into their own apps. The Touch should prompt you to download these apps (opposite page, top) when you first visit the App Store. If not, you can search them out and install them later (page 122).

Podcasts

On the Touch, if you want to download a *podcast* —
those free audio and video shows on any given topic—
you need to do it through the Podcasts app. (And when
you sync podcasts from your computer to your Touch,
they land here in the Podcasts app and not in the Music
app.)

To browse for shows, open the Podcasts app and tap
the Store button. To see all the audio and video podcasts on hand, tap either Audio or Video to sort the list
accordingly.

Tap the Categories button to find shows sorted by subject (Arts, Comedy, News & Politics, and so forth). When
you see a show that interests you, tap its thumbnail to
see an episode list, download the available installments,
or subscribe to it—iTunes automatically downloads the
new episodes to your iPod. Tap Library to return to your
Touch's collection.

To play a podcast, tap its thumbnail and then tap the
name of the episode you want to hear or see. Playback
controls at the bottom of the screen (middle-right) let
you pause, play, jump back 10 seconds, or jump ahead
30 seconds in the track. Tap the cover art to reveal
another screen of controls that let you adjust the speed
of the audio, set a sleep timer, or share your find with
friends on Twitter or Facebook—or by email or instant
message.

iTunes U

Billed as "the world's largest online catalog of free
educational content," Apple's iTunes U project offers half
a million lectures, books, courses, and other materials
from major universities. The best way to get started is to
grab the iTunes U app, open it up, and tap the Catalog
button to see what you want to learn today.

Once on the virtual iTunes U campus, you can browse
and download audio and video lectures at random—or even subscribe to online
courses, complete with weekly reading assignments. Your downloaded lectures
and course materials await you on the shelves of the iTunes U app, shown above.

What's in the Videos Menu

VIDEO COMES IN MANY forms today: movies, TV shows, music videos, and so on. If you have moving images on your Touch, they're in one of these categories:

- **Movies.** Hollywood blockbusters from the iTunes Store, movies you made yourself, and trailers you snagged off the Web all live happily here.

- **TV Shows.** Don't have time for TV the traditional way (on the couch and with a beverage)? When you grab TV shows from the iTunes Store, you see them in this part of the Videos menu.

- **Music Videos.** You find music videos you bought from the iTunes Store (or those that come with some albums) here.

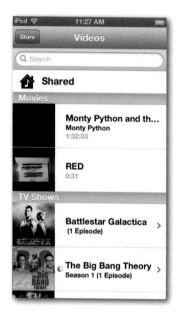

The thumbnail photo next to each video gives you a hint to its content, and information like running time and number of episodes appears here as well.

Tap a title to play a video. If you have multiple episodes of a TV show or podcast, tap the show title, and then tap the name of the episode you want to watch. Rotate the Touch to landscape view and enjoy the show. (Flip ahead to Chapter 14 if you want to know more about video *right now*.)

In addition to the stuff stored on your Touch, you can wirelessly stream videos from your iTunes library or a shared one. Tap the Shared icon at the top of the menu and select an iTunes collection to browse. You need to have iTunes Home Sharing turned on to share, so visit page 190 if you don't.

What's in the Photos Menu

WHO NEEDS TO DRAG around a photo album or laptop full of slideshows when you've got a Touch? And the current Touch offers not only a picture viewer but a whole digital camera and camcorder.

Odds are, though, you probably took most of your photos with a standard digital camera. As Chapter 15 explains, you can transfer copies of your favorite pictures and photo albums onto the Touch through iTunes or with the iCloud Photo Stream. And when you do, they land here in the Photos app.

Give the Photos icon (the happy sunflower) a tap on the Home screen, and all those pictures await you in the iPod's Photo library. Many photo-organizer programs, like Adobe Photoshop Elements and Apple's iPhoto, let you sort pictures into albums, and you can see those same albums in the Photos app if you opted to sync them over. The number in parentheses next to the album name reveals how many photos live there.

The Camera Roll album at the top of the screen collects all the photos and videos you take with the Touch itself. You can import them to your computer using your photo-organizer app. Other images that come right to the Touch—like screenshots you snap or photos you save from email messages—land here, too. Chapter 15 has all the photographic details.

Snap and Edit Photos

PHOTOGRAPHERS OFTEN SAY THAT the best camera is the one you have with you. If you rely on your Touch as an entertainment machine, odds are you have it with you. And with the Touch, you get *two* cameras—a 5-megapixel one on the back (with a flash!) and a 1.2-megapixel camera on the front. Together, they provide the hardware you need for high-def FaceTime video calls, shooting video clips, and snapping still photos.

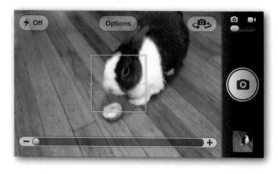

To start using the Camera app, tap the camera icon on the Touch's Home screen. Make sure the little slider in the corner is set to 📷 (still camera) and not ◼◀ (video camera). Tap ⚡Auto to toggle the flash off or on, or to have it fire automatically. Then line up your shot and press the big round shutter button (📷) in the middle of the toolbar; if you're holding the iPod like a regular camera, you can also press either volume button to take the photo. The Touch even makes a little shutter-click noise when you pop the shot.

The Touch saves your newly snapped picture in Photos→Camera Roll. A thumbnail of the last shot you snapped also appears in the corner of the Camera app screen; tap it to jump right to the photo in the Camera Roll album.

The Touch camera offers a few controls for better photos:

- **Exposure adjustment.** Here, you fiddle with the *exposure* (the overall lightness or darkness) of an image. If you have a shot lined up but part of the frame is in shadow, tap a lighter area of the image. A blue-white square appears briefly on-screen, and the Touch adjusts its exposure settings based on that area. Now snap the picture.

- **Zoom.** Touching the screen with your finger to adjust a photo's exposure brings up the zoom slider (shown above). To narrow in on your subject, drag the slider to the right until you have the framing you want. Drag the slider the other way to zoom back out.

- **Grid.** Tap the Options button to overlay the screen with a nine-square grid to help you align and compose your shots.

- **HDR.** Great for still-life and architecture shots, High Dynamic Range combines three exposures into one to bring out the best in a photo. You can turn it on by tapping Camera→Options→HDR→On.

- **Panorama.** Need a shot wider than the Touch can take? Tap Camera→ Options→Panorama. Tap the 🔘 button and then steadily move the Touch from left to right to capture the whole scene. Tap Done when you finish.

You can take photos in either portrait (vertical) or landscape (horizontal) mode. To change cameras and take a self-portrait with the front camera (circled, below left), tap the 📷 icon in the upper-right corner of the screen. The Touch's rear camera (circled, below right) sits in the corner on the back, so be careful when you shoot with it or you may get a stunning portrait of your own finger.

Editing Photos on the Touch

You can do basic image-editing on your Touch. Tap open a photo that needs fixing, and then tap the Edit button at the top of the screen. Here are your options:

❶ **Rotate.** Tap the Rotate button to spin a vertical shot into a horizontal one or flip it upside down.

❷ **Enhance.** Tap here to have the iPod analyze your picture and improve its contrast, exposure, and saturation.

❸ **Red Eye.** If your subject has glowing red demon eyes from your camera flash, tap the Red Eye button to give those devil peepers a neutral color.

❹ **Crop**. Tap here to chop out the boring, distracting, or ex-boyfriend parts of a picture. In Crop mode, tap the Constrain button to conform to standard photo sizes, like 4 x 6, and then tap the yellow Crop button.

Hate that change you just made to a pic? Tap the Cancel button to reverse it. Once you like an edited photo, tap Save to put a copy in your Camera Roll.

Shoot and Edit Videos on the Touch

CELLPHONES AND POCKET CAMCORDERS that can shoot video have boomed in popularity over the years—which could explain the noticeable increase in YouTube videos of cats riding Roomba vacuum cleaners. Thanks to its back camera that shoots high-definition video (at a resolution of 1080p and 30 frames per second), the Touch is part of the video party. Warn your pets.

Shooting a video on the Touch works a lot like shooting a still photo. And even though you can tap an area of the screen to adjust the exposure, there's no zoom feature for video as there is for still photos.

Tap the Camera icon on the Touch's Home screen to get started. To shoot videos, make sure the slider on the toolbar is set to video (■◀) and not still photos (◎).

The tiny microphone next to the camera lens on the back of the Touch records audio to go along with your video.

You can hold the Touch vertically or horizontally to shoot video. Portrait-shot clips may get shrunk or letterboxed if you upload them to a video-sharing site that uses the more cinematic horizontal orientation. When you're ready to start filming, tap the big round ● button. It flashes from dull to bright red as you record.

The time stamp in the corner of the screen shows the current length of your video-in-progress. When you're ready to virtually yell "Cut!", tap the ● button again to stop recording.

When you do, the Touch stores your clip in Photos→Camera Roll. To see what you shot without leaving the Camera app, tap the thumbnail preview at the end of the gray toolbar. Tap ▶ to play it back.

Editing Video on the Touch

Do you have a video where all the good action is in the middle? You know, the one where the first 5 minutes capture your voice trying to wheedle your toddler into dancing for Grandma—while the last 2 minutes show the inside of your shirt pocket because you forgot to turn off the camera? That stuff is easy to fix on the Touch.

Here's how to trim off the unnecessary parts on either end of a clip (you can't edit *within* a clip):

1. Open the video you want to edit.

2. Tap the screen to call up the editing controls. The frame-viewer bar at the top of the screen displays scenes from the clip.

3. Press the outer edge of the frame-viewer so it turns yellow, and then drag either end of the yellow bar to isolate just the frames you want to keep. Tap the Trim button to cut away the detritus.

After you press Trim, the Touch offers you a choice of cutting the original clip (which makes this edit permanent) or saving the edited video as a whole *new* clip—while leaving the original version intact.

TIP The Touch offers rudimentary tools for quickly chopping video. If you want a more complete pocket movie studio that lets you add titles, transitions, theme music, and more, hit the App Store and check out programs like Splice ($4) or Apple's own iMovie for iPhone/Touch ($5).

Share and Upload Photos and Videos

NOW THAT YOU'VE TAKEN all these great photos and videos on your Touch, don't you want to share them with the world—or at least your friends and relatives? No matter how you want to share (privately through email, publicly on Facebook, for example), the Touch offers several ways to show off your work:

- **Email.** Tap Photos→Camera Roll to see your photos and videos (if you have the Camera app open on-screen, tap the thumbnail preview in the toolbar to jump to your collection). If you have just one photo you want to share, tap open its thumbnail image so it fils your Touchscreen and tap the 📤 icon. A menu pops up with nine options (below left). To send the picture as an email attachment, tap Mail to create a new message with the photo already attached and ready to address.

The 📤 menu for a single selected item.

The menu options for a sharing multiple selected items.

To share multiple photos by email, stay on the thumbnails screen of the photo album and tap Edit. Next, tap the thumbnails of the photos and videos you want to send to select them with a ✔. Tap the Share button at the bottom of the screen, and then tap the mail icon in the drop-down menu (above right). A mail message appears with your files attached, ready for you to address and send. (You can also use the Edit button to select files for deletion out of the Camera Roll or to copy into a new album in the Photos app—just tap Edit, select the photos you have in mind, and then tap either Delete or Add To New Album.)

- **Message.** Tap  on a selected photo or video to send it as an instant message (page 73) to friends with iOS 5 or later devices. You send multiple images in a message the same way you send multiple photos with an email: On the album's screen, tap the Edit button, select your images, tap 📷, and then tap Message.

- **Photo Stream (Photos only).** If you use the Photo Stream feature (page 286), tap 📷 on a selected picture to send it to your stream. As with mail and messages, you can send multiple images to the Photo Stream as described above.

- **Twitter (Photos only).** Got Twitter? Select a photo and tap 📷 to get the Twitter button so you can share the image with your followers.

- **Facebook (Photos only).** If you're one of the billion people with a Facebook account and want to post a pic from your Touch right to your profile page, tap 📷 and select Facebook. You can share several images using the bulk-share method described above for mail, messages, and the Photo Stream.

- **Assign to Contact (Photos only).** Just snapped a nice picture of a friend and want to assign it to her address card in the iPod's Contacts app? Tap 📷 and then Assign to Contact. The next chapter has more on contacts.

- **Print (Photos only).** If you have an AirPrint printer (page 82), select a photo and tap 📷 for the Print option. You can print multiple photos by tapping the album's Edit button, selecting the photos, and tapping Share and then Print.

- **Copy (Photos only).** Tap 📷 and then Copy to grab the photo for pasting into a document or message. Use the Edit button method described above to copy multiple images at once.

- **Use as Wallpaper (Photos only).** To turn a selected picture into your Touch's background image, tap Tap 📷 and then tap Use as Wallpaper.

- **Upload to YouTube (Videos only).** With a video clip on-screen (right), tap the 📷 button and then tap YouTube.

> **TIP** You can transfer your Camera Roll contents to your computer. Connect your Touch to your Windows PC or Mac and use the Import command in your photo-organizer program (like Adobe Photoshop Elements or iPhoto) to copy over photos and videos. Once you have the files on your computer, you can post them to your blog or a photo site.

Play Around in Game Center

UNLESS YOU'RE PLAYING SOLITAIRE, games are usually more fun when you play with someone. Once you sign up for the Touch's Game Center, you can compete against thousands of other players around the world. You can add pals to a Friends list for quick competitions, do battle with strangers in multiplayer games, and join the race to the top of each game's leaderboard.

Here's how to get started with Game Center:

1. Tap the Game Center icon on the Touch's Home screen and sign up for an account or type in your Apple ID (page 240); games you buy and download get billed to this account. You need to tap through a few account setup screens (including one with legal terms) to create an Apple ID.

2. Pick an online nickname—it may take a few tries to find an available one. You can also add a photo to your profile. When you fire up Game Center later, your carefully constructed gamer identity greets you as shown below. (To switch to a different, more fear-inspiring photo later, tap the Change Photo button, and then select a new image from the Photos app.)

3. March through the rest of the account setup screens. You can configure your settings so you get invitations to games and so Game Center members can find you based on your email address. Game Center also asks if you'd like to add your Facebook friends to your list of recommended opponents. You can also get push notifications for game invitations and updates by configuring your iPod's Notifications (page 78).

Get Games

Not every game out there works with Game Center, but if you've already downloaded some that do, tap the Games icon to see them. If you need more games, flick down to the bottom of the screen and tap Find Game Center Games for a quick trip to the App Store.

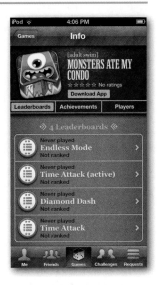

The Games screen also shows recommendations for games you might like based on previous purchases. To see the leaderboards and possible achievements (goals) in a game, tap the name of the game. The next screen has buttons that reveal who's leading and the list of achievements you earned in that game.

Find Someone to Play With

Game Center is its own social-gaming network for global competition (it's similar to the Open Feint network, which works with some Game Center games as well). Tap the Friends button at the bottom of the screen to see a list of friends you already have—or potential new ones Game Center recommends based on your common gaming interests. To see a player's profile, tap his or her name to see the games that person plays and the points scored.

You can add gaming friends two ways:

- **Tap Friends→Add Friends (or tap + in the upper-left corner).** On the next screen, type the nickname of the person you wish to send a Friend Request message. (To find friends on Game Center, you need to know the person's email address or Game Center nickname.)

- **On the Friends screen, flick through the list of Game Center-recommended potential pals.** When you see someone who looks like fun, tap the name and then, on the next screen, tap Send Friend Request.

If you've gotten friend requests, tap the Requests button to see who wants to play. To invite a friend to a multiplayer game, open that game and tap the Play button. Next, select the friends to whom you want to send invites, and when everyone accepts, start the game.

You can issue challenges to other players by tapping Games→[Name of Game]→Achievements→[Name of Achievement]→Challenge Friends; tap the Share button to brag on your achievement by email, message, Facebook, or Twitter. And to see who's thrown down the digital gauntlet at *your* feet, tap the Challenges button on the main Game Center screen.

Use Newsstand and iBooks

Even though the iPod Touch's screen is several inches smaller than the Amazon Kindle's or even the iPad Mini's, it displays electronic magazines, newspapers, books, and other reading material with a pair of Apple apps: Newsstand (which comes with iOS 5 and later) and iBooks (which you can download from the App Store, as explained below). These apps turn your Touch into a pocket reading room—and it's easier to hold on crowded trains, planes, and other tight spots.

Newsstand

This app sits quietly on the iPod's Home screen, waiting for you to download an electronic periodical so it can proudly display the material on its virtual shelves.

"Hey," you say, "That all sounds great, but how do I find and subscribe to digital magazines and newspapers in the first place?" Apple, in its quest to sell you more content, has made it extremely easy: Just launch the Newsstand app and tap the Store button in the top-right corner (right).

The Newsstand whisks you to a special part of the App Store where you can buy, subscribe to, and download electronic periodicals. The Store displays each title like an app, offering price, ratings, and other info. Tap a title to learn more, buy a single issue, or sign up for a subscription. The bill goes to the credit card linked to your Apple ID (page 240).

If you need to cancel, renew, or adjust a subscription, log into your Store account. You can do that right from the Touch by opening the iTunes Store app, flicking to the bottom of the screen, and tapping either your Apple ID (if you're signed in already) or Sign In. Tap View Apple ID, log in, and flick down to Subscriptions. Tap Manage, and then tap the title you want to change.

If you sign up for a subscription, the Newsstand app automatically grabs each new issue and sends you a notification (if you have your settings configured to do so). The app also lists the number of new e-rags in a red circle on the Newsstand icon. Tap it open to see what awaits you on the faux-IKEA shelves.

iBooks

The first time you visit the App Store, you get a note from Apple (shown at the top of page 37) asking if you'd like to download a free copy of iBooks and a few other apps. If this appeals to you, tap the Download Free button. If the time's not right, you can also go back and download iBooks later (Chapter 6).

When you open iBooks, you see that it, too, has a Store button beckoning you to tap it. Once you do, you're swept right into the ebook section of the App Store. After you find something to read, tap the price to buy it—and to have it billed to your iTunes account. If you're not sold yet, tap the Sample button to download a portion of the book to evaluate. Tap the Library button to leave the Store and return to your personal book collection.

The books you download appear on the iBooks shelves; tap the Books button at the top and choose Purchased Books to see (and re-download) all the iBooks you've ever bought. Tap a book cover to open the title and start reading. You can read your book in either portrait (vertical) or landscape (horizontal) mode.

By tapping the electronic page of an ebook, you summon iBooks' navigation and customization controls:

- Tap ☰ to go to the book's table of contents or list of pages you've bookmarked.

- Tap ₐA to make the type larger or smaller by tapping either the big A or the little A buttons. In the same menu, you can move the ☀ slider to adjust the screen brightness. Tap Fonts to pick a different typeface. Tap Themes (right, bottom) to add a light-brown sepia tone to the page to make it easier to read, or switch to the Night theme (white-text-on-a-black-background) for bedtime reading. You can also change the way the book's pages move: tap Book for the animated page-turning action or Scroll to get the text in one continuous vertical page.

- Tap 🔍 to search for text within the book—or on the Web and Wikipedia.

- Tap 🔖 to bookmark your place. If you're reading the book on different iOS devices, iBooks offers to sync your bookmarks between them.

With your fingertip, use the brown slider at the bottom of the page to skip around in the book. When you're done reading, tap the Library button in the top-left corner to close the book and return to your Library. You can also open, read, and store PDF files in the iBooks app.

Get Fit With Nike + iPod Touch

IN ADDITION TO THE stopwatch feature mentioned on page 138, the Touch has another plus for fitness buffs: the Nike + iPod software. With this built-in iTrainer beside you at the gym (and some Nike gear, mentioned below), you can record your workout statistics, pick your favorite exercise music, and upload your daily results to *www.nikeplus.com* to track your progress over time (you need to register for a free account at the Nike site to store your workout data).

Nike + iPod Touch

To use the fitness feature on the Touch, you need to buy a special set of Nike gym shoes—they include a small compartment where you stick in the iPod-compatible shoe sensor. You can find the shoes at most athletic-footwear stores.

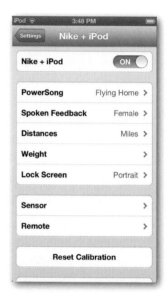

The sensor costs $19 and can be found online at *www.apple.com/ipod/nike*. It transmits your steps to the Touch, which dutifully records the information.

That information lives in the Nike + iPod app. If you don't see a red Nike icon on your Touch, tap Home→Settings→Nike + iPod→On.

Tap the Workouts screen to pick an exercise session that suits your needs. You can choose:

- A basic workout with no set goals.

- A timed workout based on 20 to 90 minutes (or a custom amount) of activity.

- A distance goal to cover a specific amount of ground (like 3K or 5 miles).

- A calorie workout that lets you target the fat you want to burn after last night's pizza-and-cookies binge.

Once you choose a workout, the Touch asks you to pick a playlist from the inspiring collection you created in the Music app. You can shuffle the songs or, if you're feeling all Zen, skip the music and work out in silence.

The first time you work out, the Touch prompts you to enter your current weight. Once you do, it asks you to "pair" (electronically link) the iPod and shoe sensor so the two can communicate. If you don't get a prompt, tap Settings→Nike + iPod→Sensor to open a dialogue between the electronics in your hand and the electronics under your foot. A screen like the one on the right guides you through the process.

Once you have the shoe sensor linked and your chosen workout ready to go, tap the green ▶ button (right, bottom) to get rolling. The Touch keeps track of the time, distance, and calories for you.

If you find your playlist of soothing classical violin favorites isn't exactly pumping you up, tap the orange Change Music button to pick something livelier.

To pause a workout session to catch your breath, press the Touch's Sleep/Wake button, and then tap Pause (II) on the Lock Screen. When you're ready to start up again, tap ▶ to pick up where you left off.

Tap Settings→Nike + iPod to further personalize your workout with a power song, spoken feedback, and your weight (it may change if you keep working out, you know). The Settings screen, shown at the top of the opposite page, also holds controls for displaying metric or imperial units of measure in case you prefer to run in kilometers instead of miles.

As mentioned earlier, the Nike software comes with several stock routines in its workout library, but you can get creative with your exercise sessions. To create your own routines, tap the My Workouts icon at the bottom of the screen. Tap + and compile a new workout by selecting the Basic, Time, Distance, or Calorie options. To calibrate the Touch to your own stride, when you finish a workout, tap the End Workout button, and then tap Calibrate. (You can recalibrate the Touch by tapping Settings→Nike + iPod→Reset Calibration.)

When your workout is over, you can send all this info to your online Nike+ account via WiFi. Just tap History→Send to Nike+ to log your daily stats.

You'll learn to:

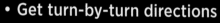

- Ask Siri to get info, launch apps, and open web pages
- Get turn-by-turn directions
- Post to Twitter and Facebook from apps
- Organize your life and appointments with apps
- Use Passbook
- Make FaceTime video calls

CHAPTER 4

Get Organized With the iPod Touch

THE IPOD FIRST MADE its mark as an entertainment device back in 2001, but as it's evolved from a humble music player to a pocket computer, it's picked up a few more capabilities. The iPod Touch of 2012 is an electronic address book, notepad, voice-memo recorder, to-do list, datebook, atlas, and dictionary. This chapter explains how to use your iPod to do all that—and to use the keyboard as efficiently as possible in the process.

Thanks to the built-in apps that come with this most versatile of iPods, you can keep your life in sync with the people in it. You can make and take video calls with FaceTime, post and read updates from pals using Twitter and Facebook, send instant messages to other iOS users, and check your Notifications Center for anything you might have missed.

The iPod Touch has other apps to keep you organized as well. You can store movie tickets, airline boarding passes, and customer-loyalty cards in Passbook, check the weather and stock market with a tap, and set the Touch's clock for multiple time zones. And if you don't have a free finger to do the tapping, you can ask Siri, the cheerful virtual assistant that comes with iOS 6 (and the latest Touch), to do the checking for you. So if you're ready to let the iPod make life just a little easier, turn the page.

Use the Touch Keyboard

THE TOUCH HAS FOUR buttons but no keys—and no physical keyboard. You type in web addresses, email messages, Game Center sign-ups, and more from the Touch's virtual keyboard. The 'board magically appears whenever you tap an area that requires typed text.

Trained typists (or those with large fingers) may find the keyboard annoying at first, but most people feel it gets easier the more they use it. To enter a letter, tap the key you want. As your finger hits the screen, a bigger version of the letter balloons briefly into view so you can visually confirm your keystroke.

The keyboard works in portrait (vertical) mode, but it's wider and easier to use in landscape (horizontal) view. It's a regular old QWERTY keyboard, with a few special keys.

1. **Shift (⇧)**. Need a capital letter? Tap this key first (it takes on an eerie white glow to show you it's in action) and then type your letter, which should appear in uppercase. After all that excitement, the ⇧ key returns to normal and your letters go back to lowercase.

2. **Backspace/Delete (⌫)**. One of the most popular keys ever. Press this one to back up and erase previously typed letters. Tap once to erase the first letter to the left. Hold the key down to have it gobble letters a bit faster, like a reverse Pac-Man. Hold it down even longer, and it whacks entire words at a time for speedier deletion.

3. **?123**. The Touch keyboard has a finite amount of space and not enough room for *all* the keys the average person uses. Tap this button when you need to type in numbers or punctuation, and the keyboard switches to a whole new set of keys. Tap the same key—which is now an **ABC** key—to return to the letters keyboard. (Want to get to a special character more quickly? Press and hold the **?123** key until the keyboard changes, and then drag your finger over to the punctuation or number you need.)

   Need even more characters? The Touch has a third keyboard tucked away. When you're on the **?123** keyboard, a **#+=** key appears. Tap it to get more obscure characters, like math symbols, brackets, and currency signs.

When you type letters into a note, an email message, a web form, or any place that's not a URL, the Touch adds a return key to the keyboard so you can jump from one line to the next. This key transforms itself to say "Join" when you type in a WiFi password, "Go" when you enter a web address, and "Search" when you enter keywords into Safari's search box.

To make up for its limited real estate, the Touch keyboard includes shortcuts that help you work faster:

- **Web addresses.** When you type in Safari's web address box, the keyboard adds a few characters to aid your URL entry, including an underscore, a slash, and a hyphen. It also provides a *.com* button so you can finish off that address fast. For URLs that end with other suffixes, like *.edu, .org, .us*, or *.net*, press and hold the *.com* button to see them all, and then slide your finger over to the one you need. Tap the Go button to take off.

- **Accented or special characters.** Need an accented letter, say an *á* instead of a regular *a*? Press and hold the *a* character to reveal a whole bunch of accented choices and slide your finger onto the one you need. This trick works on most letters that take accent marks. You can also use it to get international currency symbols by holding down the *$* key, or to get a *§* when you hold down *&*.

- **Keyboard settings shortcuts.** Tap Settings→General→Keyboard to turn on (or off) all the iPod's keyboard helper settings, like auto-capitalization (the next letter after a period gets capped), auto-correction (for catching typos), and the spell-checker that underlines suspect words in red. There's also the Enable Caps Lock setting that kicks you into all-caps mode with a double-tap of the Shift (⇧) key and the "." shortcut that inserts a period and a space at the end of a sentence when you double-tap the space bar.

If you want to communicate in another language altogether, tap International Keyboards and select the language you want—the Touch offers around 50 keyboards, including those for Arabic, Cherokee, and Korean. Tap a language in the list to add its keyboard. When you're ready to type with international flair, tap ⊕ on the keyboard (it's to the left of the space bar, as shown on the opposite page) and you can switch between languages and keyboard layouts.

You can also add text shortcuts for commonly used phrases. Just flick down to Shortcuts and tap Add New Shortcut.

Cut, Copy, Paste, and Replace by Touch

THE TOUCH HAS COME a long way as a device that can handle the conventions of modern word-processing. Yet it has no Ctrl or ⌘ key on its keyboard, so Apple incorporated tap-friendly commands for those convenient cut-copy-paste functions right into the Touch.

1. To cut or copy from text you can edit (like an outgoing email message or a note you created), double-tap a word to highlight it. A Cut | Copy | Paste box pops up. To select more words, drag the blue dots on either end of the selected word. Then tap Cut or Copy.

2. For pages you *can't* edit (like incoming emails), hold your finger down until a magnifying glass and an insertion-point cursor appear. Drag it to the text you want to copy. When you lift your finger, a Select or Select All box appears. Select gives you the blue dots you can drag to highlight more text. Select All highlights all the text. Lift your finger, and you get a Copy button.

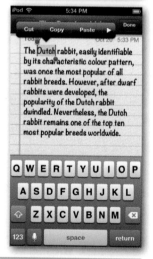

A web page works differently: When you lift your finger there, you get only a Copy button, as shown in the top-right image.

3. Tap the place where you want to paste the text—or jump to a different program and tap within it to get the Paste button.

4. Tap the Paste button to add the text to the new location.

Make a mistake and wish you could undo what you just did? Give the Touch a shake and then tap the Undo Edit button that appears on-screen.

TIP If all this tiny typing is denting your productivity when you have to do some serious text input, consider getting a wireless Bluetooth keyboard for your Touch. True, you have to haul around a big chunk of gear—unless you're at home in front of the TV. To use an external keyboard, turn on the iPod's Bluetooth chip by choosing Settings→General→Bluetooth→On, and then follow the instructions that came with the keyboard for electronically linking it to the Touch.

In addition to the Cut, Copy, and Paste options in apps where you can edit text (like Notes or Mail), you can replace a misspelled word with one that's spelled correctly—or look up its definition in the onboard dictionary by selecting it and tapping Define.

If you have the Touch's spell-check function turned on (page 26), the Touch highlights typos (and unknown words) with a red underscore so they stand out as you proofread. (You *do* proof important messages, right?) These are the words you want to replace.

You can also replace one word with a closely related one (for those times when you typed close to, but not quite, the right word).

To get the Suggest option, double-tap (or Select) a word on-screen. When the Cut | Copy | Paste box appears (top right), tap ▶ and then tap Suggest on the next part of the menu bar. The Touch offers up a few alternate words. If you see the one you *meant* to type, tap it to replace the text. If it can't find a similar word, you see a "No Replacements" message.

But enough about text—want to copy a photo or video into a message-in-progress or some other program? Hold your finger down on the screen until the Copy button pops up, as shown in the bottom right photo. Tap Copy, and then tap within the message to get a Paste button. Tap it to insert your image or video.

If you want to copy *multiple* items, like pictures out of a photo album, tap the Edit button in the top-right corner. Next, tap the photos you want to copy; red checkmarks in the corners confirm your selection. Tap the Share button in the bottom left of the toolbar, and then tap the Copy icon. Switch to the program where you want to deposit your pics (like a mail message under construction), and then press the glass until the Paste button appears.

> **TIP** Hate the Touch correcting your typing as you go? Choose Settings→General→Keyboard→Auto-Correction→Off.

Add Contacts to the Touch

PUTTING A COPY OF your contacts file—also known as your computer's address book—on your iPod is easy with the help of iTunes. (Touch owners using iCloud to sync contacts and calendars can skip to page 116.)

Windows users need to store their contacts in Outlook Express, Outlook 2003 or later, Windows Contacts, or the Windows Address Book (used by Outlook Express and some other email programs).

Mac folks need to have at least Mac OS X 10.5 (Leopard) and the Mac OS X Address Book (shown below), which Apple's Mail program uses to stash names and numbers. You can also use Entourage 2004 or later and Outlook 2011, but you have to *link* before you *sync*: In the mail program, choose Preferences, and then click Sync Services. Turn on the checkboxes for sharing contacts and calendars with Address Book and iCal (Apple's calendar program) so iTunes syncs up the info with the Touch's Address Book and iCal apps.

You need one other thing for an on-the-go contacts list: the right type of iPod. That means a Touch or Classic, or an older click-wheel Nano. Sadly, the touch-screen Nano can't display contacts, calendars, or notes.

To turn your iPod into a little black book, follow these steps:

1. Connect your iPod to your computer and click its icon in the iTunes window. (If you use Outlook or Outlook Express, launch that now, too.)

2. In the main part of the iTunes window, click the Info tab.

3. Windows owners: Turn on the checkbox next to "Sync contacts from" and use the drop-down menu to choose the program that holds your contacts. Mac owners: Turn on the "Sync Address Book contacts" checkbox. If you want to sync contact *groups*, select them from the "Selected groups" box. You can also choose to import the photos in your contacts files.

4. Click the Apply button in the lower-right corner of the iTunes window.

iTunes updates your iPod with the contact information stored in your address book. If you add new contacts while you have your iPod plugged in, choose File→Update iPod or click the Sync button in iTunes to move the new data over to your pocket player. When you decide someone doesn't deserve to be in your contacts list anymore, delete her from your computer's address book, and she'll disappear from your iPod the next time you sync up.

To look up a pal on an iPod Touch, tap the Contacts icon on the Home screen and flick your way to the person's name. Tap the name to see the person's contact info. Tap Send Message or FaceTime to directly contact your contact; tap the Share Contact button to email the info. And if you want to know more about sending Messages or starting FaceTime chats, keep reading—both of those Touch apps are covered later in this chapter.

TIP On the iPod Touch, you can sync contacts from your Google Gmail and Yahoo Mail address books. First, tap the Settings icon on the Touch's Home screen. On the Settings screen, tap Mail, Contacts, Calendars. On the next screen, tap the name of the account— Google's Gmail or Yahoo Mail. On the following screen, you can turn on wireless syncing for Contacts, Calendars, Notes, and more. If you prefer to sync over USB, import the Google or Yahoo contacts into your computer's address book and then sync the address book through iTunes. For example, in OS X 10.8 on the Mac, choose Contacts→Preferences to pull in contacts from those other accounts.

Sync Up Your Calendars

JUST AS ITUNES CAN pluck contacts out of your computer's address book, it can also snag and sync a copy of your desktop's daily or monthly schedule to your iPod Touch—*if* you use Outlook on your PC or iCal on your Mac. (You can also use Entourage 2004 or later by choosing, in Entourage, Preferences→Sync Services and turning on the option to have Entourage share events with iCal; Outlook 2011 for the Mac works similarly.) Or you could just use iCloud (page 116).

To get your calendar connected, fire up iTunes and follow these steps:

1. Connect your iPod to your computer and click the iPod's icon when it shows up at the top of the iTunes 11 window.

2. On the page full of iPod syncing options, click the Info tab. Scroll down past Contacts to Calendars.

3. Turn on the checkbox next to "Sync calendars from Microsoft Outlook" (Windows) or "Sync iCal calendars" (Mac). If you have multiple calendars, select the ones you want to copy.

4. In the lower-right corner of the iTunes window, click the Apply button.

5. If iTunes doesn't automatically start updating your iPod with your datebook, choose File→Sync iPod. If you haven't changed any sync settings and you're just *updating* contact info, iTunes' Apply button turns into a Sync button, and you can click that instead of going up to Menuville.

After the sync, it's time to check your dates. On the iPod Touch, tap the Calendar icon on the Home screen. When the current month appears on-screen, tap List, Day, or Month to see your schedule for the short or long term, or tap Today to see the current day's events.

If you synced over multiple calendars, the Touch displays events from all your datebooks on the main screen. To see one calendar at a time, tap the Calendars button in the top-left corner and select the one you want.

On any calendar, the List view shows all your upcoming appointments one after the other. In Month view, your Touch represents events with black dots and lists them by day below the calendar. Tap the black triangles on either side of the month name to go forward or backward through the months. Tap the **+** button to add an event.

A few other calendar-keeping tips:

- Turn the Touch sideways to see your calendar for the current week.

- Tap the ⬇ icon to see the meeting and event invites you've received and add them to your calendar with a tap.

- You can have your iPod remind you of upcoming events. The Touch emits a beeping on-screen alert keyed to the event reminders in your synced calendar. You can set your own alert by selecting an event and tapping the Edit button. Tap the Alert screen and pick a suitable amount of advance warning.

Map Your Way with WiFi

THE TOUCH'S RELIANCE ON a WiFi signal doesn't make it a very good navigational device when you're away from your home network or a coffee shop (unless you have a personal portable hot spot, like the Verizon MiFi). There are plenty of times, however, when getting directions and finding places on a map from the comfort of a WiFi connection comes in handy.

To plot your course, tap the Maps icon on the Home screen. With the Maps app and a network connection, you can:

- **Find yourself.** Tap the compass icon in the bottom-left corner (➤) to have the Touch pinpoint your current location within a few hundred yards. (While the Touch doesn't have a GPS chip inside it, it does have software that calculates your position based on a big database of WiFi hot spots.) To find yourself, you need to make sure you have Location Services turned on. To do that, tap Settings→Privacy→Location Services→On.

- **Find an address.** In the Address box at the top of the screen, type in an address—or tap the ⌂ icon to call up your Contacts list, where you can select the friend or business you want to map. Then tap the Search button to see a red pushpin drop onto that location.

If your location has a green car icon next to it (🚗), tap the icon to get turn-by-turn directions to there from your current location. (To get turn-by-turn directions from any two roadworthy points, see page 64.)

- **Options for map addresses.** Tap the Directions button (:≡) at the bottom of the screen. When you see your address marked on the map next to the pushpin, tap the ❯ icon to advance to a screen where you can get directions to or from that address. Your other options include adding the address to a contact file (great for filing away restaurants you want to visit again), or sharing the location details by email, iMessage, Twitter, or Facebook. You can also bookmark it for future reference. (Tap the ⌂ button to call up a screen with tabs for Bookmarks, Recents [for recent locations], and Contacts.) If you know where you're going and suspect the map is wrong (and people have criticized the Maps app in iOS 6 for inaccuracy), tap the Report a Problem button and march through the resulting screens to notify Apple.

- **Find reviews of area points-of-interest.** In iOS 6, Apple has teamed up with Yelp to provide information, photos, and reviews about restaurants, bars, stores, and other attractions on the map. When you see an icon for a local establishment—like a knife-and-fork for a restaurant or a mug for a coffee shop—tap it. If the place has been checked out by anybody on the Yelp user reviews site, you'll see a series of stars rating the place. Tap ⊙ on the place name to get to the Info tab listing its phone number, website (if it has one), and exact address. In the same box, tap Reviews (bottom left) to see more detailed thoughts from Yelp reviewers. Tap the Photos tab to see pictures taken at the location.

- **Find your view.** The Maps app offers three views of the terrain: Standard (regular old cartography with labeled streets and points-of-interest), Satellite (pictures of the area from space) and Hybrid, which puts Standard labels on Satellite photos. In iOS 6, the app now includes 3D maps in the Standard mode and the urban-friendly Flyover view in Satellite or Hybrid mode that let you zoom in and out and spin the landscape on-screen around with your fingers. To add the third dimension, tap the 3D or Flyover button (which looks like a trio of buildings) in the bottom-left corner of a map. To switch map-viewing modes, tap the curled-up corner on the bottom left to see the hidden menu (shown here at the bottom right). You can also drop a pushpin or print out your map to an AirPrint-friendly printer (page 82).

Get Turn-by-Turn Directions

The Touch may not have its own cellular connection and the ability to play GPS in the car, but you can still get turn-by-turn directions for printing out (page 82) or general reference. And if you get truly lost while you're on the road, the app can serve as a guiding beacon—just stop at a WiFi-enabled rest stop or café to have the Touch triangulate your position using hotspots.

To get the Touch telling you where to go, make sure you turn on the iPod's Location Services (page 85), and then tap the Directions button. Then:

1. In the Start box, tap to select Current Location.

2. In the End box, type in the destination address.

3. Select the driving icon (🚗). If you tap the person icon (🚶), you get walking directions. Tap the bus (🚌) and you go to the App Store to shop for mass-transit apps.

4. Tap the Route button.

5. If Maps shows you multiple paths to a destination on the Suggested Routes screen, choose one and tap Start. (You can jump right into turn-by-turn directions from any point on the map by tapping 🚗 in the place name.)

If you want to see what you're in for on any given route, select it on the Suggested Routes screen (bottom left) and tap the Directions icon (:☰) in the lower-left corner to see each turn presented in a step-by-step list (bottom middle). Once you pick a route and hit the Start button, the Touch displays each turn on the journey in a big green box on the map (bottom right). Again, this may not be so helpful unless you have WiFi access, but you can peek ahead.

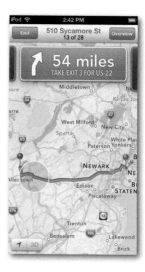

Make FaceTime Video Calls

SINCE THE EARLY DAYS of science-fiction movies and TV shows, the videophone has been a staple of fantasy communication. Cheap webcams and teleconferencing systems made the fantasy real, but they're *so* last year (and so stationary). For modern convenience, the Touch makes and takes video calls thanks to FaceTime, its built-in mobile video-chat app.

To use FaceTime, you need an Apple ID (Chapter 13) and a WiFi connection. You also need folks to talk to, namely other new Touch owners and people running around with *at least* iPad 2s and iPhone 4/4S models who have time to chat.

Once you have all that, getting started with FaceTime is easy:

1. Tap the FaceTime icon on the Home screen and sign in with your Apple ID. Fill in your vitals, like your geographic region and email address, so other FaceTimers can find and call you.

2. Once you have your account set up, tap the Contacts icon on the Home screen, tap the name of the person you want to call, and then tap the FaceTime button at the bottom of the Contacts screen. Since iPhone 4/4S/5 owners can use their phone numbers for FaceTime calls, a screen pops up asking what connection (phone digits or email address) you want to use for the call. Tap your choice. If you don't have anybody in your Contacts file, flip back to page 58, which explains how to import your computer's address book or add entries on the Touch itself.

3. When your buddy picks up the call, hold your Touch up so they can see you and start chatting. You see them, too. If the little picture-in-picture window of your face is in the way, use your finger to drag it to a new part of the screen.

4. After you wave goodbye, tap End to hang up the call.

If you need to temporarily turn off the sound during a call (like when the baby starts screaming), tap the Mute icon (🎤).

Want to show your friend what you're seeing without physically flipping the Touch around? Tap the 📷 icon in the bottom-right corner to switch to the Touch's rear camera. Tap the icon again to return the view to you.

Keep Time with the Touch Clock

THE IPOD TOUCH HAS a Clock app, but it's more than just a digital pocket watch. It's actually *four* clocks in one: World Clock, Alarm, Stopwatch, and a Timer. Here's how to work them all.

World Clock

The Touch should already have a couple of clocks: one you created when you first set up your player and selected your time zone, and one for (of all places) Cupertino, California, home of Apple HQ. To add new cities around the world:

❶ Tap Home→Clock→World Clock.

❷ Tap the **+** button in the upper-right corner of the screen.

❸ When the keyboard pops up, start typing in the name of any large city.

❹ Tap the name of the city to add its clock to your list.

If you want to rearrange your list of clocks, tap the Edit button and use the three-stripe gripstrip (≡) to drag them into the order you want.

To delete a clock, tap the Edit button, tap the ⊖ icon next to the clock's name, and then tap Delete.

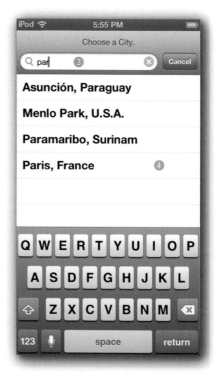

Alarm

Need a personalized wake-up call from that power nap or an alert for some other timed event? The Touch comes with its own built-in alarm clock. To set it, tap Home→Clock→Alarm. On the main Alarm screen, tap the + button and then spin the wheels (shown top right) to set the time for the alarm to sound. Tap the Sound button to pick a song or a tone to play when the alarm goes off. You can also have the alarm repeat regularly, give it a name, and even add a snooze button if you need another 10 minutes of sleep. Press Done when you finish.

Stopwatch

To get to the Touch's stylish full-screen stopwatch, tap Home→Clock→Stopwatch.

To start timing yourself, tap the green Start button. The timer starts counting, and the Start button turns into a red Stop button. (Tap that when you're done timing.) If you're running a series of laps, tap the gray Lap button each time you finish a turn on the track. The iPod records your time for that lap (shown middle right) and then starts timing your next one.

The iPod displays the time for the lap-in-progress above the overall session timer. It lists the time for completed laps below the timer, so you can track your workout. The timer keeps ticking even if you tap your way to another program. When you return to the stopwatch, it's still going.

If you need to pause the timer, tap the Stop button; to pick up where you left off counting, tap Start again. When you're finally done, tap the Stop button to halt the clock. To clear the times from the screen, hit the gray Reset button.

Timer

Want to make sure the roast doesn't burn? Tap Home→Clock→Timer and dial up a period of time (shown at bottom right) to count. Tap "When Timer Ends" and pick an alert sound, and then tap Start.

Notes, Weather, Stocks, and Calculator

THE MULTIMEDIA APPS ON the Touch may get a lot of attention, but a humble quartet of utilities adds to this iPod's usefulness and helps you stay organized with the ability to jot down quick thoughts, check the forecast, keep tabs on the stock market, and do a few calculations.

Notes

When you need to write up something in a hurry—like a grocery list or an idea for the Great American Novel—tap the Notes icon on the Home screen. The Touch keyboard slides up, ready for action (right). Tap **+** to add a new note, and tap 🗑 to delete one. To call up a previously typed note, tap its name in the main Notes list. To email or print a note, tap 📤.

If you have Google, Yahoo, or AOL mail accounts set to sync wirelessly, you can sync their Notes, too. Tap Settings→Mail, Contacts, Calendars; tap the name of your account; and tap the Notes button to On. And you can sync notes through iCloud (page 116). Hate the Notes font? Tap Settings→Notes to change it (above).

Weather

On the Home screen, tap the Weather icon to get temperatures and hourly forecasts for your favorite locations. To add cities to your list:

1. Tap the encircled **i** in the bottom-right corner of the screen to flip it around; you can delete existing cities here by tapping ⊖ and reorder them by dragging them up or down by the grip strip (≡).

2. Tap the **+** button in the upper-right corner to add towns by name or ZIP code. Tap Done when you finish.

3. To cycle through your cities when you open the weather app, swipe a finger across screen to whip through them.

If you were checking the forecast ahead of a trip to the area, tap ! in the bottom-left corner of the Weather app to get Yahoo's event info for that locale.

Stocks

When you tap open the Stock app from the Home screen, you get an eyeful of financial information—including, if you like, updates on your own market holdings.

To add your stocks to your palm-sized Big Board:

1. Tap the tiny ❷ in the bottom-right corner.

2. The screen spins around. You can whack unwanted stocks listed here by tapping ⊖ and reorder them by dragging them up or down by the grip strip (≡).

3. Tap the **+** button in the upper-right corner to type in a company name or stock's ticker symbol. Tap Done when you finish.

When you tap open the Stocks app now, you get a snapshot of current trading prices for your selected stocks, (delayed 20 minutes or so). On the main Stocks screen, flick the bottom panel to browse through three screens of information about a selected stock, including a quick-look chart of its 52-week performance, sales graphs, and recent headlines about the company. Tap ❸! to get company info from Yahoo Finance.

Turn the Touch sideways and tap to see the stock's trading price rise and fall over a day, a week, a month, 3 months, 6 months, 1 year, or 2 years, plus a quick look at the big indexes like the Dow Jones Industrials, NASDAQ, and the S&P 500.

Calculator

Need to divide the dinner bill or do some light trigonometry to unwind after a long day? Tap the Home→Utilities→Calculator to get a big, bright math machine, ready to divide and conquer.

Hold the Touch in landscape mode to get a scientific calculator for higher-level math functions.

Command Siri

IT'S A BUSY WORLD and everybody needs a little help sometime. Imagine how great it would be if you could ask your Touch to take on a task, like automatically add your next dentist appointment to your calendar or fire up a text message to remind your spouse to bring home cat treats after work—just like those people with iPhones running Apple's Siri virtual assistant software.

Now, the good news for many Touch owners: Siri has *arrived*. To use this sassy little helper program with the big personality, you need:

- The latest hardware, namely the 5th-generation iPod Touch
- The latest iPod operating system: iOS 6 or later
- An active Internet connection.

Once you have all that, you're ready to make Siri work for you. The feature is turned on and ready to go by default if you're running iOS 6, but if you want to make sure, visit Home→Settings→General→Siri and confirm Siri is set to On.

Using Siri

On the surface, summoning Siri is simple: hold down the Touch's Home button until you hear two beeps and the program appears on-screen with a cheery "What can I help you with?" note above a microphone. This indicates that Siri is listening and ready to serve.

Now it's your turn to tell her what you want. Since Siri works with a huge number of apps within iOS 6 (including the Clock, Reminders, and more), you have plenty of options. You can have Siri:

- Show you directions to a place on a map
- Post a comment to Facebook or Twitter, or send an instant message
- Look up movie times or baseball stats
- Search the Web
- Check your calendar
- Play a song by a specific artist
- Settle movie trivia arguments

In fact, Siri can do so much, you may not know where to start. If you'd just like to see what Siri can do, tap the ❶ on the right side of Siri's question box. That brings up a list of the things Siri does, with brief examples of how to ask for them in Siri-speak.

Once you ask for something, Siri does her best to perform the task or bring back the information requested. If she can't, she apologizes politely in her sincere little lady robot voice. (And don't ask her to "open the pod bay doors," either— she's a little sensitive about HAL 9000 jokes.)

Customizing Siri

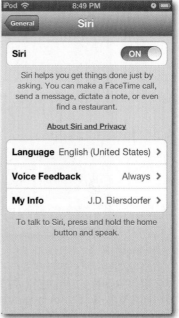

Siri works best when she understands who you are, where you live, who you're related to, and other little details about your life. When the program has this information, you can say, "Call my wife" or "What good pizza places are near work?" and Siri already knows who to call and where to look for pies.

To add your personal information, tap to Home→Settings→General→Siri→My Info. The Touch displays your own Contacts file card where you can make sure you filled in your home and work addresses. If you use Siri as a guide to nearby businesses, you need to have the iPod's Location Services feature (page 85) activated; just go to Settings→Location Services→On so Siri knows where you are.

Siri is powerful—but it can also use up a lot of power. To turn her off when your iPod's battery is feeling low, go to Home→Settings→General→Siri→Off.

Record Voice Memos

THE TOUCH DOESN'T JUST *play* sound, it *records* it, too, thanks to its Voice Memos feature. Voice Memos can be helpful when you have a sudden brainstorm, need to leave instructions for subordinates, or other situations where it's easier to talk instead of type. When you get done recording, you can share your immortalized musings by emailing them or messaging them directly from your iPod. You can also sync them back to iTunes to keep a copy on your computer.

To take a vocal memo, tap Home→Utilities→Voice Memos and then:

1. To start recording, tap the red dot. You can pause your recording by tapping the Touch's on-screen Pause icon; tap it again to continue recording.

2. Tap the black square on the right side of the screen to stop recording. To play back a recording, tap the ☰ icon and select the recording from the Voice Memos menu.

3. To delete a recording, select it on the Voice Memos menu, and then press the Delete button, as shown above-right.

The Touch has a Share button on the same screen that lets you send the recording as an email attachment or message (above, right). If you tap the recording's ⊙ icon, you get a Trim Memo button that lets you edit the clip. On this same screen, tap the recording's name to assign it a predefined label, like "Interview."

If your iPod is set to sync, iTunes offer to copy your recordings to its Voice Memos playlist the next time you make the iPod-iTunes connection.

Use Messages

THANKS TO THE MESSAGES app in iOS 5 and later, Touch owners now have a way to send free, unlimited text messages, photos, and videos to people running Messages on *their* iPads, iPhones, and Touches. It works over a WiFi connection on the iPod Touch. Setting up Messages takes just a few steps:

1. On the Home screen, tap open the Messages app. The first time you start it up, it asks you to enter your Apple ID. (If you've blown off Apple's previous 18 attempts to get you to sign up for an account, tap Create New Account and follow along on-screen.) The email address you use with your Apple ID is the one people need in order to send you iMessages.

2. To add more email addresses to your Message accounts, tap open the Settings icon on the Touch's Home screen and, in the left column of icons, tap Messages. Tap the "Receive At" line, and then type in the addresses. (The Settings screen also has a button to turn off iMessage if you don't want to be pestered.)

3. Once you sign up, you can send messages to others who have registered with Apple. Tap open Messages on the Home screen, tap the ☑ icon, and then enter the address of your recipient. Type your message in the text field at the bottom of the screen, and then tap Send.

4. Tap ◎ if you want to include a picture or video from your Camera Roll—or shoot a new pic for the occasion.

To see your previous conversations, tap the Messages button in the upper-left corner of the screen. A list of earlier chats appear on-screen. From here, you can tap open a conversation to review or restart it. To whack old chatter, tap the Edit button, select the conversations, tap the ⊖ icon next to each one, and then tap the Delete button.

Unlike a cellphone text plan, which ties your message Inbox to your mobile number, Messages works by email address. This means you can get your messages on several iOS 5 or iOS 6 devices to keep your conversations going. And, unlike a cellphone text plan, Messages is *free*—making it an affordable way to keep up with your pals, as long as they're all using recent iOS gadgets, too.

Set Up Reminders

THE IPOD TOUCH'S TO-DO List app is called Reminders, and its Home-screen icon awaits your tap. With Reminders, you can jot down tasks you need to complete in the near or far future and have the iPod alert you when you forget a chore. If you have an iCloud account (page 116), you can view your reminders on the Web as well, and Mac users running OS X 10.8 (Mountain Lion) can sync them up in the system's Reminders app.

Here's how to get started:

1. Tap open the Reminders app and tap the **+** icon to add a new task.

2. Hit the Return key on the Touch keyboard to add the reminder to the list.

3. On the main Reminders list screen, tap the **>** at the end of a line to add more information about the task and set a priority for it, as well as the date and time you want to be reminded. Tap Done when you finish.

 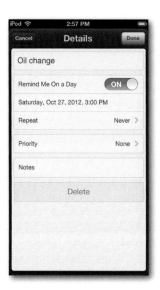

Once you complete a task, tap ☐ to put a check in the box and move the chore to your Completed list. To get to this searchable list of your past, present, and future reminders, tap the ≡ button in the upper-left corner.

> **TIP** If your email account supports Reminders, like iCloud, Yahoo, and Microsoft Exchange do, you can get pestered there, too. Tap Home→Settings→Mail, Contacts, Calendars→[Your Mail Account] and flip on Reminders.

Use the Passbook E-Wallet App

MOVIE TICKETS AND AIRLINE boarding passes were some of the first things to move from paper to pixels, and now Apple hopes to help you keep track of 'em. In iOS 6, the iPod Touch now sports an app called Passbook out on its Home screen, designed to be a holding pen for those digitized tickets, boarding passes, customer-loyalty cards, coupons, and other chunks of wallet-filler.

To use Passbook, you need a two things:

- **A Passbook-enabled app.** The first time you open Passbook, it offers to take you to the App Store to find some. Several companies, including American Airlines, Starbucks, Walgreen's, Fandango, were early in with Passbook-ready apps. The Web is another place to get *passes* (like digital loyalty cards or electronic concert tickets) from retailers.

- **An iCloud account (page 116).** You need to be signed in to iCloud to add passes to Passbook. You also need make sure Passbook and Documents & Data are enabled. To do so, go to Home→Settings→iCloud→Passbook→On and Home→Settings→iCloud→Documents & Data→On.

After you accept an app's offer to add a pass (shown below on the left), the pass joins your Passbook app. To open the pass, say, when you're buying toothpaste at Walgreen's and want to earn purchase points, tap open the Passbook app (shown below on the right) and tap the name of the pass. The cashier scans it right on your Touch. If you have a WiFi signal and Location Services turned on, your pass for that store may appear on the Touch's screen automatically.

To delete a pass from Passbook, tap ❶ in the corner, and then tap 🗑.

Add Twitter and Facebook Accounts

SOCIAL NETWORKING, PRIMARILY IN the form of Twitter and Facebook, has become so ubiquitous that Apple built support for these two services right into iOS 6. If you have an account with either site, here's how to set it up on your Touch. Once you do, you can quickly share links, photos, and more to your followers and friends online by tapping ➦ within the Safari, Photos, or other compatible app and choosing Twitter or Facebook from the menu.

Twitter

Twitter, for those who haven't been paying attention the past few years, is a microblogging service; it lets you update friends about your activities or musings. Millions of people use it to report what they see or feel, check for public announcements, and share links to photos and web pages. You have 140 characters per message to express your thoughts. And it's free.

Technically, Twitter is not a built-in app, but so many iPod programs offer a tweet option that it's best covered in this part of the book. To get full use of the Twitter experience with your iPod apps and see reactions to the things you share, you can install the Twitter app right from the Settings screen:

1. Tap Home→Settings→Twitter.

2. Tap the Install button to snag the program from the App Store. (You need to have an App Store account and password to get the app, so check out page 122 if you don't.)

3. If you already have a Twitter account, you don't need to install the app if you just want to tweet out links and photos from your Touch. Type in your Twitter user name and password on the settings screen and tap Sign In.

4. If you're new to this Twitter thing but want to take the plunge right on your iPod, tap the Create New Account button and follow along.

So now that you have Twitter installed and your personal Twitter account set up, what do you do with it on your Touch? If you're an experienced Twitter user, you've probably already put this book down and gone off to post a few tweets to your pals.

If you're brand-new to Twitter, you should take a spin over to the Support area of Twitter's site. The company offers an online guide to the service and its search feature so you can find out what everyone is tweeting about. The guide is at *http://support.twitter.com/groups/31-twitter-basics*.

Facebook

Like, Twitter, Facebook is also more tightly integrated into the iPod's apps in iOS 6. For example, if you're in the Photos app and want to post a picture to Facebook, just tap the Action Menu (📤) and select Facebook—instead of having to open the Facebook app, tap the Add Photo button, navigate to the picture in your Photos app, and *then* upload it. Quickly posting links to Facebook from Safari works the same way.

To take advantage of all this convenience, you need to install the Facebook app on your Touch and configure your Facebook account. Fortunately, you can do it all in the same place:

1. Tap Home→Settings→Facebook.

2. If you don't have the Facebook app installed already, tap the Install button, This takes you to the App Store, where you can download the free app. (You do need an Apple ID for this, see page 240 if you haven't signed up yet.)

3. If you're one of the few people in the civilized world without a Facebook account to begin with, tap Create New Account and follow along.

4. Once you install the Facebook app, go back to Home→Settings→Facebook and enter your Facebook user name and password. A privacy notice appears, identifying the personal information on your iPod that Facebook can access, like the info in Photos and Contacts. If you have privacy issues, turn off access to certain apps, like Contacts and Calendars, here. If you don't have issues, you can even sync your Contacts with Facebook.

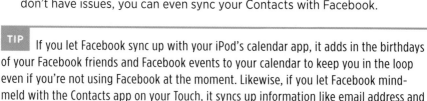

TIP If you let Facebook sync up with your iPod's calendar app, it adds in the birthdays of your Facebook friends and Facebook events to your calendar to keep you in the loop even if you're not using Facebook at the moment. Likewise, if you let Facebook mind-meld with the Contacts app on your Touch, it syncs up information like email address and phone numbers your Facebook pals have posted on their profiles.

Use Notifications

THE IPOD'S NATIVE APPS can keep track of your life, from bugging you about meetings to reminding you to buy milk on the way home. And once you visit Settings→Notifications and turn on alerts for the apps you want to hear from, you'll get little on-screen notifications no matter what you're doing on the iPod.

But wouldn't it be great to have just *one* place where you can review pressing matters, like calendar appointments, email messages, or pending to-do list items?

Thankfully, there is such a Dashboard of Your Life. It's called the Notifications screen. To see it from anywhere or any app on your Touch, just place your finger at the very top edge of the screen and drag downward, like you're pulling down a miniature window shade. The Notifications screen appears.

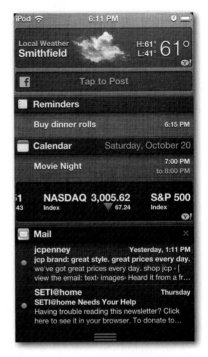

You can get a quick hit of data and jump to any listed app or message by tapping it. Notifications also appear on the iPod's Lock Screen so you don't miss anything when you're not using your Touch. To go right to a notice, put your finger on the app's icon or message and slide it to the right. This simultaneously unlocks the Touch and opens the app that's badgering you for attention.

Customizing Notifications

By default, the Notifications screen shows you basic info-nuggets, like pending reminders, calendar appointments, stock prices, and any new email messages that have arrived. But like most things on the Touch, you can customize your Notifications screen by adding apps to it, removing them, or resorting them.

To do all this, tap Settings→Notifications. As shown at the top of the opposite page, you can sort the displayed apps manually or by time (meaning the newest notices appear highest up). To manually sort the apps, tap the Edit button in the top-right corner and use the grip strip (≡) to drag them into a new order. Tap an app's name to turn its notifications on or off—or to further customize its display with one of two on-screen styles (a small, top-of-the-screen "banner" or a larger, middle-of-the-screen "alert").

No matter when a notification pops onto your screen, you can always review it by dragging down the Notifications screen. To dismiss the screen, place your finger at the bottom of it and flick upwards. Consider yourself notified.

The "Do Not Disturb" Setting

The Touch can alert you to all sorts of events, but if you want to lock in a little peace and quiet, hang out the iPod's "Do Not Disturb" sign.

1. Tap Settings→Notifications→Do Not Disturb→On.

2. On the Do Not Disturb screen (shown here), tap to enter a time range when you regularly do not want to be interrupted by alerts and calls. You can allow a specific group of contacts to still call you anyway, as well as someone who may be calling repeatedly.

3. If you just want a temporary respite from alerts without formally scheduling hours, tap Settings→Do Not Disturb→On. Reverse the process to restore alerts.

Use the iPod Dictionary

AS YOU MAY HAVE noticed from tapping text to cut, copy, paste, or replace misspelled words, a Define option can also appear in the pop-up menu. This launches the iPod's global dictionary, a built-in reference that works with most apps. It defines words in real time, so you need an Internet connection for it to work.

Using the dictionary is easy—when you see a word you don't recognize in a text-oriented app like Safari or Mail, tap it twice (or press and hold it for a second) to select it. Then tap the Define option from the pop-up menu (below left). The dictionary looks up the word and presents the definition on a new screen (below right). When you're done with the dictionary, tap the Done button in the top-right corner to dismiss it and return to your previous screen.

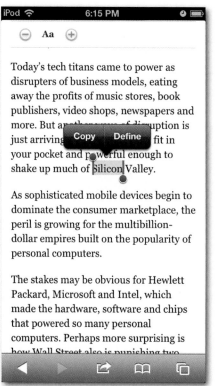

Some words may have long and varied definitions, so flick down the box to see all the noun, verb, adjective, and adverb forms. And some words, like "superior," may double as place names, as in Superior, Wisconsin.

Search the iPod Touch

ONCE YOU GET YOUR Touch fully loaded, you may actually want to find something on it—a certain song in your music library, a calendar appointment you need to reference, or someone's address, for example. If you have your 64-gigabyte Touch filled to the max, you may not want to wade around looking for that needle-in-a-data haystack. You can, however, shine the *Spotlight* on it.

Spotlight is the iPod's built-in tool for introspection and self-searching. It scans your Touch for words, apps, phrases, names, titles, and more. You can call up songs, appointments, email messages with directions to a house party, and all sorts of other things. You get to Spotlight a few ways:

- If you're on your first Home screen, press the Home button to call up Spotlight.

- If you're a few Home screens deep, flick backwards from left to right until you *pass* your first Home screen and arrive at the Spotlight screen, where you can flick no further.

Once you're on the Spotlight screen, type the name or words you're looking for ("Doctor Rosado" or "Harrigan" or "Pensacola"). Spotlight searches as you type, narrowing its results as you continue. On the results screen, tap any item to open it. You can even launch one of your apps from the list—which is a great way to fire up programs after you fill up your 11 Home screens with icons and don't have any place to display new app icons.

Flick to the bottom of the list and you get the option to search for your topic on the Web and Wikipedia via Safari. And with iOS 6 on a 5th-generation Touch, you can get Siri to do the searching for you (page 70).

TIP Tired of songs by The Smiths popping up when you search for messages from your cousins—also named Smith? You can fine-tune your Spotlight search results to weed out certain types of files. Just tap Home→Settings→General→Spotlight Search and turn off the checkmarks next to items like Music or Videos.

Print from Your Touch

YOU PRETTY MUCH HAVE two ways to print messages, photos, and other documents from your iPod Touch: apps or AirPrint.

The App Store (Chapter 6) offers dozens of utility programs that let you print files from your iPod on your home printer. Some may be more elegant than others, but odds are you can find something in the Store that'll have you printing for less than $10.

If you've never searched the Store for an app, page 123 shows you how; just type *print* into the App Store's search box and go to town. When you find an app that appeals to you from its description and reviews, buy it, install it, and follow the app's directions for printing.

The other way to print uses Apple's *AirPrint* technology. This approach can be more expensive—you need a compatible printer—but ultimately easier to use because the technology is built into your iPod, so you're not at the mercy of a third-party app.

AirPrint works with more than 75 printer models—many of them made by HP, with assorted entries from Brother, Canon, Epson, and Lexmark playing along. So if you don't have an AirPrint printer in the house, you have to buy one, which can cost at least $90. You can see a list of AirPrint printers at *http://support. apple.com/kb/ht4356*.

AirPrint has become much more widespread than it used to be. Here's how it works:

1. Find an AirPrint-ready printer. If you just bought one to use with your iOS devices, follow the printer's setup instructions for adding it to your wireless network. (You may have to upgrade certain models, like the HP Photosmart D110a, with a firmware update from the manufacturer; check the printer's manual for specific steps.)

2. Pick a file on your iPod Touch that you want to print. AirPrint works with Mail, Safari, Maps, iBooks, and pictures from both the Photos and Photo Booth apps. Other apps from the App Store, like iWork and the note-organizing Evernote, also offer the Print option. With a file open, tap ➦ and choose Print. (In Mail, tap ↰; in Maps, tap the bottom-right corner to get to the Print command .)

3. Tap Select Printer. The iPod searches your network for all the AirPrint machines it can locate and presents you with a list of the ones it finds. Tap the name of your printer to select it.

4. With your printer now selected, tap the Printer Options arrow to go back to the main Print box. Tap the + and - buttons to increase or decrease the number of copies you print.

5. Tap the Print button and listen for the sound of your printer whirring.

Once you configure AirPrint the first time, the Touch remembers your printer and offers it as the default choice the next time you need to make paper. If you add additional AirPrint printers to your network and want to switch to one of those, tap its name next to Printer in the Printer Options box.

Managing Print Jobs

Like other computers, the iPod Touch shows you how many print jobs you have lined up. It also gives you the chance to cancel a job if you change your mind—or you realize you just told the Touch to print 22 copies instead of two.

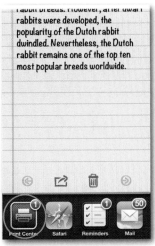

To see the jobs in your print queue, double-click the Home button and swipe through the apps panel until you see the Print Center icon (circled). Tap it to see a summary of your print jobs (below right). Tap Cancel Printing to stop a job and save that ink and paper for another time.

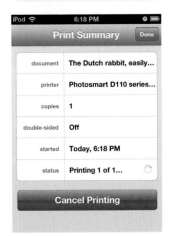

TIP If you don't have or want an AirPrint printer, hit the Web. For example, Netputing's AirPrint Activator for Mac OS X (*netputing.com/airprintactivator*) lets iOS devices see and use a network printer; you can find a Windows version with a quick Web search. These solutions might require trust and technical fiddling, but they often get the job done fine.

Set Privacy Settings on the Touch

SOME PEOPLE MAY NOT care what information app developers and social-networking sites collect about them or what personal data these groups can grab off your Touch. If you're one of them, feel free to skip this section. However, if you want to know if that fun photo app you got from the App Store is grabbing a copy of your Contacts list for itself or what apps can see the physical location of your iPod Touch (and therefore, *you*) read on.

New to iOS 6, the Privacy settings page is a centralized place where you can see all the apps that request access to certain parts of your iPod. These include both built-in *and* third-party apps that want access to the contents of your Photos app, your contacts and calendars, your location settings—even your Facebook and Twitter accounts.

Most of the time, these requests are perfectly fine and necessary for an app to function. After all, how is the Maps app supposed to give you directions unless it can tap into the iPod's Location Services and pull in your coordinates from its great big database of WiFi hotspots and other data it used to figure our where you are? Still, some apps may be a little sneakier about the data they peek at (often for advertising reasons).

So, to see who's looking at what on your iPod (and turn off access to stuff you don't want to share), tap Home→Settings→Privacy.

Privacy and Location Services

The iPod's quasi-GPS function, known as Location Services, pins your presence on a map by way of its WiFi signal. While useful for getting Siri to figure out where you are and for Maps (and Yelp check-ins at restaurants in places that have WiFi access), you may not always want to be located. To turn off the tracker, tap Home→Settings→Privacy→Location Services→Off.

The Location Services screen also shows you a list of apps requesting your whereabouts. As shown below on the left, you can tap the On or Off button next to each app's name to approve or deny the request.

You can also see what iOS 6 *functions* use your location data. On the Locations Services screen, tap System Services (shown below on the right) to see a list with an On/Off switch next to each service. Denying your location information to a system service may impede the iPod from things like finding your correct time zone based on your current location, but you do have the power to say No if you want to.

If you'd prefer not to have on-screen advertisements in apps stalking you as you travel around, you can flip off the setting for Location-Based iAds here as well. And if you're curious about what triggers an app to use your location, a list on the System Services screen explains (below right).

> **TIP** You can make the Touch tell you when an app wants your location information without having to burrow through the Privacy settings. Tap Settings→Privacy→Location Services→Status Bar Icon→On to have the tablet display the ➚ icon in its status bar when an app taps into your coordinates.

You'll learn to:

- Get your Touch online
- Use Safari's new features
- Create and sync bookmarks
- Post links to Facebook and Twitter
- Write, send, and recieve email
- Set up an iCloud account

CHAPTER 5

Surf the Web and Manage Email On the Touch

IF YOU HAVE AN iPod Touch, you know that it can download and run apps from the App Store (Chapter 6). But your Touch comes with a pre-installed app that, in terms of cool factor, is the equal of anything you can find in Apple's online emporium: Safari, Apple's versatile web browser, scaled down and redesigned for your Touch. Safari lets you comfortably surf the World Wide Web from wherever you can hop onto a WiFi connection.

You may already use Safari on your Mac, so using it on your Touch will feel familiar. But browsing on the Touch is a little different from surfing on a full-size computer screen, with *little* being the operative word here. Never fear—this chapter shows you the techniques, tips, and tricks you need to get big results out of that small window to the Web.

Surfing with Safari isn't the only advantage of a WiFi-enabled Touch. You can use Apple's free online storage locker, iCloud, to keep your contacts, calendars, and other personal information in sync across your computer and all your devices running iOS 5 and later.

Get Your WiFi Connection

TO JUMP ONTO THE Web with your Touch, you first need to *get connected* to the Internet. That's pretty easy, thanks to the sheer abundance of wireless networks these days—in homes, coffee shops, airports, hotels, college campuses, libraries, and more. WiFi, like love, is all around.

WiFi is geekspeak for *wireless fidelity*, a networking technology that lets you connect to the Internet over radio waves instead of wires. Also known as 802.11, it's the same technology that lets desktop PCs, laptops, game consoles, and other devices connect to the Web over the air. When you come across a network you can tap into, you've found what's called a *WiFi hotspot*.

Odds are you jumped on your home WiFi network when you activated your brand-new Touch (page 16). If you didn't, here's what to do:

1. Fire up a 'Net-needy app like Safari or Mail. Your iPod scans the airwaves for a WiFi signal and presents you with a list of available networks. If you don't get one, tap Home→Settings→Wi-Fi→On.

2. In the "Select a Wi-Fi Network" box, tap the name of the network you want to join.

3. If you select one with a small lock icon (🔒) next to its name, you need a password to join it. Type in the password when the Touch prompts you (on the next screen), and you're ready to start surfing. The 📶 icon at the top of the Touch means you're network-connected.

Thankfully, the Touch remembers your network name and password. So if it detects a previously used network that's up, running, and in range, it jumps back onto that network without fuss, and the 📶 icon at the top of your screen confirms your connection.

If the Touch can't find a previous network, it pops up the "Select a Wi-Fi Network" screen again, listing nearby hotspots, and you start the first-time connection dance all over again. See the next page for directions.

At home and confused about why your own network didn't link your Touch (review your typing) or isn't showing up in the list of hotspots? Check your network's modem and wireless router (the box with the blinking lights that broadcasts the network signal from your modem) to make sure everything's working.

Find More Hotspots

The Touch is great at suggesting nearby networks, and you may quickly find one you can join. But you'll see only a couple of them in the "Select a Wi-Fi Network" box, usually the ones with the strongest signal and no password requirement—the iPod tries to provide a solid, simple connection.

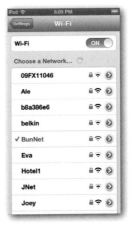

While that keeps the list short and tidy (especially in big cities with lots of networks), it's not the full list of nearby nets. And the list also doesn't show *hidden* networks, where the owner has decided to not publicly broadcast the network's name for security reasons.

To see a list of *all* nearby *visible* networks, go to the iPod's Home screen and tap Settings→Wi-Fi. On the list that comes up, tap the name of the network you want to join.

Don't see the network you want in the list? Odds are it's one of those "hidden" ones. Tap Other and move on to the next screen. In the box, type in the exact name of the network. You also need to know the type of security the network uses (like WPA2 or WEP; you may have to ask the owner, if that's not you) and its password so you can join your pal's network for gaming or other WiFi fun.

Use Commercial Hotspots

Although your home and office WiFi networks are free, that's not always the case when you're on the go. Airports, hotels, and other places offer *commercial* hotspots. When you try to join one of these pay-to-play networks, you get a screen requesting your billing information before you can do anything online. (Before you start typing, make sure you're in a legitimate hotspot by checking the network name posted in the hotel room or airport waiting area. Fake hotspots are out there, so be careful.)

If you travel a lot, getting a long-term, discounted account with a hotspot vendor like Boingo, T-Mobile, or AT&T may save you money in the long run.

TIP Tired of the Touch bugging you to join hotspots when you don't need to—or even want to? From the Home screen, tap Settings→Wi-Fi. At the bottom of the screen, tap the Off button next to "Ask to Join Networks." You can reverse this process later if you decide you do want to be 'Net-connected.

Take a Safari Tour

READY TO SURF? ON the Touch, Safari is your on-ramp to the Web. By default, it occupies the third icon on the Home screen's bottom row (below left), but you can put it anywhere (page 21). The first time you tap open Safari, a blank browser window appears (below middle). Tap its address bar to summon the Touch keyboard (below right) so you can type in a Web address. Once you do, hit the keyboard's blue Go button to jump to that site.

So how do you use Safari once you get out on the Web? Here's a guided tour of the program's bars and buttons, starting from the upper-left:

- **Address bar.** As shown in action on the right-most screen above, this narrow strip of typeable turf is where you enter a page's web address (also known as its *URL* or Uniform Resource Locator—a term that dates back to the early days of the Web, when programmers and scientists were its big users.)

- **✕, ↻ (Stop, Reload).** See a typo after you enter an address or change your mind about going to a site? Click the ✕ button in the address bar to stop loading the page-in-progress.

NOTE The iPod Touch runs pretty much the same operating system (OS) as the iPhone, and Apple usually releases OS updates a few times a year. While some updates are simply security fixes, the company does occasionally make bigger overhauls, like redesigning the Safari interface. If your copy of Safari doesn't look exactly like the one pictured here, odds are you're running a version of the Touch's OS released before or after iPhone/iPod Touch OS 6.0.1. You can see what flavor OS you have by tapping Home→Settings→General→ About→Version.

After you tap Go, a Blue Progress Bar of Loading displays the page's download status. Once the page appears on-screen, Safari converts that ✖ button to a ↻. Tap this circular-arrow icon to reload the page if, say, you're checking sports scores or election results and want the absolute latest news—or if the page doesn't look right and you want to download it again.

- **Search box.** The lilliput search box in the upper-right corner of the screen is now a staple of most desktop browsers, and mini-Safari follows suit. Tap the box and type in your keywords, and then tap the blue Search button that appears in the bottom-right corner. (See page 103 to select a search engine—you have your choice of Google, Yahoo Search, or Microsoft Bing.)

- **◄, ► (Back, Forward).** The first two icons on Safari's bottom toolbar let you navigate backward and forward through the pages you visit during an Internet session. Tap ◄ to go back to the page you were just on. When you do that, you now have the option to return to the page you just left with a tap of the ► button.

- 🖼 **(Share menu).** Tap here to do one of nine things. You can bookmark the current page, add the page to your Reading List for later consumption, or add a shortcut to that page on your Home screen. If you're in a sharing mood, you can also send a link to the page in an email message (which brings up the Touch's mail app with the link already embedded) or a message over Apple's iMessage network, share it with your Facebook or Twitter pals, or print out a copy with your AirPrint-compatible printer. Page 104 explains this menu in detail.

- 📖 **(Bookmarks).** By tapping this icon, you can see all the bookmarks you've added to the Touch (page 97), along with any you synced over from your desktop or laptop computer (page 98).

- ⬚, ⬚ **(Pages).** You're not stuck with just one active web page at a time, and this icon (in the bottom-right corner) tells you how many pages you currently have open. See page 106 for more on multiple web pages.

Zoom and Scroll Web Pages

WHEN THE IPHONE AND iPod Touch first appeared in 2007, many new owners spent hours zooming and scrolling through web pages because it was cool, fun, and novel. It was also useful, because a lot of websites hadn't yet developed easy-to-read mobile versions of their sites, with type and graphics designed to maximize readability on the small screen (see page 101).

Thanks to the global invasion of smartphones, many sites have jumped on the mobile bandwagon, so the problem isn't so bad anymore. But even when a site offers a mobile edition, you sometimes need to see the full-size version. Happily, when you type in the address of a "desktop" website today, the Touch scrunches down the site's pages into palm-size replicas.

So now you can see a whole web page at once, but can you read it? Probably not, unless you have extremely good (even microscopic) vision. Here's where Safari on the Touch shows its versatility, because it offers multiple ways to make that page readable:

- **Rotate the Touch.** Need just a bit of a size boost? Turn the Touch 90 degrees to the left or the right so you get a wider viewing window, which is known by its formal name, *landscape mode*.

- **Zoom and pinch.** Place your thumb and forefinger (or whichever fingers you prefer) together on the screen and slowly spread them apart to zoom in on (enlarge) the part of the page between your fingers. To go in the opposite direction and *reduce* the size of the selected area, move your spread fingers closer together in a pinch formation (the same way you harassed your siblings in the back of the car on family vacations).

- **Double-tap.** Web pages are made up of different sections, and Safari can isolate each one and magnify just that part. Find the section of a page you want to read and double-tap it to expand it to the width of the Touch's screen. Double-tap the area again to reduce the section to its original size.

Double-tap

When you zoom in on a page and want to read a part that's out of view, simply drag your finger on the glass to pull that section to the center. You can also scroll around a page quickly by flicking your finger. As your finger flies around, you'll pass over links, but Safari knows you're in transit and doesn't open them. To actually click a link, stop scrolling and tap the link with your finger.

> **TIP** Ever hit one of those page-within-a-page situations (also known as a *frame*), where the inner window has its own scroll bar but you can't scroll inside it without scrolling the outer page? Don't you just hate that? Never fear, Safari Touch can handle it. Just place *two* fingers on the frame and gently drag them up or down to scroll through just that part of the page.

Surf with Safari

USING SAFARI ON YOUR Touch, you can freely roam around the Web in several ways:

- **Typing.** As mentioned earlier, you can go to just about any page on the Web as long as you can type in its address correctly.

- **Bookmarks.** These shortcuts to favorite sites work like they do on desktop and laptop PCs, except that you tap them instead of clicking them.

- **History.** Yes, Safari for the Touch keeps a record of your page-browsing activity. It's in the History folder under the Bookmarks icon, and you can easily tap your way to a page from your recent past.

- **Links.** It wouldn't be the Web without links. And all you need to do is tap.

The next few pages look into each of these surfing moves in detail, but first consider the address bar—and its handy shortcuts:

- **Jump back to the top.** No matter how many miles down a page you've scrolled, you can quickly bop back up to the top by tapping the Touch's black status bar, the one with the clock and battery icon on it. That brings you to the top of the page *and* to Safari's address bar, where you can type in a fresh address to surf to another site.

- **Delete an address all at once.** You don't have to hold down the delete key to whack a web address so you can type in a fresh one—just tap the ⊗ button at the right end of the bar to obliterate the address. To get to the ⊗ icon (and pull up the keyboard), tap inside the address bar.

In recent versions of the iPod Touch software, tapping the URL inside the address bar also brings up the Select and Select All buttons so you can copy a web address to the Touch's clipboard (Chapter 4). Once you do that, you'll see a Paste button.

- **Don't over-type.** As with most modern browsers, you can skip pecking out *http://* and *.com* in web addresses, since Safari is savvy enough to stick those on for you. So, instead of typing *http://www. amazon.com*, just type *amazon* and hit Go. (If you need the suffix *.net*, *.edu*, *.org*, or *.us*, press and hold the *.com* button and slide across to the suffix you need, as shown at right.)

If you flipped immediately to this chapter because you wanted to start using Safari to roam the Web as soon as possible, flip back to Chapter 4 for tips and tricks on using the Touch keyboard for browsing, email, and other typey tasks.

Create and Use Safari Bookmarks

YOU CAN ADD BROWSER bookmarks to Safari for the Touch two ways: right from the Touch as you search, surf, and discover new places around the Web, or by syncing your desktop bookmarks with the Touch (flip ahead to page 98 to do that).

No matter how you save 'em, you find your Touch's bookmarks in the same place: tap 🔖 at the bottom of the Safari screen.

Depending on how you organize your web addresses, you may see a collection of single bookmarks (as shown at right), or you may see them grouped into folders, just as you had them in your desktop browser. Tap a folder to open it, and then tap a bookmark inside to visit the corresponding site.

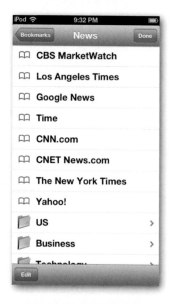

Add a New Bookmark

To add a cool new site to your Bookmarks list, tap the ↗ icon at the bottom of the screen, and then tap the Bookmark icon. On the Add Bookmark screen, you have these choices:

- **Rename it.** Some websites have hideously long names, like "Uncle Earl's Good-Time Five-String Finger-Pickin' Jam Session," but you can change that. Tap the top box on the Add Bookmark screen and rename the site to something shorter, like "Banjos."

  The box right below that—which you can't mess with—displays the site's official web address.

- **File it.** The third box down lets you file a bookmark in a folder (see opposite page). Tap the Bookmarks link to open Safari's list of bookmark folders. When you find the one you want, tap the folder's name to deposit your bookmark there.

The ↗ menu also offers an Add to Home Screen option. Tap that icon and you get an icon on your Touch Home screen to take you back to the site.

Edit and Organize Bookmarks and Folders

SAFARI LISTS BOOKMARKS IN the order in which you save them, and that may not be the easiest way to find them. Touch Safari is ready for this inevitability, as well as the probability that you'd like to delete old bookmarks every once in a while.

Editing your bookmarks and bookmark folders is quick and efficient on the Touch. To do either, tap the 🕮 button and then tap Edit. To edit bookmarks *inside* a folder, tap 🕮, tap open the target folder, and then tap Edit. Here's what you can do with the bookmarks and folders:

- **Delete them.** When it's time for that bookmark or folder to go, tap the ⊖ button, and then tap Delete to confirm. (You can't delete the History folder, however.)

- **Edit them.** Need to rename a bookmark or folder? To edit a bookmark, tap it to get to the Edit Bookmark screen, where you can change its name and address. Tap a folder to get to the Edit Folder screen so you can change the folder's name. Tap the Bookmarks button in the upper-left corner when you're done.

- **File/refile them.** To make, name, and file a new folder, tap the New Folder button in the upper-left corner of the Edit screen, then name the folder and tap Bookmarks to file it. You move an existing folder by tapping it, tapping Bookmarks on the Edit Folder screen, and then choosing a new location.

- **Rearrange them.** Need a new order for your bookmarks or folders? As shown at right, drag the grip strip (≡) up or down the list to move them to a new place. (You can't move the History folder, however.)

Tap 🔲 Done when you finish.

Sync Bookmarks with iTunes

OVER THE YEARS, YOU'VE probably built up a considerable collection of bookmarks on your desktop and laptop computers. In fact, you're probably very attached to some of those links. The good news is you *can* take them with you—at least on the iPod Touch.

To copy your entire Internet Explorer or Safari bookmark library from your computer to your Touch, all you need to do is turn on a checkbox in iTunes. Connect your iPod, click its icon in the iTunes window, and click the Info button at the top of the screen. Scroll down past things you can sync, like contacts, calendars, and mail accounts, until you get to the section called Other. Now, do the following, depending on the type of computer you have:

- Windows PCs: Turn on "Sync bookmarks with" and then choose either Internet Explorer (or Safari, if you still have the discontinued PC version installed) from the menu. Click Apply or Sync.

- Macs: Turn on "Sync Safari bookmarks" and then click Apply or Sync.

If you use Mozilla's Firefox browser, drop into the App Store (Chapter 6) and search for "Firefox." You can find mini-programs, like Firefox Home, Mozilla's own free app, to port your Firefox faves over to the Touch.

Any bookmarks you create on your iPod can make the trip *back* to your computer when you sync, too. But if things start to get too messy on the Touch, you can wipe out all its bookmarks and start over. In iTunes, scroll down to the Info screen's Advanced area (under "Replace information on this iPod") and turn on the checkbox next to Bookmarks. Click Apply or Sync to have iTunes replace all the bookmarks on the Touch with those from your computer.

The Safari History List

THE HISTORY BUTTON ON desktop browsers has saved many a soul who can't remember the name of that really informative site from the other day. Safari on the Touch doesn't let you forget your history, either (well, not without some work), and it, too, keeps a list of the sites you've surfed recently.

To see your web trail, tap ⬚ and then tap the History folder, where Safari collects your past sites in tidy subfolders with names like "Yesterday." Tap a bookmark within one of the subfolders to go back in time—or at least back to that site. The link won't be in the History folder forever (time does march on, and so does the History list), so you may want to bookmark it for real before it slips away.

Erase the History List

Don't want to leave a record of your browsing history in case someone picks up your Touch? One way to prevent that is to set up a Passcode Lock. Then, anyone who wants to get into your Touch will need a four-digit code to unlock the screen; see page 26 for more.

Another way to clean up after yourself is to erase your whole History list. To do that, open the History folder (below left), tap the Clear button in the bottom-left corner (below middle), and then tap the Clear History button (below right). You've just wiped away History. Many politicians are probably envious.

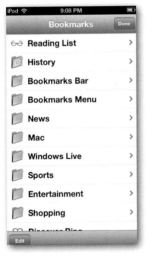

Tap Links

LINKS ON THE TOUCH work just like links on any other computer, except that on the Touch, you tap a link with your finger instead of clicking it with your mouse. While websites traditionally display links in blue, that's not always the case—you can find links of just about any color online, and oftentimes pictures, logos, and other graphics turn out to be links as well.

If you want to know where a link points to before you click it (not a bad idea in these days of rampant bad behavior and evildoing on the Web), hold your finger on the link for a second or two. A box like the one below-right slides up, offering you four options: open the page right away, open the page in a new window ("Open in New Page") so you can switch back and forth among pages, add the page to your Reading List (see page 105), and copy the link.

If you prefer to keep your original pages on-screen when you click links, you can tell Safari to open new pages in the background, where you can find them later by tapping the ⬚ icon. To do that, tap Settings→Safari→Open Links→In Background. When you do, the pop-up menu options change accordingly.

Want to stash the linked page away for later? Tap Add to Reading List. The Copy option lets you paste the link into a Notes document so you can save it (page 68) or pop it into an email message so you can share it. Speaking of email, when you tap a link in a Touch mail message (page 112), Mail closes and Safari opens to take you the site. Yes, these hyperlinks are a pretty nifty invention.

RSS Feeds and Mobile-Friendly Sites

AS COOL AS TOUCH Safari is about showing you full websites on a tiny screen (well, except for sites that use Adobe Flash, an interactive technology the Touch doesn't support), they can sometimes be a lot of work to read. That's especially true if you just want to get a quick look at the news or find out the basics of a story. That's where two really wonderful parts of the Web come in: RSS feeds and mobile-friendly sites. Here's how to use both:

RSS Feeds

Depending on which nerd you're taking to, RSS stands for Rich Site Summary or Really Simple Syndication. No matter what you call it, RSS is a fabulous technology for your Touch (or any mobile device with a browser). It lets you subscribe to short text dispatches called *feeds* sent out by thousands of sites and news sources around the world.

Feeds, like the one shown at right, provide a linked headline and a short summary of the related story. In iOS 6, you can read RSS feeds with services like Google Reader (shown at right). If you want better graphics and more control, you can also buy, download, and install an RSS app like the free Feedler or the $5 NewsRack. With an RSS feed, there are no ads, flashing banners, or dancing hamsters clogging up the works—just straightforward text. When you want to read more about a story, tap its link.

Mobile-Friendly Sites

Many major news organizations and other companies have noticed that this whole smartphone/mobile browser thing has caught on with the public, and they offer versions of their sites optimized for the small screen, using smaller graphics and bigger type. These sites save time since you don't have to constantly pinch and zoom to see what's on the page.

When you surf on the Touch, you'll likely get served up the mobile edition of a site automatically. If that doesn't happen, try exchanging the *www* in the URL with an *m*, as in *m.cnn.com*. (The *m* stands for *mobile*.) When you land on a mobile site, your eyes will be much happier.

Search the Web

IMAGINE TRYING TO FIND anything on the Web *without* search. At more than 10 billion indexed pages and counting (according to *www.worldwidewebsize. com*), the Web would be a pretty hard place to pinpoint information unless you knew exactly where to find it. And how many of us can say that?

Fortunately, the Web offers search engines. And fortunately for iPod Touch owners, three of them are built right into Safari. You can use any one as your Sherlock of the 'Net.

The next page explains how to set your default search engine, but no matter which one you use, they work the same way. To search the Web, tap the search box on the upper-right side of the Safari window and then, when the keyboard appears, type in your keywords. Tap the blue Search button in the bottom-right corner to start the hunt.

Mobile web search has come a long way since 2007, when the original iPhone and iPod Touch hit the scene; back then, their browsers didn't even have a search box. Nowadays, many search engines come in mobile-friendly versions that round up not just general results, but news stories, video clips, and images. As you can see below, Google and Bing let you tap different tabs on the search results page (or under the **Q** menu on the Yahoo screen) to see the various types of information the search engine has thoughtfully rounded up.

Change Your Default Search Engine

Google is the default search engine for many people, both at the desk and on the go, but it's not like you *have* to use it. Yahoo and Microsoft also offer smooth-running engines that can bring back slightly different results from what the Big Goog might give you. In the case of search, the more choices, the better, and you can change things up any time you want by switching Safari's default search engine.

To try Yahoo Search or Microsoft Bing (or to go back to Google if you switched before), visit the Home screen and tap Settings→Safari→Search Engine. On the Search Engine screen (shown bottom-right), tap the name of the service you'd like to use.

Tap the Safari button in the top-left corner to go back to the previous screen to adjust other settings (like turning on the Autofill feature that lets Safari automatically fill in your contact info and user name and password on web forms), or press the Home button to bail out of the Settings area and get back to surfing.

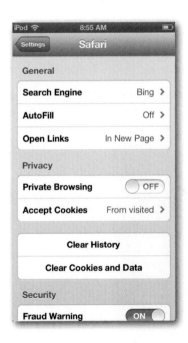

TIP Search engines do more than find web pages—they can also act as electronic crib sheets for quick data points. Need the weather forecast for Boston? Type *weather 02114* into the search box. Movies in Manhattan? Type *movies 10018*. You can also get stock quotes by typing in a company's ticker symbol, unit conversions (*kilometers in 6 miles*), and dictionary definitions (*define bildungsroman*).

Use the Safari Action/Share Menu

IT MAY NOT BE obvious at first, but Safari in iOS 6 is a very sharing web browser—just tap the Action/Share menu icon (⤴) in the Safari toolbar and see for yourself. Here's what each does with the web page currently open:

- **Mail.** Tap here to fire off a link to the page by email.

- **Message.** Tap this icon to send a friend a link to the story over the iMessage network (page 73).

- **Twitter.** Tap the birdie to share the page's link in a tweet to your Twitter followers (page 76).

- **Facebook.** Tap this icon to post a link to the article on your Facebook page.

- **Add to Home Screen.** Tap here to make a bookmark icon on the Home screen.

- **Print.** Need hardcopy? Tap here to send the page to your AirPrint-compatible printer (page 82) and output a version on treeware.

- **Copy.** Tap the Copy button to paste the link into a text app like Notes.

- **Bookmark.** Tap here to make a regular Safari bookmark (page 96).

- **Add to Reading List.** Tap here to save the page so you can read it later, as the next page explains.

Use Safari Reader and Reading List

LIKE TO READ? THE Touch software brings a couple of treats to Safari for serious browsers of the Web: Reader and Reading list. Here's what each one does:

Reader

Hate web pages full of distracting graphics and ads? The iPod Touch has a wonderful feature called Safari Reader that works with many sites (but not all) around the Web. Like its cousin-in-code for the desktop, Safari Reader strips away all the distracting and nonessential graphics and other elements on a page, and presents that article in a nice, easy-to-read format. It's like a pair of comfy slippers for your eyes.

To tell if a web page supports Safari Reader, look up in the address bar for a Reader icon. If you see one, tap it. Like magic, the distracting ads melt away, and only the essential text and images appear front-and-center. You can even adjust the font size in the Reader version of a page by tapping the ₐA icon until you're satisfied with the way things look. Under the 🖅 menu, you find options for mailing and printing the page in the sleek, streamlined Reader format. Tap Done to return to the page's regular view.

Reading List

No time (at the time) to read? When you're browsing around in Safari and find an article that you just don't have time to fully explore, tap 🖅 and choose Add to Reading List. That saves the article to your personal reading list in your browser, where it waits for you.

Later, when you have time to read, tap ⛛ and choose Reading List from the menu. You see a tidy set of all your saved articles.

To read one, tap its entry. Safari divides the Reading List into two parts, All and Unread. All, as you may have guessed, shows every article you added to the list. Unread shows just the stories you haven't opened yet. As you open, read, and move on with each saved article, the link for it automatically moves from the Unread list to the All list—saving you the trouble of remembering what you have and haven't read.

Use Multiple Web Pages

TABBED BROWSERS, LIKE INTERNET Explorer and Firefox, have changed the way people surf. If you need to compare two pages or flip back and forth between them, you no longer have to open them in two separate windows. Tabs let you easily click back and forth between pages using the *same* window, making your own personal space-time continuum much more efficient.

Safari on the iPod Touch gives you a variation on that concept. You can push older pages off to the side when you need to open a new one but still have both within a finger's reach. Here's what you can do:

- **Open a new page.** Need to check something on another site? Tap the ⬚ button in the lower-right corner of Safari and your current page shrinks into the background. Tap New Page in the lower-left corner to get a fresh blank page to address. You can open up to eight pages this way. To see how many pages you have open at once, check the ⬚ icon, which now has a tiny number inside it. If you see ⬚, for example, you have three pages open.

- **Switch to another open page.** Go back and tap ⬚ again. See those dots (• • •) underneath the mini-page (circled)? The number of dots equals the number of web pages you have open, with the white dot highlighting the current page. Flick through and tap a mini-page to expand it full-screen.

- **Close a page.** Tap that useful ⬚ icon again and flick to the mini-page you're ready to close. Then tap the ⊗ button in the top-left corner.

Use iCloud Tabs

THE WORLD WIDE WEB is more than 20 years old now, and there's still no shortage of things to read on it. The only shortage you may find is *time*—as in no time to read all this cool stuff online. Thanks to the new iCloud Tabs feature in iOS 6, though, you might be able to squeeze in a little more reading wherever you happen to be by spreading it out among multiple devices.

That's because the latest version of Apple's Safari browser keeps tabs on your tabs (no matter what device you're using to read web pages at the moment) and syncs them across all your compatible iOS devices and Macs hooked into the same iCloud account. So you can start reading a long article on your iPod Touch at home, pick it up on your iPad on the train to work, and finish it on your iPhone while waiting to pick up pizza for dinner.

To use iCloud Tabs, you need:

- An iPod Touch, iPad, or iPhone running iOS 6, or a Mac running OS X 10.8 (Mountain Lion) and the latest version of the Safari browser.

- An iCloud account.

- A WiFi connection.

When you have tabs open in Safari on one device, tap ⏏ and then tap the iCloud Tabs folder to see a list of the tabs you have open on your other connected devices. Tap a tab in the list to call it up on your current screen. Now, isn't that a lot easier than emailing links to yourself?

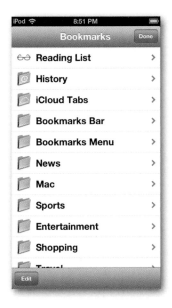

Play Online Audio and Video

IN THE EARLY DAYS of the Touch, streaming audio and video from the Internet was an exercise in frustration, mainly because many sites used media formats, like RealPlayer and Flash, that the Touch couldn't play. While there are still plenty of sites that don't work with mobile Safari, more and more do. And on its own, the Touch can play MP3, WAV, and QuickTime audio files right off the Web. It also plays QuickTime movies in certain formats, like H.264.

Here are a few audio news sites that play well with Safari on the Touch:

- **BBC News.** The Beeb's podcasts stream nicely, and you can search shows by radio station, genre, or get an A-to-Zed list. *www.bbc.co.uk/podcasts/*

- **National Public Radio.** This is a whole page of news shows and podcasts that start streaming when you tap the Listen link; you can also get NPR's official apps as well. *www.npr.org*

But you're not just stuck with Safari—you can stream audio or video through apps like the ones below, all available in the App Store (Chapter 6):

- **Last.fm.** With a free account and the free Last.fm app from the App Store, you can build your own streaming radio station. *www.last.fm*

- **Pandora Radio.** Another option for personalized radio, also with its own desktop site and App Store offering, Pandora analyzes your music taste and streams similar, but new, tracks. *www.pandora.com*

- **Netflix.** Stream high-quality movies and TV shows to your Touch. All you need is an unlimited plan from Netflix ($8 and up) and the Netflix app, available free in the App Store. *www.netflix.com*

- **Hulu Plus.** A mere $8 a month in subscription fees and the free Hulu Plus app from the App Store sets you up with thousands of TV episodes from old and new series. *www.hulu.com/plus*

Don't want to pay for streaming video? You can always download Google's stand-alone YouTube app for iOS (shown at left) for something truly entertaining—or just plain weird. And Apple hosts a huge collection of current movie trailers at *www.apple.com/trailers*. Tap a movie poster to get started; there's also an app version called iTunes Movie Trailers.

Use Safari Security

THE WEB IS FULL of wonders—it's like the collective consciousness and accumulated knowledge of everyone who's ever used it, right there for you to explore. The Web is also full of jerks, criminals, and general-purpose evildoers, so you have to take care to keep your *personal* information safe in this Playground of Information. To see how Safari can help protect you, go to the Touch's Home screen and tap Settings→Safari. Your defenses include these:

- **Private Browsing.** Tap this setting to On and you can surf incognito because Safari won't store browser history or other surfing evidence. The Safari window changes from gray to black during a private session.

- **Accept Cookies.** A cookie is a file that helps a website recognize you. This can be good—you get a personal greeting from sites you revisit, for example—or bad, because some cookies track and report (to paying third parties) the ads you respond to. Here, you can choose to have Safari take a cookie Never, Always, or only from sites you actually visit.

- **Clear History.** Tap this button to erase your Safari history (page 99).

- **Clear Cookies and Data.** This info cache is where your Touch stores cookies, downloaded graphics, and other web-page parts to speed your surfing. You can jettison these files by tapping the Clear button here.

- **Fraud Warning.** Some websites aren't what they appear to be; their main purpose is *phishing*—using a masquerade to get you to enter personal information, like a Social Security number. Make sure this setting is on so Safari can warn you when a site stinks like bad phish.

- **JavaScript.** Developers use this tool to run little programs within web pages. Many are innocent, and most people leave JavaScript on. But some are not, and JavaScript can also slow down page loads a bit. Turn it off or on here.

- **Block Pop-ups.** Once a web surfer's lament, these unwanted extra windows (usually filled with ads) have largely been shattered by pop-up blocking controls in most browsers. Still, you may *need* a pop-up window here and there to order concert tickets or fill in web forms. You can block or unblock pop-ups here, but it's a universal setting for all sites.

- **Advanced.** Tap Website Data to see and delete info that websites store on your 'Pod, or to turn on Web Inspector to track programming errors.

Set Up Mail Accounts

WHEN YOU'RE NEAR A WiFi hot spot, the Touch is a traveling email machine that lets you read, write, and send messages. And just as there are two ways to get apps on the Touch, there are two ways to set up your email accounts.

- **Sync mail settings with iTunes.** You get email on your computer, right? If you're using a dedicated program, like Microsoft Outlook or Apple Mail, you can copy those account settings over to the Touch. Connect the Touch to your computer, click its icon in iTunes, and then click the Info tab. Scroll down to Sync Mail Accounts and turn on the checkbox next to it. All the email accounts on your computer are listed underneath, so turn on the checkboxes next to the ones you want to tote around on the Touch. Click Sync or Apply to copy the settings—but not your computer-based messages—over to the Touch.

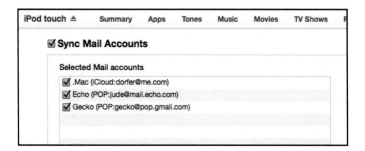

- **Set up mail accounts on the Touch.** Tap the Mail icon. You can set up a free iCloud account (page 116) or, if you use Exchange, Gmail, Yahoo, or AOL, tap the appropriate icon. If you don't use any of those, tap Other. On the next screen, type in your name, email address, password, and a brief description ("Gmail," say). If you tapped Other, type in the account settings you got from your Internet provider when you signed up. Click Save, and the program fetches your mail. Need help sorting through email geekery, like the difference between IMAP and POP? Check out this book's Missing CD page at *http://missingmanuals.com/cds/ipodtmm11/*.

Adjust Mail Settings

LIKE MOST PROGRAMS, THE Touch's mail app comes with standard settings for things like the size of the text that appears on-screen. If you don't like the way the type looks or you want to tweak the program in other ways (like how many lines of a message appear in the Inbox preview), take a trip to Home→Settings→Mail, Contacts, Calendars. From here, you can:

- **Add a custom signature.** You can add a personalized tag to the bottom of each outgoing message, with a different one for every mail account. Popular signatures include your contact information, Twitter handle, or quotes from *Star Wars*.

- **Show more (or less) preview in your message list.** Out of the box, the iPod's mail program shows you a two-line preview of each message so you have some idea of what it contains. You can change this to one to five lines, or select None to turn it off entirely.

- **Set a default mail account.** If you have multiple email accounts on your Touch, use this setting to designate one of them as your default for all outgoing messages (and for messages you create by tapping mail links in other programs). Remember, you can still tap the From field to switch to a different account on the fly.

- **Load remote images (or not).** Some people don't like embedded graphics in messages, as they can transmit a signal to the sender that you opened the message. Turn off images here.

- **Organize by thread.** Hate threaded messages clumped together under one subject line? Turn it (and those ❸ › icons) off here.

- **Increase quote levels.** Mail indents sections of the original message when you reply to it. If you hate that indenting stuff, turn it off here.

- **Delete unwanted mail accounts.** Need to ditch an account because it's become too spam-laden or you want to streamline things? Flick up to the Accounts section, tap the name of the doomed account to get to its settings, and then tap Delete Account.

Use Email on the Touch

MAIL ON THE TOUCH looks and works pretty much like any other email program. You can:

- **Check mail.** Tap the Mail icon on the Home screen. If you have just a single account on your Touch, you see just one Inbox. If you're juggling multiple mail accounts, the Inboxes area of the Mailboxes screen displays the name of each account, the number of new messages in each, and the total number of new messages. You can get to the individual mailbox folders for each account (like Sent and Saved) by tapping their names in the Accounts list. Tap the ↻ button in the bottom-left corner to check for new messages.

- **Read mail.** When you have an Inbox open on the screen, tap a message preview (pictured bottom right) to open it. A blue dot means you haven't read that message yet. If you open the message and want to remember to read it again later, tap Details on the From line, and then tap the blue Mark Unread link that appears.

- **Write mail.** To compose a new message, tap the ☑ icon in the bottom-left corner of the mailbox screen or in an open message. An empty message form and the Touch's keyboard appear, ready for you to write and send mail. To format text, select it, tap the ▶ icon on the menu, tap **B**/U, and then pick a style.

- **Delete mail.** Tap the 🗑 icon at the bottom of the screen to trash an open message. Delete a message without opening it by swiping your finger across its Inbox preview and tapping the red Delete button that appears. To trash bulk mail in bulk, tap the Edit button in the upper-right corner of the Inbox screen. Tap the preview of each message so a red checkmark appears, and then tap Delete to whack them all at once.

On the Edit screen, you can also move messages to another mail folder, tap the Mark button to flag messages (🚩) for later, or mark them as unread or read, depending on their current state; see page 115.

Add Picture and Video Attachments to Mail Messages

One of the more popular uses of email (besides the sending and unfortunate receiving of spam) is as a delivery mechanism for pictures and videos. Images of grandkids, puppies, and kittens fill the Internet. If the photo or video is in your iPod's Photos app, you can mail it. (See Chapter 15 for more on shooting, syncing, and storing photos on your Touch. Chapter 14 tells you how to have the same kind of fun with videos.)

In iOS 6 for the iPod Touch, you can stick a photo on an outgoing message—even if you've already started the message. With the message open, press your finger on the screen where you want to add the photo or video. A menu appears. Tap "Insert Photo or Video," as shown below left.

A box with your Camera Roll and other photo albums appears. To select a photo or video you shot with your iPod, tap Camera Roll, and then tap the thumbnail of the image or clip you want to attach. Tap Choose in the bottom-right corner (below middle) to insert the item into the message (below right).

To mail a photo right from the Photos app, select the picture, then tap and choose Mail to create a new message with the photo attached.

To select multiple photos for mailing, open the album and tap the Edit button. Tap the photos you want to send (up to five at a time) to select them. Tap the Share button, and then tap Mail.

If you already have a message started, you can paste in a picture. Double-click the Home button and select Photos in the app panel that appears at the bottom of the screen. Tap open the album that has the photo you want to use. Press the thumbnail until the Copy button appears. Tap Copy, then press the Home button and go back to the Mail app—where you can press down on the open message and tap Paste to stick the image into the message.

Set Up a VIP Mailbox

EMAIL IS A GREAT way to exchange information, but it's easy to get over-whelmed with trying to find the messages you want among the spam, newsletters, and other stuff in your mailbox. Wouldn't it be great if the Touch would notify you when someone you *want* to hear from zaps you a note?

In iOS 6, this dream comes true. Thanks to the VIP Mailbox feature baked into the latest version of the iPod's Mail app, you can set up a list of all the important people in your life—spouse, offspring, parents, business partners, Amazon customer service—and have the Touch collect those messages in the VIP mailbox and notify you (page 78) when they arrive.

Here's how to set up a VIP Mailbox:

❶ Open the Mail app and tap VIP in the Mailboxes list.

❷ Tap Add VIP.

❸ When your Contacts list appears, flick around and tap the names of the people to whom you want to assign VIP status.

❹ To have the iPod alert you when one of your VIPs has dropped you a line, tap VIP Alerts. This takes you to the Notifications settings. Next to Notification Center, tap the On button and choose an alert style (discreet screen-top banners or middle-of-the-screen alerts like the one on the bottom right). Choose what kind of sound you want the iPod to play, whether you want to see a message preview, and if you'd like the notification to show up on the iPod's Lock Screen, too. (Page 78 has more about configuring Notifications for Touch apps.)

Now, whenever one of your VIPs sends you a message, it arrives in style and with a star (★). To add new VIPs to your list, tap ❷ in the VIP Inbox, and then tap Add VIP on the next screen. You can remove people by tapping open the VIP list, hitting the Edit button, and then tapping ❸ next to The Unworthy.

Flag Messages for Later

THE MAIL APP GIVES you a couple of ways to deal with messages at a later time. You can *flag* certain messages, which makes them stand out in the Inbox with a snappy orange flag. Or you can mark messages as *unread*, which restores their blue "unread" dot and makes them seem like new messages all over again. Here's what to do for:

- **One message.** If you have the message open on-screen, tap the flag icon (⚑) at the top of the Mail window. Select Flag or Mark as Unread from the menu.

- **Multiple messages.** If you're cruising down your Inbox and see several pieces of mail you want to flag or mark as unread at once, tap the Edit button at the top of the column. Tap each message you want to either flag or mark as unread, and then tap the Mark button at the bottom of the screen. Choose Flag or Mark as Unread to change the selected messages.

If you already have a message flagged and you hit the Flag/Mark menu, you get the option to *unflag* the item and remove its Marker of Importance. Likewise, if you have mail you haven't read—and you don't *want* to read—the menu gives you a "Mark as Read" option. Tapping it whacks the "unread" dot (●) from your message so it sinks back into the pile of mail you've already read.

The Flagged Mailbox

Those snappy orange flags do a good job of making those deal-with-me-later messages stand out in your mailbox, but what if you have a ton of messages in your Inbox—do you really want to scroll up and down the list looking for that one flag in the bunch? Or maybe you have multiple mail accounts and can't remember where you planted the flag about that upcoming meeting.

The iPod gives your flagged messages a whole mailbox of their own. It's like a To Do List for messages that need responses.

You don't see the Flagged mailbox until you stick that first flag on a message. But once you do, it pops up proudly in your iPod's Inbox panel, right under your VIP list. It even displays the number of messages in the box. When you unflag or delete the last message in the list, the Flagged mailbox disappears from view—only to return when you let your mail flag fly once again.

Set Up an iCloud Account

BACK BEFORE ICLOUD FLOATED into view, if your iPod Touch got broken or lost—and you hadn't backed up its files to your desktop computer—you were out of luck.

But Apple's free iCloud service backs up all your stuff, including music, apps, personal info, and more, to a great big server in the sky. Providing, that is, that you have iCloud turned on and actually set to back up your data. You also need iOS 5 or later installed on your iPod and on any other iOS devices you want to keep synced up. If you didn't create an iCloud account when you first set up your iPod (page 16), here's what to do:

1. Go to the Home screen and tap Settings→iCloud.

2. Create an iCloud account. Tap the Account button and fill in your Apple ID (page 240) and other requested info. Along with an iCloud account, you get a free email account on Apple's me.com servers to add to your address collection.

3. Now it's time to tell iCloud what you want it to back up and sync. The first batch of apps in the list are the Touch's personal information and organizer programs: Mail, Contacts, Calendars, Reminders, Safari bookmarks, Notes, and your Passbook documents; except for Safari and Mail, all the apps are explained back in Chapter 4. Tap the button to On for each one you want iCloud to sync for you. You also get online versions of the Mail, Contacts, and Calendars apps that you can tap into, read, and edit using any web browser (see page 119).

4. Once you have these files secure, it's time to get your photo stream flowing. If you want iCloud to automatically transfer photos you take with your Touch to your computer, Apple TV, and other iOS devices (like your iPhone or iPad), tap Photo Stream settings to On. Page 286 has more on using Photo Stream.

5. Thanks to the iWork apps for the iPhone, iPod Touch, and iPad, you can edit and review documents, spreadsheets, and presentations on your various iOS 5-and-later devices, and iCloud keeps those files in sync across your gadgets—and backed up to the Web as well. To make sure that happens, go to the iCloud settings page, tap Documents & Data, and then tap the On button. Flipping this setting to On also syncs up your Safari Reading List (page 105) between your iOS 5 gadgets and any computers running Safari.

6. Another benefit of iCloud is its Find My iPod feature. You can use it to track down a missing Touch, whether it's just lost in the house somewhere, back at the office, or hijacked by an evildoer. Tap the On button here if you want to Find Your iPod. Later, when you need to locate the errant 'Pod, go to *www. icloud.com/find* and log into your account. If your iPod is still on a WiFi network somewhere, you see it on a map—with the option to send a sound alert or message to display on its screen, like "Yo, this is my lost iPod" along with your contact info. To protect personal data, you can also lock the screen or erase the iPod's contents from afar.

7. Although your iTunes Store purchases and your Photo Stream pictures don't count against iCloud's free 5 gigabytes of storage, you may need more room if you have a lot of documents and other data to back up. If you suspect things are getting tight, tap the Storage & Backup button on the iCloud settings screen to see how much space your stuff currently takes up. If you don't want to delete anything, tap the Buy More Storage button. On the next screen, you can tap to sign up for an additional 10 GB ($20 a year), 20 GB ($40 a year), or 50 GB ($100 a year) of space. All of this is on top of your free 5 GB. The extra gigs get billed to your iTunes Store account.

8. Finally, if you want to back up your iPod's system settings, app settings, and Camera Roll photos, pop down to the "Back Up to iCloud" line on the Settings screen and tap it to On. iCloud now copies your Touch's housekeeping settings and pics daily via your WiFi connection. You can trigger a backup session right away by tapping Back Up Now. (Remember, all your other data—iTunes purchases, personal info, and documents—are taken care of by other parts of the iCloud service.)

iCloud does its deep-in-the-background backup thing when you have your iPod connected to a WiFi network, plugged in to a power source, and locked. (You can perform a similar backup through iTunes on your computer, as page 306 describes.) When setting up a new Touch (or one you restored to its factory settings), you get the option to restore all that backed up data.

If you ever need to adjust your backup settings, add more online storage, or even delete your account, just return to Home→iCloud→Settings.

Use iCloud on Your Computer

SOME PEOPLE WILL NEVER sync their Touches to a computer, and for them, the iCloud setup process concluded on the previous page. But what if you want to bring the cloud down to earth, namely, to your desktop or laptop computer? When you loop your computer into iCloud, it can download content from your account, like permanent copies of pics from your Photo Stream.

You can also update the iPod's address book and calendar by typing new information into relevant programs, like Microsoft Outlook or iCal. Once you make a change on the computer, iCloud pushes it out to your iPod Touch and other iCloud-connected devices—as long as you have everything set up on your computer as well as on your iPod.

If you haven't signed up for an iCloud account, go to *www.icloud.com* and click Sign Up. If you have an Apple ID, enter your user name and password to log in.

Windows users must download a setup program for iCloud's control panel from the site first. Once you install the Apple iCloud software on your computer, go to Start→Control Panel→Network and Internet→iCloud and log in with your user name and password.

In the window that pops up (shown right), turn on the checkboxes for the stuff you want to sync from your computer, including mail, contacts, calendars, and bookmarks. Windows users need Microsoft Outlook 2007 or later to sync their mail, contacts, and calendars over iCloud. You can also turn on Photo Stream here; page 286 has more on that.

Mac OS X 10.7 (Lion) and 10.8 (Mountain Lion) users just need to visit →System Preferences→iCloud to get to the options for syncing Mail accounts, Mac OS X Address Book contacts, iCal calendars, and Safari bookmarks.

Once you have iCloud configured on both your iPod (described on the previous two pages) and your computer, you're syncing. Want to know where else you can see your iCloud info in a pinch if your computer or iPod isn't within reach? The Web, of course. Read on.

Use iCloud on the Web

YOU CAN GET TO your iCloud mail, calendars, contacts, and more through just about any Internet-connected computer. Being able to get to your iCloud data through the Web is great for those times when you don't have access to it through your home computer or iPod Touch—like when you're on your office PC, or on the road without electronics.

To see your iCloud mail, for example, just grab a web browser and go to *www. icloud.com*. Type in your iCloud user name and password to get to your Inbox on the Web. (If you had an old MobileMe or .Mac account, you can see your messages from those, too, providing you converted your old account to an iCloud account at Apple's persistent prompting.)

As shown below, the main dashboard on the iCloud site also offers clickable icons for your contacts and calendars—both of which you can update here and have those changes show up on your Touch and computer back home. The Notes and Reminder apps sync up here as well. And although iCloud calls its iPod locator (free in the App Store!) Find My iPhone, click the radar-screen icon to log in and locate the whereabouts of a missing Touch.

Do you use Apple's iWork suite of productivity programs on, say, both your iPad and iPod Touch, and want to keep your documents up to date on both gadgets? Click the iWork icon here to see (and transfer) copies of those files from your online iWork file cabinet, where the latest version is always on file. It's also probably one of the most tidy file cabinets you'll see online.

You'll learn to:

- Find and download new apps for your Touch

- Arrange and organize apps

- Keep your mini-programs up-to-date

- Delete unwanted apps

- Switch between apps

CHAPTER 6

Add More Apps to the Touch

AS THE PAST THREE chapters have shown, the iPod Touch comes preloaded with colorful little programs that let you do a lot of stuff, like email, Web surfing, and personal-organization tasks. But you're not limited to the Touch's standard-issue software—thanks to the iTunes App Store, you can turn your Touch into a personalized pocket computer with its own games, productivity programs, ebooks, and more.

That's what this chapter is about: finding new programs in the App Store that expand the powers of your Touch beyond what it comes with out of the box. Here, you'll learn how to shop the App Store from iTunes on your computer and on the Touch itself.

Having a ton of apps turns your Touch into the electronic equivalent of a Swiss Army knife with a tool for every occasion, but having those apps strewn all over the home screen can make your iPod look like a miniature episode of *Hoarders*. In this chapter, you'll learn how to organize your apps into logical order, or even stash them in a series of tidy folders for fast and easy access. Because, after all, what's the point of buying that app if you can't find it when you need it?

Buy iPod Touch Apps

THE APP STORE HOSTS more than 700,000 little programs you can add to your iPod Touch to make it a tiny pocket computer as well as a stylish media machine. Currency converters, 3-D video games, newsreaders, ebooks, blogging tools, guitar-chord programs, and mobile versions of popular sites like Buzzfeed and eBay are among the many offerings.

Buy Apps in iTunes

Click the App Store link on iTunes' main Store window to see program categories like Sports and Finance. From this menu (shown at right), you can jump to any category and browse away for that video editor or sports-score app you've decided to add to your Touch arsenal. Many apps are free (each category's page has a list of freebies), and most for-pay programs cost less than $10.

When you see an app you simply must have in iTunes, click the price tag or Free button under the app's icon to start the purchase process. The bill goes to the credit card linked to your Apple ID (page 240).

After you download your new app, you can sync it over to the Touch through iTunes:

1. Connect your iPod to your computer.

2. Click the iPod icon in the iTunes window.

3. Click the Apps tab to see all your purchases.

4. Turn on the checkboxes next to the apps you want to sync to your Touch.

5. Click the Apply and Sync button in the corner of the iTunes window.

If you turned on the "Automatically sync new apps" checkbox in iTunes (circled right), the media manager copies all your new purchases to the Touch the next time you sync up.

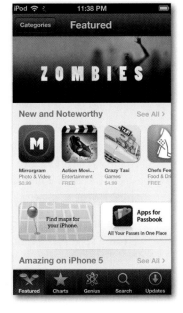

Buy Apps on the Touch

When you've got a WiFi connection, you can browse and buy new apps directly on the Touch. Start by tapping the blue App Store icon on the Home screen.

At the top of the Featured screen, you can see what's new and hot. In the top-left corner, tap the Categories button to see apps grouped by category, like Finance or Games.

Tap an app to find out more about it. The Charts button (★) at the bottom of the screen displays the most popular paid, free, and top-grossing apps. As with music, browsing the charts gives you an idea of what everybody else is buying or downloading. Tap the Genius icon (✳) to have Apple suggest new apps for your collection based on apps you already bought. A Search icon (Q) awaits if you're looking for something specific. The Updates button (◉) alerts you to a new version of an app you've previously purchased; the next page has more on that.

When you find an app you want, tap the price icon, which turns into a Buy button. Hit that, type in your iTunes Store name and password (even if you're getting a free application), and the download begins. After the program finishes loading and installing, tap its icon to launch it.

Update Apps

SEE A RED, CIRCLED number on the App Store icon on your Home screen? You've got updates waiting for that number of apps. As mentioned on the previous page, the same number also shows up on the Updates icon when you're in the App Store itself.

From the iPod's Home screen, tap the App Store icon to pop into the e-boutique. On the Updates screen, you'll see the list of apps that need refreshing—there may be a new version of the app, for example, or bug fixes. Tap the Update button next to an app to download and install the new version. If you have a bunch of apps on the list, tap the Update All button at the top of the screen to upgrade them all at once.

Although earlier versions of the App Store required you to type in your Apple ID each time you updated an app (to prove you bought it), the App Store in iOS 6 assumes you're updating your own apps and doesn't pester you for the info.

Uninstall Apps

IT'S A FACT OF life: Sometimes apps don't work out. They're not what you thought, they're buggy (it happens), or they take up too much precious Touch space. Here are two ways to uninstall an app:

- **Remove apps in iTunes.** Connect the Touch to your computer, click its icon in iTunes, and then click the Applications tab. In the list of apps, deselect the ones you want to remove, and then click Sync to uninstall them from the Touch.

- **Remove apps on the Touch.** As shown here on the Home screen, press and hold the unwanted application's icon until it starts wiggling, and an ⊗ appears in the corner. Tap the ⊗, confirm your intention to delete the app, and wave goodbye to it. Press the Home button to return to business as usual.

Remember, even if you uninstall an app by syncing it off through iTunes or deleting it directly from the Touch, you can always download and install it again from the Purchased list in the App Store; tap the Updates button to see it.

Manage Apps in iTunes

AFTER YOU GO ON a few shopping sprees through the App Store, you may have a *ton* of groovy new app icons all over your Touch—but not in the order you want them. Sure, you can drag wiggling icons all over the 11 pages of your Home screen (page 21), but that can get a little confusing and frustrating if you accidentally drop an icon on the wrong page.

Fortunately, iTunes lets you arrange your Touch icons from the comfort of your big-screen computer:

1. **Connect the iPod to your computer**. Click its icon in the window.

2. **Click the Apps tab**. You now see all your applications—plus giant versions of each page of your Touch Home screen, all lined up vertically on the right side.

3. **Select the icons you want to move**. Once you click an icon on the large screen, drag it to the desired page thumbnail along the right side of the screen. It's much easier to group similar apps on a page this way—you can have, say, a page of games or a page of video and photography apps. You can even change the four permanent icons in the gray bar at the bottom of the Touch's screen.

4. **Click Apply or Sync**. Wait just a moment as iTunes rearranges the icons on your Touch, so they mirror how you have them in iTunes.

Organize Apps in Folders

AS MENTIONED EARLIER IN this book, you can have up to 11 Home-screen pages on your Touch and flick across them to find the apps you want. But some app-loving folk can quickly fill up all 11 screens with icons. Also, some people would prefer a tidier way to group their apps than dragging them around to different pages.

That's where Home screen *folders* can make everything better. You can have up to 12 apps in a single folder—which looks like an icon with little icons nestled inside it (right). Putting apps in folders saves screen space and keeps them corralled. By default, most new Touches come with one folder from the start: the Utilities folder, which contains the Contacts, Calculator, and Voice Memos apps.

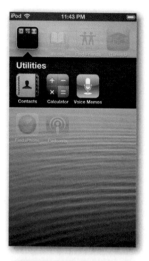

To create a folder, press and hold an icon until it wiggles, and then drag that icon on top of another one that you want in that folder as well. When you do, you automatically create a folder with a generic name on it, like "Games" (bottom-right). You can keep this name or replace it with one of your own. Once you set up a folder, you can drag up to 10 more apps into it to fill it up. Tap the screen to close the folder.

To launch an app inside a folder, tap the folder to open it, and then tap the app you want to use.

If you change your mind and want to pull an app out of a folder, open the folder and press and hold the app's icon to start the Wiggle Dance. Now you can drag it out of the folder and back to its place on the Home screen proper.

To get rid of a folder altogether, press an icon to get them all wiggling. Drag *all* the apps out of the folder and back to the Home screen. When the last app is out, the folder disappears.

TIP Can't remember what folder you stuck an app in? From the Touch's first Home screen, flick to the left, type the app's name into the Spotlight search bar, and then tap the app open when it appears in the results list.

Multitask on Your Touch

PUTTING APPS IN FOLDERS helps you organize your Touch screen more precisely, but it doesn't save you a lot of time when you're in the middle of one thing and want to switch over to use another app real quickly—like when you're reading email and want to nip out and turn on your Pandora radio app to hear some tunes as you work. Who wants to go all the way out to the Home screen for that?

Fortunately, the Touch has a shortcut. When you're in an app, click the Home button twice. A row of four icons sprouts from the bottom of the screen, shoving the app you're currently using up to the top of the screen (top right).

These four icons represent apps you've recently used. Tap one to quickly switch to it. Turn on Pandora, check your sports scores, do whatever it is you wanted to do. When you finish, double-click the Home button again. When the row of icons appears again, tap the icon of the app you were previously using to return to it.

If the app you want isn't in this initial row of four, flick the icons from right to left until you find the one you want.

To kill apps in the hidden row that you haven't used in forever (because they may be hogging memory), press down on an icon until the ⊖ symbol appears. Tap it to remove the app from the recently used list—but not from the Touch itself. Press the Home button when you're done.

In addition to your most recently used apps list, the Home button double-click offers another time-saver. Instead of flicking right to left to see recent apps, flick left to right to get to the music playback controls (bottom right). They can save you the trouble of going all the way back to the Now Playing screen to skip a playlist track. And if you get agitated when the Touch reorients itself into landscape view when you try to read an ebook in bed, tap the first icon, the circular arrow in the left corner. This locks the Touch into portrait mode no matter which way you hold it—until you tap this icon again to unlock the screen.

You'll learn to:
- Set up your Nano
- Load it up with music, movies, and podcasts
- Play music and spoken-word recordings
- Tune the FM Radio
- Track your workouts with the Nike+ software

CHAPTER 7

Tour the iPod Nano

IF THERE'S AN IPOD that's been around the design block a few times, it's the Nano. Since its debut in 2005, Apple's mid-range media player has gone from looking like a pack of Trident gum with a tiny screen and click wheel to a small square of metal and glass resembling a high-tech pocket watch that plays music.

In between those versions, Apple molded the Nano into a squat version of the iPod Classic, and then stretched it out into a long, thin player that forced you to hold it sideways to watch videos. 2012 brings the latest rendition of the Nano, the seventh generation of Apple's small-but-powerful media player.

While it now looks like an iPod Touch Mini, the newest Nano brings together many of the most popular features of Nanos Past. As this chapter explains, music, photos, and videos are all a tap away. The Nano is also the only iPod with a built-in FM radio and a pedometer that counts your steps as you strive for fitness. So when you're ready to give this year's model a spin, this chapter shows you the way.

Set Up and Autosync the Nano

YOU DON'T HAVE TO do much to keep your Nano's music and video collection up to date with what's on your computer. That's because iTunes has a nifty *autosync* feature that automatically makes sure that whatever is in your iTunes library also appears on your iPod once you connect 'Pod to desktop PC.

The first time you plug in your Nano, iTunes takes you through the setup process. Earlier versions of iTunes offered to automatically copy all your music and photos to your new 'Pod, but in iTunes 11, manual management is the default option. If you have a music library that's small enough to fit on the Nano, click the Nano's icon in the iTunes window, click the Summary tab on the next screen, and then turn off the checkbox next to "Manually manage music and videos." Finally, click the Apply button, which turns into a Sync button.

You can selectively sync content by clicking the tabs (Music, Movies, etc.) along the top of the iTunes window on the iPod management screen.

Chapter 14 explains playing Nano-sized videos and Chapter 15 can fill you in on the photo business. If you generally like the autosync feature but want more control over what goes onto your iPod, check out the next page.

NOTE If you have a small-capacity iPod, you may already have more music than can fit on your player. If that's the case, *your* automatic option is the Autofill button at the bottom of the iTunes window. Skip ahead to page 168 to learn more about Autofill, which lets iTunes decide what to put on your 'Pod.

Manually Load Your Nano with Media

IF YOU DON'T HAVE enough room on your Nano for your whole iTunes library, or if you plan to load music onto your iPod from more than one computer (say your work PC and home computer), you'll want to *manually* manage your songs and other media. If you set up your iPod in iTunes 11, odds are the program automatically put you in manual-management mode. You can tell by clicking the iPod's icon in the iTunes window and then clicking the Summary tab to see the Nano's sync settings.

When "manually manage" is selected, iTunes does not automatically dump everything onto your iPod. "But," you ask, "*how* do I get my music (or videos or podcasts) there by myself?" Easy—you just drag it:

1. **Under the Library pop-up menu in iTunes, select a media type, like Music, Movies, or TV Shows.** Click the buttons at the top of the window to sort your collection, say by Albums in the Music library, as shown below.

2. **Click the items you want to copy to your iPod.** Grab multiple songs, albums, or videos by holding down the Ctrl (⌘) key while clicking.

3. **Drag your selections to the right side of the iTunes window.** As you do, a panel slides open to reveal your connected iPod and your playlists. Drop the dragged items on the iPod icon to add them to the player. The number of songs you're adding appears inside a red circle.

You can manually load any items in your iTunes library—movies, audiobooks, whatever—this way. To copy just *some* but not all items (like new podcast episodes), you can selectively sync files. Page 24 explains how to do this for the iPod Touch, and it works the same way for the smaller iPod.

iPod Nano Buttons and Ports

THE IPOD NANO IS not a complicated media player, but its buttons and ports handle very specific functions. Here's how to work the Nano:

❶ **Volume**. The Nano has buttons on its left edge to control playback volume through the headphones. Press the top button (+) to increase the sound and the bottom button (-) to lower it.

❷ **Play/Pause.** Nestled between the two volume buttons is a flat indentation. This is the Nano's Play/Pause button. Its easy access lets you quickly stop the music should someone come up and talk to you. The button has other uses, too: press it again to resume playback. Press it twice to skip to the next song on the current album or playlist. To jump back a track, press Play/Pause three times.

❸ **Home button.** Deep in a photo slideshow and want to get back to the main screen with all the Nano's apps on it? Press the Home button, that round indentation on the front of the iPod.

❹ **Sleep/Wake**. The Tic Tac–shaped button on the Nano's top-right edge turns its touchscreen on or off. Press it gently.

❺ **Lightning connector**. This tiny jack is where you plug in the iPod's USB cable so you can connect 'Pod to computer to sync up your iTunes library or charge up the Nano's battery.

❻ **Headphone jack**. The small, round jack on the bottom of the Nano (below) is where you plug in your white Apple EarPods or other headphones.

Control the Nano by Touch

IN ADDITION TO ITS hardware buttons, the Nano has a sensitive multitouch screen that responds to specific movements from your fingertips. Here's how you move your digits to get the Nano singing (or speaking or showing photos):

- **Tap.** Gently press your finger on an icon to open its menus, or on a song title to play it.
- **Double-tap.** Tap two times to zoom in on a photo—repeat to zoom back out.
- **Swipe.** Lightly whip your finger side to side on the glass to move through Home screen icons or back and forth through menu screens.
- **Flick.** Whip your finger up and down to scroll through long playlists.
- **Drag.** Hold down the on-screen volume control button and slide your finger left or right to adjust the sound.
- **Pinch and Zoom.** You can selectively enlarge an area on the screen by placing your thumb and index finger on the glass and spreading them apart. To zoom back out, reverse the move and "pinch" your digits together.

The iPod Nano's Home Screen

LIKE THE IPOD TOUCH, the Nano uses a grid of icons on its *Home screen* (the Nano's main screen, where all your apps live) to organize its content. No matter where you are or how many menu levels deep, you can always return Home by pressing the Nano's Home button (opposite page).

Each icon on the Nano's Home screen represents the top menu for the app bearing its name. Want to hear a podcast you recently synced over from iTunes? Tap the Nano's Podcasts icon to see a list of all the podcasts you copied over. From that menu, tap a podcast title to see a list of the episodes available, and from that list of episodes, tap the one you want to hear.

The Home screen displays six icons at a time, but the Nano has more than six icons. To accommodate them all, the Nano gives you a second Home screen. Put your finger on the first Home screen and flick from right to left to see it. When you're deep in an app's menu, you flick from left to right to page back through the menu screens. To learn what each icon on the Nano's Home screen actually does, turn the page.

The iPod Nano's Menus

ON THE MODERN NANO, you get to your songs, photos, FM radio, pedometer, and other fun stuff by tapping your fingers—or sliding, dragging, and flicking them, as described on the previous page. The Nano's all about touch.

And here's what you'll find under those touchable icons:

- **Music.** Tap here to see a list of icons for all the ways you can sort your song lists. You see tappable categories for Genius mixes (page 205), playlists (Chapter 12), artists, albums, songs, genres, composers, and compilations. If you have them, you can also see a list of your audiobooks, podcasts, and iTunes U lectures. Tap a category to see its related tracks. For example, tap Artists to see all the songs and albums by that singer or band.

- **Videos.** If you copied movies and TV shows from your iTunes library to your Nano, tap the Videos icon to see the list of viewing possibilities sorted by Movies, TV Shows, or Music Videos. Tap a category to see the list of movies or shows, and then tap the title of the video you want to watch. Chapter 14 has more on watching videos.

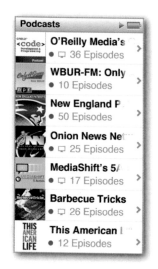

- **Fitness.** The iPod Nano isn't just an audio player. It's a pedometer and a pocket workout coach as well. Page 50 has more on those features.

- **Podcasts.** If you subscribe to *podcasts*, those free audio and video shows from the iTunes Store, you'll find them under this icon. If you have a lot of podcasts, you'll see a menu that looks like the one pictured here.

- **Photos.** If you synced digital photos from your computer, you can view them by tapping the Photos icon, and then tapping a photo album or image thumbnail. Chapter 15 has more on photo-viewing.

- **Radio.** Tap here to fire up the Nano's built-in FM radio. Page 136 has more on using the radio and its features.

- **Clock.** Tap the faux-clockface icon to see an even bigger clock on-screen, one with the real time. Flick the screen left to get to the Nano's stopwatch, and flick left again to see its timer.

- **Settings.** Tap here to adjust the way your Nano works. See page 140 for more on what you can customize.

- **Audiobooks.** If you synced over any audiobooks from your iTunes library, you see an orange Audiobooks icon on the second page of the Nano's Home screen. Page 137 has more on audiobooks.

- **iTunes U.** Likewise, if you transferred any free audio lectures from iTunes U, Apple's big free digital university, they appear under this icon.

- **Voice Memos.** If you plugged in a headset and mic and recorded some audio notes (page 72), you'll see a blue Voice Memos icon as well. Tap the icon to get to the next screen, where you can tap Record and say your piece. Tap the Memos button on the recording screen to see a list of your audio notes and play them back. When you plug the Nano back into your computer to sync, iTunes offers to copy the clips back to its Voice Memos playlist.

Play Music

As described on the opposite page, the Music menu holds all the albums, playlists, and Genius mixes you copied over from your iTunes library. Once you find a song and tap it to play it, you see the Now Playing Screen, with the name of the song, the artist, and other info on it.

The bottom part of the screen contains the usual music playback controls: Rewind (I◀◀), Play (▶), Pause (II), Forward (▶▶I), and there's a volume slider along the bottom that you can drag with your finger if you don't feel like pressing the physical buttons on the Nano.

Tap the screen again to see more icons, as shown here. Here's what each of the glyphs does:

- **Loop (⟲).** Want to play that album again? Tap the Loop button so that it turns blue (⟲). To repeat a *song*, tap it twice so it looks like ⟲.

- **Genius playlist (✳).** Tap here to build a Genius playlist around the current song. Page 224 has more on the Genius.

- **Shuffle (⤬).** Tap here to play the current set of tracks in random order. To stop the shuffle, tap ⤬ again.

- **Track listing (☰).** Tap here to see the list of tracks on an album or playlist.

Above all these icons sits a scrubber bar, which lets you manually jump to a certain point in a song. Just put your finger on it and drag to the good part.

Play FM Radio

FORGET ABOUT THOSE BOXY transistor radios of yore—your sleek new iPod Nano can pull down FM signals and bring live broadcasts right to your ears. For stations transmitting RDS (Radio Data System) information, the Nano even displays the name of the song, the artist, and the station's call letters on-screen. One thing: You need to listen to the radio through headphones or a set of connected external speakers, because the connecting wire doubles as the radio antenna. Here's how it all works:

- **Tune and play the radio.** Tap the Radio icon on the Home screen, and then tap ▶ at the bottom of the screen. Tap I◀◀ or ▶▶I to sample stations up and down the dial, or flick the on-screen tuner bar with your finger to manually find a station. You can also press and hold the I◀◀ and ▶▶I buttons to scan FM stations. Tap ■ to stop the radio.

  To see a list of local stations, tap the screen to call up the Nano's Live Pause and other controls. Tap ≔ on the right side of the screen, and then tap Local stations to have the Nano round up a list of all the stations in your area. Tap a station to listen to it. Tap the radio-tower icon in the top-right corner of the Local Stations list to return to the radio screen, or tap Refresh to have the Nano scan the airwaves again (in case you changed locations).

- **Add favorite stations.** When you land on a station you really like, tap the star icon (★) next to the station number in the middle of the screen to turn it blue (★); tap it again to "unfavorite" the station. To see your list of favorite stations (which also appear as orange markers on the tuner dial), tap the screen, tap ≔, tap Favorites, and then tap a station in the list to hear it. To edit the list, pull down on the Favorites list with your finger and tap the Edit button that appears. Tap ⊖ next to the station you want to ditch, and then tap Delete to confirm.

- **Pause live radio.** To pause a broadcast, tap the Radio screen to call up the Live Pause controls, and then tap II. Tap ▶ to resume playing. A progress bar at the bottom shows you how long you've been in Pause mode. Like TiVo, you can fast-forward or rewind through the audio stored in the progress bar—just tap  or ▶▶ to jump forward in 30-second blocks, or press and hold the ▶▶ icon to skip ahead in 10-second hops. You can pause radio up to 15 minutes before the Nano begins to delete the earliest recorded section.

- **Tag songs.** If you see a little tag icon (circled on the opposite page), the station supports iTunes tagging. When you hear a song you *have* to have, tap the tag icon. To see a list of your tagged tunes, tap the Radio screen, tap ☰, and then tap Tagged Songs. When you sync your Nano to your computer, the songs appear in a Tagged playlist in the Store area of the Source list. You can listen to previews there—and *buy* the songs, naturally.

Play Spoken-Word Recordings

Playing audiobooks, podcasts, and iTunes U lectures on your Nano works pretty much like playing music (page 135): tap the menu, tap a title, and then tap play.

In fact, these types of recordings even appear in the Nano's Music menu. But if you want a shortcut to your favorite audiobook, podcast, or iTunes U recordings, the Nano gives you a Home screen icon for each.

While the spoken-word playback controls are the same as they are for songs (described on page 135), spoken-word recordings offer a few more options when you tap the Now Playing screen.

These controls, especially tailored for voice narration, include:

- **Repeat the last 30 seconds.** Tap the 🔄 icon to jump back half a minute in the recording to repeat a line you missed.

- **Playback speed.** By default, the narration matches the speed at which the track was recorded, signified by a 1X icon on the screen. If you find the narrator talking too slowly for you, crank that speed up to double-time by tapping 1X until you see 2X. If you find the narrator talking too fast, tap the icon until you hit ½X, which slows the narration to half-speed.

The iPod Nano as Personal Trainer

WITH ITS SLIM SIZE and easy-to-read screen, the Nano has always been a natural for runners and gym fiends who need a lightweight music player to exercise by. Thanks to its included sporty software, the Nano's also a workout coach.

The Nano as Stopwatch

The Nano has a stopwatch feature, but it's tucked away where you may miss it: on the second screen of the Clock app. To summon the stopwatch, tap the Clock icon on the Home screen and flick from right to left past the standard clock to get to the stopwatch.

To start timing yourself, tap the green Start button. The timer starts counting, and the Start button turns into a red Stop button. (Tap that when you're done.) If you're running a series of laps, tap the gray Lap button each time you finish a turn on the track. The iPod records your time for that lap, and then starts timing your next one.

The Nano displays the time for the lap-in-progress above the overall session timer. It lists the time for completed laps below the timer, so you can track your workout. The timer keeps ticking even if you tap your way to another program to, say, play some jogging music. When you return to the stopwatch, it's still going.

If you need to pause the timer, tap the Stop button; to pick up where you left off, tap Start again. When you're done with your exercise, tap Stop to halt the clock. To clear the times from the screen, hit the gray Reset button.

Nike + the iPod Nano

On the iPod Nano, tap the Fitness icon on the Home screen to open the app. The Nano has a built-in pedometer, so you don't need the Nike+ shoes and shoe sensor to track your steps, as you do with the Touch. (If you want more accuracy, however, you can still buy the $19 Nike + iPod shoe sensor at *store.apple.com*; on the main Fitness screen, tap ❸ in the lower-right corner to get to the Nike + iPod Sport Kit menu for linking the sensor, a remote control, or even a Bluetooth heart-rate monitor.)

On the Fitness screen, you have two main options: Walk and Run. When you tap Walk, the Nano turns into a musical pedometer as described on the next page. If you tap Run, you get the same choice of goal-oriented workouts as you do with the Touch: Basic, Time, Distance, and Calorie. Page 50 describes these workouts and how to add your own music to the mix. Each type of workout lets you pick a playlist when you select it for action.

You can use the Nano's Play/Pause button (page 132) to momentarily pause a workout in progress. The workout screen itself displays buttons for changing the music, playing your "PowerSong" (page 50), or ending the exercise. When you stop a workout, the Nano recites the statistics (like distance and calories burned) for that session into your earbuds; if you're using the fancy Apple EarPods with the built-in remote control, hold down the center button to hear your current statistics at any given point in the workout.

Later, when you tap the small clock icon in the bottom-left corner of the screen, you see a menu of your past personal bests and overall workout statistics. To upload your info to the Nike+ website, connect your Nano to iTunes. A box pops up asking if you'd like to send your data to Nike; if you do, you're taken to the site to set up a free Nike+ account. You can find out more about how the Nike software works with the iPod at *http://www.apple.com/ipod/nike*.

Counting Steps With the iPod Nano

If walking is more your speed, take the Nano, with its colorful pedometer, along on your strolls so you know how many steps you took.

To set up the pedometer for the first time:

1. On the Home screen, tap Fitness→Walk.

2. Use the on-screen wheels to spin up your height and weight.

3. Tap Start to begin counting your steps, Nano-style (this also turns the Start button into a Stop button). A little shoe in the Nano's menu bar tells you that the pedometer is on and counting away.

4. Tap the Stop button when you're done so you can see the total number of steps you took (plus the distance walked and calories burned) for the day. Swipe the screen from left to right to see your daily, weekly, monthly, and overall stats.

If you need to change your weight, pick a daily step goal for your walks, or want to change the distance measures from miles to kilometers (or vice versa), tap ❶ in the bottom-right corner of the screen.

The Nano Settings Menu

The Settings icon on the Nano's Home screen has submenus so you can tweak your iPod experience. Here's what you can do:

Bluetooth

Tap here to turn on the Nano's Bluetooth receiver so you can pair the player with wireless accessories like a heart-rate monitor or Bluetooth stereo speakers. When the name of the gadget appears on the Nano's screen, tap it to pair it.

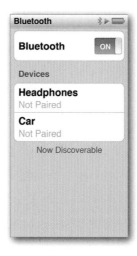

General

Several settings live under this menu, including:

- **About.** Find out how many songs and photos your Nano holds, the player's format (Windows or Mac), the amount of space left, and its serial number.

- **Brightness.** Use the slider to make the Nano's screen dimmer or brighter.

- **Wallpaper.** Tap here to pick a different background for the Home screen.

- **Date & Time.** Set the date, time, and time zone here. You can also opt for the military-style 24 Hour Clock, have the Nano display the time when it wakes up from sleep, and pick a new clock-face style from six options. You can add a World Clock showing the time in three time zones by tapping Settings→General→Date & Time→Clock Face→World Clock. Once you select this clock face, you get a World Clock line in the Date & Time settings. Tap World Clock here and then, on the next screen, select two other cities for time display along with your home zone.

- **Language.** Select the default language for the Nano's menus here.

- **Accessibility.** Turn on the VoiceOver function that speaks menus and item names out loud, or invert the screen colors for a high-contrast look. You can also switch the audio from stereo to mono and program the Home button to toggle VoiceOver or the Inverted Colors scheme when clicked three times.

Music

Turn on Shake to shuffle songs kinetically (you get a new song each time you shake your Nano-clenching fist), even out song volumes with Sound Check (or lock them in with Volume Limit), improve tracks with equalizer presets, or cross-fade from one song to another.

Video

Have your videos pick up where you left off or always start from the beginning here, and also turn on alternate audio, closed captioning, and subtitles.

Radio

If you travel a lot and want to pick up local stations wherever you may be, duck into the Radio settings to pick your current geographic area. You can also turn on (or off) the radio's Live Pause feature here (page 136).

Photos

The Nano puts photo slideshows right in the palm of your hand. Tap into the Photos settings to set the time each slide stays on-screen (from 2 to 20 seconds). You can also choose to repeat a slideshow once its played through, or shuffle the photos in an album as it plays.

Reset Settings

Choose this option to blow away all those custom settings you've been fiddling with and start fresh with the factory defaults.

Customize the Nano's Home Screen

YOU'RE NOT STUCK WITH the iPod's stock icon positions or menu items. On the Nano, you can rearrange icons across the Home screens. So if, for example, you want the Radio and Podcasts icons to appear first, you can make it so.

To redecorate your Home screen, press and hold your finger down on any one icon until they all start wiggling. While they're wiggling, drag the icons into your preferred order. You can also drag an icon off the screen's right edge to drop it on its own empty Home screen page. When you're happy, press the Home button to stop the shaking and lock in the new arrangement.

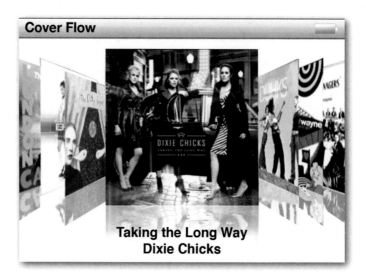

Cover Flow

**Taking the Long Way
Dixie Chicks**

You'll learn to:

- Set up your Classic
- Navigate its menus, jacks, and switches
- Load your Classic with music
- Customize its settings
- Turn the Classic into an external hard drive

CHAPTER 8

Tour the iPod Classic

INTRODUCED IN THE FALL of 2001, the original chunky white iPod changed the world of portable entertainment, melding form and function into an easy-to-use pocket media player. Eleven years later, the iPod has evolved into several different versions, but the essence of original model lives on today as the iPod Classic.

As with the original iPod, today's Classic is still simple to operate—five buttons and a click wheel take you to all your songs, movies, games, audio books, and everything else parked on your 'Pod. Even though the player doesn't have a mouse, its controls work just like those on a desktop computer: You highlight an item on-screen and click the Classic's center button, which either takes you to another menu of options or triggers an action—like playing a song, calling up a calendar, or displaying the time in Paris.

This chapter gives you a tour of the Classic's many features and shows you how to load up the player with music. When you're ready to put the *multi* in multimedia, visit Chapter 14 to learn how to watch video and Chapter 15 to load up photos. While this iPod may lack Internet connectivity and the small size of other iPods, its storage space (a whopping 160 *gigabytes*) and versatility make it well-rounded and, well, *Classic*.

Set Up the iPod Classic

UNLIKE ITS DESCENDANT, THE iPod Touch, the iPod Classic needs to connect to your computer—and iTunes—as part of the setup process. So if you haven't installed iTunes on your Windows PC or Mac, flip back to page 7 for instructions.

Once you have iTunes up and running, take a look inside the box your Classic came in. It should include these items:

1. Apple's newly engineered white headphones.

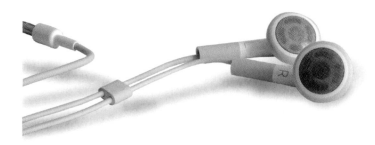

2. A USB cable to connect your Classic to your computer. Although other iPods use Apple's new and smaller Lightning port, the Classic still gets its power and media files via the original 30-pin Dock Connector cable, shown below.

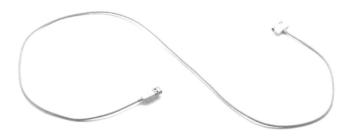

3. A little pamphlet of quick-start information that's not nearly as fun or as colorful as this book.

What you want right now is the USB cable. Connect the small, narrow end to your computer's USB port and the wide, flat end to the iPod Classic. (Thanks to the USB connection, the iPod's battery begins to charge when you plug it into the computer.) If it's not open already, iTunes leaps into action, popping up on your screen, ready to walk you through the Classic configuration process.

Use iTunes to Configure Your Classic

The iTunes Setup Assistant now takes over. It walks you through a few screens that format your new Classic for use with a Windows PC or a Mac, and then it loads music and other content onto your 'Pod.

If this isn't your first iPod—maybe you had a Nano or a Shuffle and decided you needed *a lot* more room for your music collection and only a 160-gigabyte Classic would fit—you might already have music tracks and other files in your iTunes library. If that's the case, iTunes can copy all those audio tracks over to your new Classic and you're good to go.

But if this is your first visit to Apple Land and you've never used iTunes to load up an iProduct, you can have iTunes automatically copy over your media to your iPod; see page 152 for details. Alternatively, you can pick and choose (or "manually manage") what goes onto your iPod; see how on page 153.

In addition to formatting the Classic, the Setup Assistant offers to register your new iPod with Apple. These screens take a few minutes to click through, but can pay off later, as your iPod's serial number is linked to your name in Apple's database—and that can speed up technical support at the Genius Bar or an Apple-autorized provider since there's a record of your purchase.

When you finish setting up and registering your new Classic, its icon appears at the top of the iTunes window, under "iPod." Click the iPod's icon to see details on your new media player—and, as you will soon see, to copy files to it.

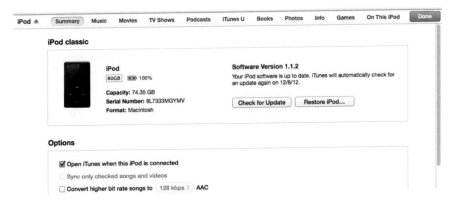

> **NOTE** Windows PCs can't read the Mac disk format, but a Mac can read a Windows-formatted iPod Classic. If you want to use your iPod with both systems—say a Windows PC at work and a Mac at home—plug your 'Pod into the Windows PC first and let iTunes format it for Windows.

iPod Classic Ports and Switches

ALTHOUGH THE BIG WHEEL on the front of the Classic gets all the attention, the top and bottom edges of the player handle all your connections for power and sound. Here's what each port and switch does:

On the top edge of the iPod Classic, you have:

❶ **Hold**. The Classic is the only iPod left with a physical Hold switch. Slide it to the On position (with the orange background visible) to lock down the Classic's controls so your iPod doesn't accidentally get bumped on or off when it rattles around in your pocket or bag.

❷ **Headphones**. The small, round jack on the top of the Classic is where you plug in your white earbuds. And if you don't like white earbuds or want to use a different style of headphones altogether, just plug them in here—as long as your new cans use the standard 3.5mm plug.

On the iPod Classic's bottom edge, you have:

❸ **Dock Connector**. This flat, thin jack is where you plug in one end of the iPod's USB cable so you can connect to your computer to sync up your iTunes library, charge up your Classic battery, or connect external speakers and docks.

> **TIP** In addition to locking the Classic's controls with the Hold switch, you can lock this iPod's screen to keep out prying eyes. To freeze it, go to Extras→Screen Lock and enter a four-digit passcode. Once set, the iPod's screen is locked until you supply the code.

Control the iPod Classic

JUST AS WITH THE original Classic, you still drive today's model with that great big ring of controls on the front of the player. Commonly called the *click wheel*, this where you control your Classic's playback functions for music, video, games, and photo slideshows. To turn on the Classic, push any button on the wheel. From there, you control the player like so:

① **Menu**. Tap this button to return to any screen you just viewed. For example, if you visited Music→Playlists→My Top Rated, you'd press Menu twice to return to the Music menu.

② **Next/Fast-Forward (▶▶I)**. Press here to jump to the next song in a playlist (Chapter 12), or hold the button down to zip through a song that's playing.

③ **Play/Pause (▶II)**. This button starts a song; push it again to pause the music.

④ **Previous/Rewind (I◀◀)**. Press and release this button to play the song before the current track, or hold it down to "rewind" within a song.

⑤ **Center button**. Press here to choose a highlighted menu item. When you have a song title highlighted, pressing Select begins playback. If you press the Select button while a song plays, you cycle through the Classic's options. You can scrub (fast-forward through a song's audio) to a certain part of the song (page 154); assign a star rating to the song by sliding your thumb over the wheel until you see one to five stars on-screen; choose song and album shuffle options; and turn on the iTunes Genius for automatic playlist-creation (page 224). If you pasted lyrics into your song files in iTunes (page 202), you can press Select until you see the words on-screen.

If you get no response when you push a click-wheel button, check to make sure the Classic's Hold switch (previous page) isn't on and that the iPod's battery hasn't run down. (Page 10 has more on charging up the battery.)

Navigate the iPod Classic's Menus

LIKE ANY MODERN GADGET, the iPod uses a series of menus and submenus to control it. You can recognize the Classic's top-level, or main, menu because it says "iPod" at the top of the screen. No matter how deeply you burrow into the player's submenus, you can always get back to the main menu by repeatedly pressing the Menu button on the click wheel.

Think of Classic navigation like this: Press the center button to go deeper into menus and press the Menu button to back out, retracing your steps along the way. The contents of your iPod menu vary a bit depending on what you're doing at the time and whether you changed any of the default settings, but here's the basic lineup. The next page shows you how to mix and match menu items:

- **Music.** The Music menu holds all the submenus that let you organize your collection—Cover Flow (page 36), Playlists, Artists, Albums, Compilations, Songs, Genres, and Composers. Audiobooks and a Search feature live here, too. Select a submenu, say Albums, to see your music grouped by album.

- **Videos.** The Classic stores your movies, TV shows, and music videos under the Videos menu, as it does any iTunes movies you rent or video playlists you create. The Video Settings menu, which lets you connect the Classic to a TV so you can see photos and movies on the big screen, is here, too.

- **Photos.** Pictures and photo albums you sync from your computer (page 274) are here, as well as the timing and music settings for slideshows.

- **Podcasts.** Those free audio and video shows you download from the iTunes Store live under this menu.

- **Extras.** You'll find things that make the Classic more than a media player—clocks, calendars, games, and notes—under the Extras menu; they're described beginning on page 156.

- **Settings.** As with your desktop computer, you can tweak and fine-tune your iPod's settings to your heart's content. Page 150 explains what each item in the Settings menu can do for you.

- **Shuffle Songs.** Want to mix up the music? Scroll to the Shuffle Songs menu to have your Classic spin tunes in random order.

- **Now Playing.** You only see the Now Playing option if you have a song currently playing. Scroll down and select it if you can't remember the name of that song wafting into your ears.

Customize Your iPod's Menus

The iPod Classic lets you customize both your main menu and your music menu so you see only the options you like. For example, you could add "Calendar" as a main menu item so you don't have to dig through the Extras menu to get at it.

To do that, choose iPod→Settings→Main Menu. As you scroll down the list of menu items, press the center button to add (or delete) each one from the main menu. You might, for example, consider adding these commands:

- Clock, for quick checks of the time.

- Games, for quick killing of time.

- Contacts, to look up phone numbers and call people to pass the time.

To see the fruits of your labor, press Menu twice to return to the main screen. Sure enough, in addition to the usual items, you see the formerly buried menus right out front, ready to go.

Now that you've got your Classic's main menu squared away, you can customize your iPod's music screen by choosing Settings→Music Menu.

Want to learn more iPod settings? Turn the page.

Adjust The iPod Classic Settings

THE SETTINGS MENU HAS more than a dozen options for tailoring your iPod's look and sound.

- **About.** Look here for your iPod's serial number; the number of songs, videos, and photos on it; your model's hard drive size; and how much disk space you have left. Click the center button to go through all three screens of info.

- **Shuffle.** Turn this feature to On to shuffle songs or albums.

- **Repeat.** Repeat One plays the current song over and over; Repeat All repeats the current album, playlist, or song library.

- **Main Menu.** Customize which items appear in the Classic's main menu here.

- **Music Menu.** Customize which items appear in your music menu here.

- **Volume Limit.** Keep your (or your child's) eardrums from melting down by setting a volume limit. The bar on the screen shows the iPod's maximum volume. Slide the scroll wheel until the indicator on screen shows a new, less-loud maximum volume. Press the Play button to lock in the volume limit.

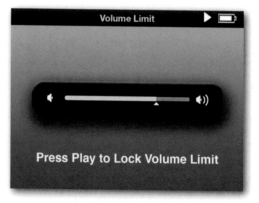

- **Backlight.** Specify how long your screen's backlight stays on each time you press a button or turn a dial—from 2 seconds to Always On.

- **Brightness.** If your iPod movies seem a bit dim (and not just because of Hollywood's standards), use this setting to brighten the screen.

- **Audiobooks.** Having trouble catching all the words as you listen to an audiobook? Visit this setting, where you can speed up or slow down the narration.

- **EQ.** Choose from more than 20 equalizer presets for acoustic, classical, hip-hop, and other types of music. Chapter 5 has more on equalization.

- **Sound Check.** Turn on Sound Check to level out the song volume as you go from one tune to the next. Chapter 11 has more.

- **Clicker.** Some people think the clicker noise the Classic makes during a long scroll sounds like ants tap-dancing. Others like the audio cue. Decide for yourself and turn the sound off or on here.

- **Date & Time.** Adjust your iPod's date, time, and time zone here. If you want your iPod to always display the time at the top of the screen, flip the "Time in Title" setting to On here.

- **Sort By.** This setting lets you change the sort order of the contacts in your iPod's address book (first name first or last name first).

- **Language.** The iPod can display its menus in most major European and Asian languages. Pick the one you want here. If your Classic gets set to a language you can't read (accidentally or by the hand of a prank-minded associate), you can restore your native tongue to the menus a couple of ways.

    For one, you can scroll all the way down to the end of the menu to the Reset All Settings option and select it. Although this pops you back to the iPod's original pick-a-language screen, it also wipes out any other settings you custom-configured.

    The second method saves your settings but requires some careful counting: Start by clicking the Menu button until you get back to the main iPod menu.

    Next, scroll down to the sixth line on the main screen and select it. This calls up the Settings menu, even if you can't read it. On the Settings menu, scroll all the way down, select the third line from the bottom (as shown above) and press the center button. That takes you to the big list of languages, with English right there on top. Select your language of choice, press the center button to set it, and return to business as usual.

- **Legal.** The Legal screen contains a long scroll of copyright notices for Apple and its software partners. It's not very interesting reading unless you're studying intellectual-property law.

- **Reset All Settings.** This command returns all your iPod's customized sound and display settings to their factory defaults.

Load Music onto the iPod Classic

NOT EVERYONE WANTS TO haul around their entire iTunes library—and some people can't even if they wanted to because they have too much stuff. Here are the various ways to load music onto the Classic from iTunes.

Automatic sync

If you want iTunes 11 to automatically load a copy of all the music and videos in your library, you can make it so. Just connect the Classic to iTunes, click the iPod icon that appears at the top of the iTunes window, and then click the Summary tab on the next screen. Once you turn off the checkbox next to "Manually manage music and videos" and click the Apply/Sync button, your Classic gets the works.

Selective sync

If you want more control over what goes on your iPod, click the iPod icon at the top of the iTunes window. Along the top of the next screen, you see a row of tabs marked Music, Movies, TV Shows, and so on. Now:

1. Click the Music tab and turn on the checkbox next to Sync Music.

2. Click the button next to "Selected playlists, artists, albums, and genres" and in the list that appears below, turn on the checkboxes next to everything you want to copy to the iPod. Turn on the checkbox next to "Automatically fill free space with songs" if you want to top off the iPod's tank with extra music after iTunes copies over your selections.

3. Click Apply and then Sync to make it so.

Selectively syncing your iPod lets you automatically copy certain items (the ones you choose in step 2 above) each time you connect your player. But you can still manually drag new items from your iTunes library onto the iPod when you want (see next page).

Manual management

If you don't have enough room on your Classic for your whole iTunes library, or if you plan to load music onto your iPod from more than one computer—say your work PC and home PC—you'll want to *manually* manage your songs and other media. (If you've already chosen autosync, click the iPod's Summary screen when it's connected to iTunes and turn on the checkbox next to "Manually manage music and videos.") iTunes now refrains from automatically dumping everything onto your iPod. "But," you ask, "*how* do I get the music on there by myself?" Easy—you just drag it:

1. **In iTunes, click the Music icon under the Library pop-up menu**. Click the Songs button to see all the songs in your music library. You can also click Ctrl+B (⌘-B) to go into Column Browser view (page 176), where iTunes lists your music by genre, artist, and album.

2. **Click the songs or albums you want to copy to your iPod**. Grab multiple songs or albums by holding down the Ctrl (⌘) key while clicking.

3. **Drag your selections to the right side of the screen, onto the iPod icon that appears**. The number of songs you're dragging appears inside a red circle.

You can manually load any items in your iTunes library—audiobooks, movies, whatever—onto your iPod this way.

Jump Around Within Songs and Videos

SOMETIMES, YOU JUST HAVE to hear the good part of a song again or watch that scene in a movie once more because it was so cool the first time. If that's the case, the iPod gives you the controls to make it happen.

This jump-to-the-best-part technique is called *scrubbing*, so if a fellow iPod-der tells you to scrub over to 2:05 in a song to hear a great guitar solo, he's not talking about cleaning the bathtub. It's all about having a fast-forward/reverse control with a visual guide.

Here's how to scrub on the iPod Classic:

1. When a song or video is playing on the screen, hold down the Rewind/ Previous or the Fast Forward/Next buttons on either side of the click wheel to zip back and forth through a song or video clip.

2. To get to a specific time in a song or video, press the Classic's center button and then use the click wheel to scroll over to the exact spot in the track's on-screen timeline. For an audio file, a small diamond appears in the timeline when you press the center button so you can see where you are in a song.

3. For video files with DVD-style chapter markers (which look like small vertical lines along the timeline bar), press the Rewind/Previous or Fast Forward/ Next button to retreat or advance chapter by chapter.

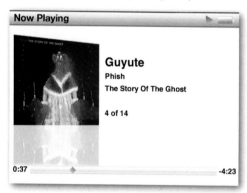

TIP Scrubbing through a track makes fast work of finding a particular spot in a song, and the Classic has a couple other time-related goodies. For one, there's the Sleep Timer feature to lull you to sleep. Choose Extras→Alarms→Sleep Timer and then pick the amount of time you want the Classic to play: 15, 30, 60, 90, or 120 minutes. (You can choose to turn the timer *off* here as well.) Once you pick a time, press Play and relax. And if you really like timers, go to Extras→Stopwatch→New Timer to track your laps or time your presentations.

Search for Songs on the iPod Classic

AS YOUR MUSIC COLLECTION grows, scrolling to find a song or album can leave you thumb-weary. Sometimes, you may not even remember if you *have* a certain song on the Classic, given its 160 gigabytes of storage. The Classic's Search feature lets you drill down through your massive library to locate specific songs, albums, and so on with a few spins of the click wheel. It works like this:

1. Choose iPod→Music→Search.

2. On the screen that appears, use the click wheel to high-light a letter from the alphabet. Press the center button to select the letter.

3. The iPod immediately presents a list of matching titles, winnowing the list further as you select more letters. Use the iPod's Rewind/Previous key as a backspace button to wipe out letters you don't want.

4. Once the title you want appears on-screen, click the Menu button (to jump up to the results list), and then scroll down to select your song.

Search Visually With Cover Flow

SEARCHING BY SONG NAME is one way to find the music you're looking for, but you can visually search your Classic's music collection, too. Press iPod→Music→Cover Flow to see all your music displayed as miniature album covers (or gray music notes if you haven't added art; see page 201).

To take a stroll through the music, slide your thumb along the iPod's scroll wheel to see the covers sail by. When you see an album you want to play, press ▶❙❙. To see the tracks on the album, press the center button to flip the cover around. Scroll to the desired song and press ▶❙❙ to play it.

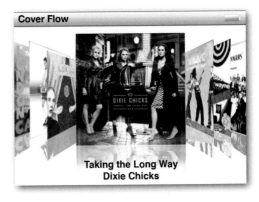

Taking the Long Way
Dixie Chicks

The iPod as Address Book

PUTTING A COPY OF your contacts file—also known as your computer's address book—on your iPod is easy with the help of iTunes.

Windows users need to store their contacts in Outlook Express, Outlook 2003 or later, Windows Contacts, or the Windows Address Book (used by Outlook Express and some other email programs).

Mac folks need to have at least Mac OS X 10.5 (Leopard) and the Mac OS X Address Book (shown below), which Apple's Mail program uses to stash names and numbers. You can also use Entourage 2004 or later and Outlook 2011, but you have to *link* before you *sync*: In the mail program, choose Preferences, and then click Sync Services. Turn on the checkboxes for sharing contacts and calendars with Address Book and iCal (Apple's calendar program) to have the shared info synced up with Address Book and iCal.

To turn your iPod Classic into a little black book, follow these steps:

1. Connect your iPod to your computer and click its icon in the iTunes window. (If you use Outlook, launch that now, too.)

2. At the top of the iTunes window, click the Info tab.

3. Windows owners: Turn on the checkbox next to "Sync contacts from" and use the drop-down menu to choose the program that holds your contacts. Mac owners: Turn on the "Sync Address Book contacts" checkbox. If you want to sync contact *groups*, select them from the "Selected groups" box. You can also choose to import the photos in your contacts files.

4. Click Apply in the lower-right corner of the iTunes window.

iTunes updates your iPod with the contact information stored in your address book. To ditch a person, delete him or her from your computer's address book, and the contact disappears from your iPod the next time you sync up.

To look up a pal on an iPod Classic, choose iPod→Extras→Contacts and scroll to the name of the person. Press the center button, and you'll see his address card pop up on-screen.

The iPod as Calendar

JUST AS ITUNES CAN pluck contacts out of your computer's address book, so it can snag and sync a copy of your desktop's daily or monthly schedule to your iPod Classic—*if* you use Outlook on your PC or iCal on your Mac. (You can also use Entourage 2004 or later by choosing, in Entourage, Preferences→Sync Services and turning on the option to have Entourage share events with iCal; Outlook 2011 for the Mac works the same way.)

To get your calendar connected, fire up iTunes and follow these steps:

1. Connect your iPod to the computer and click the iPod icon in the Devices list.

2. In the main part of the iTunes window, click the Info tab. Scroll down past Contacts to Calendars.

3. Turn on the checkbox next to "Sync Calendars." If you have multiple calendars, select the ones you want to copy.

4. In the lower-right corner of the iTunes window, click Apply.

5. If iTunes doesn't automatically start updating your iPod with your datebook, choose File→Sync iPod. If you haven't changed any sync settings and you're just *updating* contact info, iTunes' Apply button turns into a Sync button, and you can click that instead of going up to Menuville.

To look up your busy schedule on a Classic, choose iPod→Extras→Calendars. Select the name of the calendar you want to examine and press the center button. You get a blue-and-gray grid with tiny red flags planted on the days you have something scheduled. Use the scroll wheel to navigate to a particular day, and then press the center button to see the details.

If you use the To Do list function in your calendar program, your action items appear in their own place on the Classic. Choose iPod→Extras→Calendars→To Do's. You can also have your iPod remind you of upcoming events. To turn on Nag Alerts on the Classic, choose iPod→Extras→Calendars→Alarms. You have your choice of Off, Beep, or None (the last displays a silent message on-screen).

Set the iPod's Clock

WHEN YOU CONNECT YOUR iPod to your computer, the player's clock syncs up with the one on your Windows PC or Mac. If you don't sync that often or you travel between time zones, you may need to reset the clock.

To adjust your current clock for things like daylight saving time, the current date, the time zone—or to opt for the military-style 24-hour clock display—choose iPod→Settings→Date & Time.

To change the city a clock represents, click it with the Classic's center button and then select Edit. Pick the geographic area you want from the Region menu, and then choose a city on the next screen. The clock adjusts itself to the new time zone.

You aren't stuck with just one clock on the Classic. Your iPod can also serve as a world timekeeper, showing the hour in places faraway. Here's how to add multiple clocks:

1. **Go to iPod→Extras→Clocks.** Press the iPod's center button.

2. **You'll see your local clock.** Press the center button again to select Add. (Choose Edit if you have just one clock but want to change it.)

3. **On the next screen, select a world region, like North America, Europe, Africa, or Asia.** Some categories on the Region menu are less obvious: Select Atlantic if you live in Iceland or the Azores; choose Pacific if you live in Hawaii, Guam, or Pago Pago.

4. **Once you select a region, a new screen displays a list of major cities and the current time in that part of the world.** Scroll and select the city of your choice. Once you do, the iPod creates a clock named after the city, displays the local time, and adds the timepiece to the Clocks menu.

If you want to change a clock, select it and press the iPod's center button to bring up the Edit and Delete options. Choose Edit, which takes you back through the whole "pick a region, pick a city" exercise.

If you decide you have too many clocks and don't need that Bora Bora timepiece after all, select the unwanted clock from the list. Press the center button on the iPod, scroll down to Delete, and then press the center button again to erase time.

Use the iPod Classic as an Alarm Clock

IT MAY NOT HAVE the booming wake-up powers of a bedside alarm clock, but the iPod Classic's alarm can give you a gentle nudge when you need it.

To set your alarm:

1. **Choose Extras→Alarms→Create Alarm**. Press the center button. The alarm gets set to On, and you land on a screen full of choices, described below.

2. **Choose Date**. As you turn the click wheel, you change the date for your wake-up call. Press the center button as you pick the month, day, minutes, and so on.

3. **Choose Time**. Repeat the wheel-turning and clicking to choose the hour, minute, and AM/PM setting for the alarm. When you get back to the Create Alarm menu, click Repeat if this is a standing alert, and then choose the alarm's frequency: daily, weekly, and so on.

4. **Choose Alert Sound**. It's time to decide whether you want "Beep" (a warbling R2-D2–like tone that comes out of the iPod's built-in speaker) or music from a selected playlist. If you choose music, it plays through your headphones (assuming they haven't fallen out) or to an external set of speakers if you have some (Chapter 16).

5. **Choose Label**. What's alarming you—a class, a meeting, time to take a pill? Pick a name for your alarm here.

If you wake up early and want to turn off the alarm so it doesn't bother anybody else, go to Extras→Alarms→[Name of Alarm]→Alarm and press the center button to toggle it off. You can also delete an alarm with the Delete option at the bottom of the menu.

Voice Memos: The iPod as Audio Recorder

THE IPOD CLASSIC DOESN'T just *play* sound, it can *record* it, too, thanks to its Voice Memos feature. You do need to invest in an external microphone for the player first, though—Apple's optional Earphones with Remote and Mic (available for $29 at *www.apple.com/ipodstore*) or a compatible third-party microphone. In fact, you need a microphone *connected* to even see the Voice Memos menus on the Classic.

Once you have your microphone in place, you can start your recording session:

1. Choose iPod→Voice Memos.

2. To start recording, choose Voice Memos→Start Recording. You can pause your recording by pressing ▶︎II on the Classic's click wheel. Press ▶︎II again to pick up recording where you left off.

3. When you're finished recording, press the Menu button, and then choose Stop and Save. To play back a recording, choose iPod→Voice Memos→Recordings and select the recording.

To erase a recording from the Classic, press the center button to select it, and then choose Delete from the menu. The next time you sync your iPod, iTunes copies your recordings to its Voice Memos playlist. You can find audio files on Classics enabled for disk use (described below) in the iPod's Recordings folder.

The iPod as Portable Hard Drive

AS IF BEING A portable entertainment system and organizer isn't enough, your iPod Classic can also serve as a portable hard drive to shuttle documents, presentations, and other files from one computer to another.

To give your iPod these file-toting powers:

1. Plug your iPod into your computer.

2. When its icon shows up the iTunes window, select it, and then click the Summary tab on the next screen.

3. Turn on the checkbox next to "Enable disk use" in the Options area of the Summary screen.

4. In the lower-right corner of the iTunes window, click Apply. If you forget and try to move on to something else, iTunes reminds you that you modified an iPod setting and prompts you to OK the change.

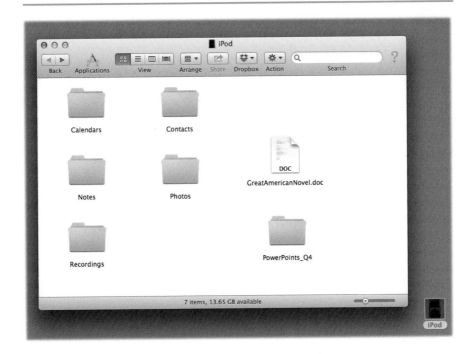

Your iPod now shows up as an icon in the My Computer area of Windows or on the Mac desktop. You can drag files on and off the icon just as you would files for any other drive connected to your computer. You can also double-click the iPod icon to create folders for your files.

File Management on the iPod Hard Drive

Like all hard drives, you'll eventually want to clean up stuff you stashed on the iPod. Delete files by dragging them to the Recycle Bin or the Trash. Steer clear of the folders labeled Photos (and, on the Classic, the folders tagged Calendars, Contacts, and Notes); the iPod uses them to store the eponymous items. (Turn the page to see what else you can do with the Notes folder.)

Keep in mind that once you turn your iPod into an external hard drive, you have to treat it like one by formally ejecting it from iTunes before disconnecting your iPod. Do so by clicking the Eject icon next to the iPod's name in the iTunes Devices list and you'll avoid huffy alert boxes from your operating system about improper device removal.

Your iPod keeps music, movies, and other iTunes stuff in a special, invisible area of the player, so you can enjoy all that media even when you use your 'Pod as a file courier. (And syncing your music with a Windows PC or Mac doesn't affect the computer files, either.) But remember that the more you fill up your iPod with data files, the less room you have for entertainment—and vice versa.

Read Text Files on the iPod Classic

IT'S A LITTLE-KNOWN FEATURE, but the iPod Classic and older click-wheel Nanos can display basic text files on-screen. You create these iPod notes as plain text files (those with a *.txt* extension), like those from Windows Notepad or TextEdit on a Mac. (You can't read full-fledged word-processing documents from Microsoft Word or Apple's Pages unless you save them as plain text files.)

To use the iPod's Notes feature:

1. Connect your iPod to your computer as an external drive (flip back a page to find out how).

2. Once you save your files in the plain-text format, open your iPod by double-clicking its icon in the Computer window in Windows Vista/Windows 7/ Windows 8 (the My Computer window for Windows XP) or on the Mac desktop.

3. Drag the files into the Notes folder on your iPod.

4. After you copy your files, eject the iPod from iTunes by clicking the Eject button next to its name in the Devices list, or use the Eject button in the corner of the iTunes window.

5. When you're ready to start reading, choose Extras→Notes. You'll see the names of your text files listed in the Notes menu. Scroll to the one you want, and then press the iPod's center button to bring it up on-screen.

As you read, you can use the scroll wheel to page up and down through the file. Press the Menu button to close the file and return to the list of notes.

Using the iPod as a text reader is a handy way to bring your grocery list with you so you can rock while you shop. But to browse prose more challenging than "Buy Pampers," swing by Project Gutenberg's website at *www.gutenberg.us*. Here you can download thousands of public-domain literary works as plain text files and transfer them to your iPod's Notes folder. (The iPod can display files up to only a measly 4

Boswell's Life of Johnson highlights.txt

Mr. Cambridge, upon this, politely said, 'Dr. Johnson, I am going, with your pardon, to accuse myself, for I have the same custom which I perceive you have. But it seems odd that one should have such a desire to look at the backs of books.' Johnson, ever ready for contest, instantly started from his reverie, wheeled about, and answered, 'Sir, the reason is very plain. Knowledge is of two kinds. We know a subject ourselves, or we know where we can find information upon it. When we enquire into any subject, the first thing we have to do is to know what books have treated of it. This leads us to look at catalogues, and the backs of books in libraries.'

kilobytes in size; to read longer files, see the list of shareware programs on this book's Missing CD page at *www.missingmanuals.com/cds/ipodtmm11/*.)

 # Play Games on an iPod Classic

THE IPOD CLASSIC IS a personal entertainment machine on many levels, and it comes with three games: Klondike, iQuiz, and Vortex. To find them, go to iPod→Extras→Games.

Klondike

The iPod has a Vegas-style Klondike solitaire game. To play, you get a row of seven card piles, on which you alternate black and red cards in descending numerical order. Use the click wheel to pass a virtual hand over each stack. Click the center button when you get to the card you want to move to the bottom of the screen. Then scroll the hand to the pile where you want to place the card and click the center button again to make the play. Click the facedown card (upper left) for three new cards to play.

iQuiz

Complete with colorful flashing graphics and a cheesy, '70s-style game show soundtrack, iQuiz picks your brain with contemporary multiple-choice questions in several trivia categories like music, movies, and TV. The game brings its own questions to the screen, but it also taps into your iPod to find out how much you know about your own library.

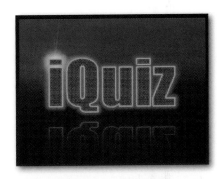

Vortex

Most computers and handheld devices wouldn't be complete without some brick-bashing version of the old Pong-against-the-wall game. Vortex scales up the basic concept to 360 degrees of brick-smashing 3-D fun. Use the scroll wheel to move the bat around the edges of the circular Vortex and audibly smash through the rotating bricks.

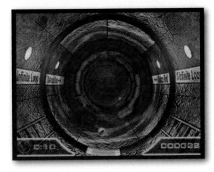

You'll learn to:

- Get your Shuffle up and running

- Automatically fill it with music, audiobooks, and podcasts

- Make the Shuffle announce song titles

- Use the Shuffle as a flash drive

CHAPTER 9

Tour the iPod Shuffle

AS THE SMALLEST MEMBER of Clan iPod, the Shuffle is often overshadowed by the more full-featured members of the family. Sure, the Shuffle has no WiFi access, apps, or even a screen—but who needs any of that when you're out on a 10-mile run at 6 a.m.?

The Shuffle's simplicity is perhaps its greatest asset: It's just there to play music, audiobooks, and audio podcasts and not distract you while you're working out or sitting quietly. At 1.24 inches wide by 1.14 inches high and grazing the scales at 44 ounces, this featherweight iPod won't distract you physically because it comes with a built-in clip that lets you attach it to your collar, t-shirt, or bag strap.

Although the Shuffle has no screen, that doesn't prevent it from giving you feedback about the song or playlist currently coursing through your earbuds. Thanks to its optional VoiceOver feature, the Shuffle announces the title of your current selection at the touch of a button.

This tiny iPod runs on stable flash memory—the same kind used in pocket USB drives. With a couple of clicks, you can convert your Shuffle into file-toting flash drive, too. This chapter shows you how to get the most out of your Shuffle in, shall we say, a flash.

Control the iPod Shuffle

AS MUSIC PLAYERS GO, the iPod Shuffle is a breeze to operate. The ring on the front handles all your playback moves, with a button and switch on the top edge to provide the eponymous shuffle function and VoiceOver feedback.

Here's what each part and port on the Shuffle can do for you:

➊ The control ring rules the content on this iPod. Press a button to play and pause tracks (▶︎❙❙), jump ahead to the next track (▶︎▶︎❙), or back to the previous one (❙◀︎◀︎). Adjust the Shuffle's volume by pressing the top of the ring to make things louder (**+**) or the bottom (**-**) to lower the level.

➋ The earbuds/USB adapter jack sits on the left side of the top edge. You need to unplug one to use the other, so when the Shuffle's battery gets low, disconnect the earbuds and plug in the skinny end of the USB adapter (shown right). Plug the flat end into your computer or a compatible AC adapter (page 8) and charge away.

➌ The tiny status light shows green when the battery charge is good (●), amber when it's dipping low (●), and red when you need to recharge soon (●). A flashing yellow light when you have the Shuffle connected to your computer means Do Not Remove until it finishes copying your songs and files.

➍ The Shuffle's VoiceOver button is in the middle. Push it to hear the Shuffle announce the name of the current song or playlist. (There's more on VoiceOver on page 170.)

➎ The Shuffle's On/Off switch, here in the Off position, is on the right side. Slide it one notch to the middle to play tunes in order (⟳) or slide it over all the way over to shuffle them (⤨).

Set Up and Sync the Shuffle

AS WITH ANY IPOD (except for the Touch), you need to connect the Shuffle to your Windows PC or Mac and fill it up with music, podcasts, and other audio through Apple's iTunes program. If you haven't installed iTunes yet, see page 7. If you don't have any music either, see Chapter 10.

Once you have iTunes installed and some music ready to go, plug in the Shuffle's USB adapter to the headphone jack and connect the bigger end to your computer's USB port. If you have an iTunes library smaller than 1.88 gigabytes, you can sync all your content to the Shuffle by clicking its icon on the main iTunes screen and then clicking the Summary tab. Turn off the checkbox next to "Manually manage music" and then click the Apply/Sync button.

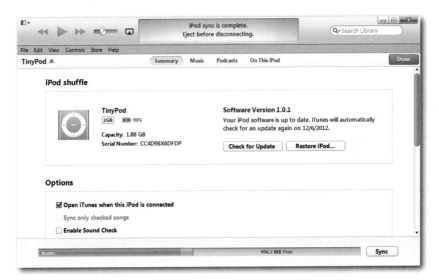

If you have an enormous music collection, though, all your songs may not fit, and you'll get a message saying iTunes will copy as much music as it can. If you have high-quality audio tracks (page 180), you can have iTunes auto-matically convert the Shuffle versions to smaller files so you can squeeze more of them on. With the iPod connected to iTunes, clicks its icon under "Devices," and then click the Summary tab. Scroll down to Options, turn on the checkbox next to "Convert higher bit rate songs," and select a lower bit rate from the pop-up menu, like 128 kbps. Click Apply and Sync. The trade-off here is audio fidelity—while your songs may not sound as rich, it's a case of quantity over quality.

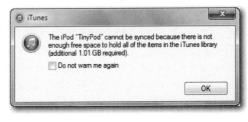

Autofill Your Shuffle with Songs

IF YOU LIKE ALL the music in your collection but don't feel like manually managing it all the time, you can have iTunes randomly load your Shuffle using Autofill. Go to View→Show Sidebar (if it's not already visible) and click the triangle next to the Shuffle icon to spin open its audio libraries. Click the Music icon there. The Autofill bar appears at the bottom of the iTunes window.

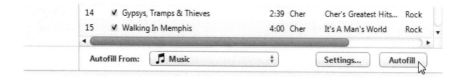

In the "Autofill From" pop-up menu, tell iTunes to snag songs from your entire library or just a particular playlist (see Chapter 12). Click the Settings button and in the box that pops up (shown below), have iTunes pick random tracks or select highly rated songs more often. ("Ratings?" you say? Check out Chapter 11.)

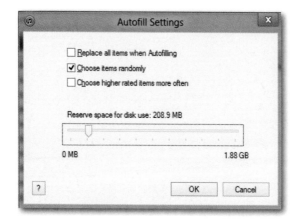

After you Autofill for the first time, when you return for another batch of songs, you can turn on the checkbox next to "Replace all items when Autofilling" to have iTunes wipe the first batch of songs off your iPod and substitute new tracks.

Once iTunes fills up your 'Pod, you see an "iPod sync is complete" message at the top of the screen. Click the Eject button next to your iPod's icon, unplug the player from the computer, clip it onto your shirt, and head out with your little metal square full of music.

Manually Fill Your iPod Shuffle

IF *YOU* WANT TO decide what goes onto your Shuffle, opt for manual updates instead of letting iTunes choose. As with any other iPod on manual control, you drag songs and playlists you want from your iTunes library and drop them onto the Shuffle icon that appears when you drag files to the right edge of the iTunes window..

To see what's on your Shuffle, click the iPod's icon in the iTunes window and then click On This iPod. Feel free to rearrange individual songs in the order you want to hear them—just drag them up or down. The info at the bottom of the iTunes window tells you how much space you have left on your Shuffle.

To delete songs from the On This iPod screen, select one or more tracks and then press the Delete key on your keyboard. This action deletes the song from your Shuffle only, not from your iTunes library; see page 208.

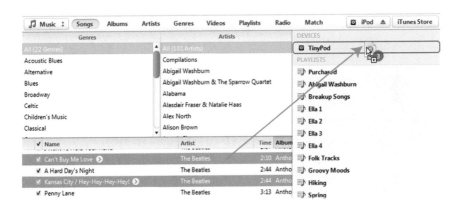

You can also mix and match your song-loading methods. Start by dragging a few favorite playlists over to the Shuffle, and then click Autofill to finish the job. Just make sure you turn the "Replace all items when Autofilling" checkbox off, or iTunes will wipe out the tracks you already added.

TIP The Shuffle may be tiny, but it can produce big sound—so big that it may cause hearing damage if you crank it up too high. Because of its easy interface and low price, children often use this iPod, and they may not realize the potential for injury.

To help prevent this sort of thing, you can limit the Shuffle's loudness. Connect the player to iTunes, click the Shuffle's icon on the left side of the screen, and click the Summary tab at the top of the iTunes window. Scroll down to Options, and turn on the checkbox next to "Limit maximum volume." Use the on-screen slider to lower the top volume the Shuffle can reach—and click the lock icon to set a password that prevents small hands from undoing the favor you just did their ears. Click Apply and then Sync.

Use VoiceOver on the Shuffle

THE SHUFFLE MAY NOT have a screen, but it has a voice—which announces the names of your songs when you push the VoiceOver button its top edge. To get the Shuffle yapping, though, you need to turn on the VoiceOver feature in iTunes. Connect the Shuffle to your computer with its USB cable, click its icon on the left side of the iTunes window, and then click the Summary tab at the top of the screen.

Scroll down to the options area, turn on the checkbox next to Enable VoiceOver, and choose the language you want the Shuffle to speak (it knows 29 of them) from the pop-up menu. Click Apply and Sync.

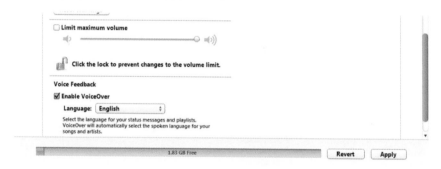

Sync Podcasts and Other Audio

The iPod Shuffle isn't limited to playing music—it can also play audiobooks, recorded iTunes U lectures, and audio podcasts from the iTunes Store. Once you download these spoken-word files to iTunes, you can sync them over to your iPod. Plug in the Shuffle, click its icon on the left side of the iTunes window, and then click the tab describing the content you want to sync—Podcasts, iTunes U, or Books—to get to those settings. (If you don't have any iTunes U content, you don't see an iTunes U tab; ditto for Podcasts and Books.)

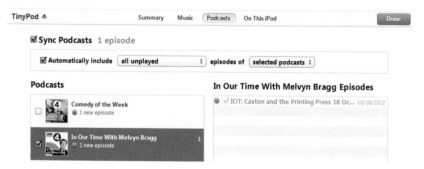

As shown at the bottom of the previous page, you can automatically refresh podcasts, which often have daily, monthly, or weekly episodes, each time you connect the Shuffle to your computer. Just click the Podcasts tab and use the pop-up menu at the top of the screen to control which episodes (new, recent, or unplayed) get copied automatically. In the lower part of the window, you can choose specific episodes to sync. Click Apply and Sync when you finish.

Use the Shuffle As a Flash Drive

AS IF BEING A miniature entertainment system and organizer isn't enough, your Shuffle can also serve as a portable hard drive to shuttle documents, pre-sentations, and other files from one computer to another.

To give your iPod these file-toting powers:

1. Plug your Shuffle into your computer.

2. When its icon shows up in the iTunes window, select it, and then click the Summary tab on the next screen.

3. Turn on the checkbox next to "Enable disk use" in the Options area of the Summary screen. To set a limit for non-music storage on the storage-shy Shuffle, spin its triangle open, click the Music icon, and then click the Autofill settings button (page 168). Drag the slider to the desired amount of space.

4. In the lower-right corner of the iTunes window, click Apply.

Your iPod now shows up as an icon in the Computer area of Windows or on the Mac desktop. You can drag files on and off the icon just as you would files for any other drive connected to your computer. You can also double-click the iPod icon to create folders for your files. Delete files by dragging  them to the Recycle Bin or the Trash and electronically emptying the receptacle.

Keep in mind that once you turn your iPod Shuffle into an external flash drive, you have to treat it like one by formally ejecting the drive from iTunes before disconnecting your 'Pod. Do so by clicking the Eject icon next to the iPod's name in the iTunes Devices list and you'll avoid huffy alert boxes from your operating system about improper device removal.

You'll learn to:

- Navigate the redesigned iTunes 11
- Convert music from CDs
- Customize iTunes' look
- Browse and search media
- Shuffle your music
- Relax with the Visualizer

iTunes Basics

IF YOU READ CHAPTER 1 to find a speedy way to get your iPod set up and ready to play, you've already dipped a toe into the iTunes waters. But as you may have guessed, beneath its pretty surface, iTunes is a deep well of media-management wonders.

Even if you haven't bought any music from the iTunes Store yet, you can use the program to import music from your CD collection. Once you check everything into your iTunes library, the program makes it easy to browse and search through your media treasures. You can add song ratings, lyrics, and artwork to your music files, too.

Yes, iTunes is a powerful media organizer. So powerful, in fact, that this chapter focuses on its most basic and useful functions—like what its controls do and how to import music from CDs. Chapter 11 focuses on advanced iTunes features, and Chapter 12 tells you how to create customized song playlists. Chapter 13 is all about blowing your bucks at the iTunes Store, and Chapter 14 spotlights the video side of iTunes.

Even if you've used iTunes before, Apple overhauled the program in November 2012 to give a fresh look, new features, and a bit of zip under the hood. So turn the page to get to know iTunes 11 better.

The iTunes Window: An Introduction

ITUNES IS YOUR IPOD'S best friend. You can do just about everything with your digital files here—convert songs on a CD into iPod-ready tunes, buy music, listen to Internet radio stations, watch videos, and more. Here's a quick tour of the main iTunes window and what all the buttons and sliders do.

The small drop-down menu on the left side of iTunes displays all your media libraries. Click an item in the panel to see its contents in the center of the main window, like so:

➊ From the Library drop-down menu, you can see the types of media in your various libraries. As you add music, movies, and other stuff to iTunes, click the appropriate link to find what you're looking for—songs, TV shows, and so on. Programs you buy for the iPod Touch land here under Apps. Want to change what iTunes lists? Press Ctrl+comma (⌘-comma) to call up iTunes' Preferences menu, and then click the General tab. In the "Sources" area, turn on (or off) the checkboxes for, say, Tones or iTunes U.

➋ If you have a music CD in your computer's drive, it shows up in the Library menu as well. Click the gray Eject icon (⏏) next to the disc name to safely pop it out.

➌ In the Shared area, you can browse the media libraries of other iTunes fans and stream their music if you have iTunes' Home Sharing feature turned on (page 190). When you're fully set up with Home Sharing, you can copy music and videos between machines.

The outer edges of the iTunes window are full of buttons and controls. Here's what they do:

● Play and pause a song or video—or jump to the next or previous track. The volume slider adjusts the sound level. If you see a ▣ icon, you have an Apple TV or set of AirPlay-enabled speakers on your network through which you can play your iTunes music (Chapter 12 has more on that). The Windows version of iTunes has a small square icon in the upper-left corner, as shown here. Click the triangle next to it to turn iTunes' menu bar (File, Edit, View, and so on) on or off.

● The center of the upper pane shows the song currently playing. Click the album cover to see a larger picture of it pop up on-screen, complete with its own set of playback controls (there's an example on this chapter's opening page). This window has a few other icons of note. Click the Loop icon (⟳) to repeat the current album or playlist and click it again so it looks like ⟳ to repeat the current track. Click the ✕ icon to shuffle your music and click it again to return to normal song order. To see what's in your Up Next list (page 227), click ≡.

● A search box awaits your keywords. Page 183 has more on searching.

Next, there's the horizontal row of buttons under the iTunes playback controls.

● After you select a library from the drop-down menu on the left (Music, in this case), click any of the first four buttons to sort that library's items into groups, like song titles, albums, and genres. Click Playlists to see all your customized song lists; Chapter 12 is all about those. Click the Radio button to stream any of the hundreds of Internet radio stations through iTunes, and click the Match button to see your iTunes Match collection (page 194).

● If your iPod is connected to iTunes, click the iPod button to sync new files, change the iPod's settings, or see how much room you have left on it.

● Feel a shopportunity coming on? Click the Store button to dive right into Apple's online emporium, described in detail in Chapter 13. When you're in the Store, this button changes to say Library—click it to go back home.

Change the Look of the iTunes Window

With iTunes 11, Apple radically overhauled the look of its all-purpose jukebox for the first time in nearly 10 years. For many people, it was a makeover long overdue. For newcomers to iTunes, well, they had to learn the program anyway. But for some long-time iTunes fans, the facelift was a jarring change that instantly lead to the question, "Hey, where's all my stuff?

If you're in that last group and long for the days of the Source panel that vertically listed all your libraries, connected devices, playlists, the iTunes Store, and everything else iTunes handled, fear not—Apple hasn't abandoned you. With just a few quick trips to the View menu, you can get back to familiar territory:

- To restore the Source list, that vertical pane along the left side of the window, choose View→Show Sidebar.

- iTunes' old multi-pane column browser in the Songs list sorted your music by genre, artist, album, composer, and grouping (the latter plays standalone but related tracks together—think movements in classical music). To restore it, click View→Column Browser→Show Column Browser and pick your options.

- To see the information bar at the bottom of the iTunes window (the one that revealed the size of your iTunes library), choose View→Show Status Bar.

If you give iTunes 11 a retro look like the one described here, you can push and pull columns and panes by clicking their edges and dragging them with your mouse. You can also right-click (Control-click) any column header to add a category you can sort, or click and drag the columns into a new order.

Use the iTunes 11 MiniPlayer

LOVELY AS ITUNES IS, it takes up a heck of a lot of screen real estate. When you're working on other things, you can shrink it down.

1. *Full size.* Here, iTunes shows you a lot of information about your media collection. This can be helpful when you're making playlists (Chapter 12) or just poking around in different genres (shown below) for music that matches your mood. (You can even expand the playlist to full-screen view by clicking the standard "maximize" icon in the top-right corner of the Windows window, or the full-screen icon (▣) in the top-right corner of the Mac version.)

2. *MiniPlayer.* It's nice to see your collection so prominently, but if you're just listening to music while working on a spreadsheet, you probably don't need iTunes hogging up your screen. In that case, switch to the MiniPlayer by pressing Ctrl+M (Shift-⌘-M) or by choosing View→Switch to MiniPlayer. The MiniPlayer displays the name of the current track—until you pass the mouse cursor over it and then it switches to playback controls (below).

Tired of losing your iTunes mini-player among an array of windows on your screen? Make it *always* visible, so that it sits on top of other open windows, documents, and assorted screen detritus. Open iTunes Preferences (Ctrl+comma

[⌘-comma]), click the Advanced tab, and then turn on the checkbox next to "Keep Mini Player on top of all other windows." Now you won't have to click frantically around the screen trying to find iTunes if you get caught listening to your bubblegum-pop playlist at work.

Import Selected Songs from Your CDs

IN CHAPTER 1, YOU learned how iTunes simplifies converting (also called *rip-ping*) songs from your compact discs into small, iPod-ready digital files: Pop a CD into your computer's disc drive and iTunes walks you through the process. If you're connected to the Internet, iTunes downloads song titles and other album info. A few minutes later, you've got copies of those songs in iTunes.

If you need time to think about *which* songs you want from a CD, no problem. Summon the Preferences box (Ctrl+comma [⌘-comma]), click the General tab, and then change the menu next to "When you insert a CD" to "Show CD."

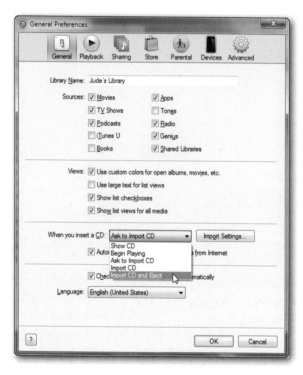

So now, if you don't want to rip an entire album—you may not want anything from Don McLean's *American Pie* besides the title track, for example—you can exclude songs you *don't* want by removing the checkmarks next to their names. Once you pick your songs, click the Import CD button in the bottom-right corner of the screen.

TIP   If you know you want all the songs on that stack of CDs next to your computer, just change the iTunes CD import preferences to "Import CD and Eject" to save yourself some clicking.

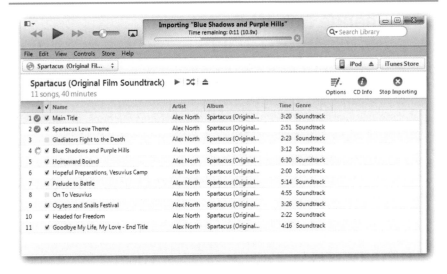

You can Ctrl+click (⌘-click) any box to deselect all the checkboxes at once. To turn them all on again, Ctrl+click (⌘-click) a box next to an unchecked song. This is a great technique when you want only one or two songs from a CD; turn off *all* the checkboxes, and then turn on only the tracks you want.

As the import process starts, iTunes moves down the list of checked songs, converting each one to a file and, in Windows 7/8, dropping it in your Music→iTunes→iTunes Media→Music folder. On Mac OS X systems, songs go in the Home→Music→iTunes→iTunes Media→Music folder. (If you've had iTunes for years, your iTunes Media folder is probably still called iTunes Music, and there's a separate Music folder inside it.)

An ✳ icon next to a song name means that iTunes is currently converting the track. Feel free to switch to other programs, answer email, surf the Web, or do any other work as iTunes rips away. If you skipped the chance to download song titles when you inserted the disc, click the Options icon on the right side of window to get them manually. Click the CD Info button to see the disc's name and title. If you decide to abandon your mission, click the Stop Importing icon.

Once iTunes finishes ripping, each imported song bears a green checkmark, and the program signals its success with a melodious little flourish. Now you have some brand-new songs in your iTunes music library.

TIP   Don't like all those checkboxes next to song titles cluttering up your screen? Turn them off in the Preferences box shown on the opposite page. Press Ctrl+comma [⌘-comma] to get the box, and then click the General tab. Turn off the checkbox next to "Show list checkboxes" (ironic, huh?). If you want an all-over streamlined look, turn off the little icons next to Source-list items by turning off the checkbox next to "Show source icons."

Change Import Settings for Better Audio Quality

IF YOU'RE HAPPY WITH the way your music sounds on your iPod or through a pair of external speakers, feel free to safely ignore this page. But If you find the audio quality lacking, you can change the way iTunes encodes, or *converts*, songs when it imports them from a CD.

iPods can play several digital audio formats: AAC, MP3, WAV, AIFF, and one called Apple Lossless. In iTunes' Import Settings box (Edit [iTunes]→ Preferences→General, and then click Import Settings), you get two main options. They are:

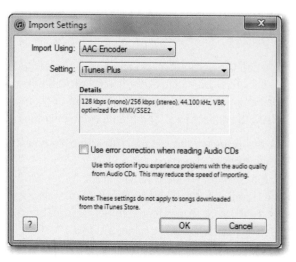

- **Audio format (use the drop-down menu beside "Import Using").** Some formats tightly compress audio to save space. The trade-off: lost sound quality. Highly compressed formats include AAC (iTunes' default setting) and MP3. Formats that use little or no compression include WAV and AIFF; they sound better, but they take up more space. Apple Lossless splits the difference: better sound quality than AAC and MP3, but not as hefty as WAV or AIFF.

- **Bit rate (beside "Setting").** The higher the number of bits listed, the greater the amount of data the file contains, and the larger the file size. The advantage? Better sound quality.

To see a song's format and other technical info, click its title in iTunes, press Ctrl+I (⌘-I), and then click the Summary tab in the Get Info box. (See your name and Apple ID listed on iTunes Store tracks? Apple *does* keep a record of these things.)

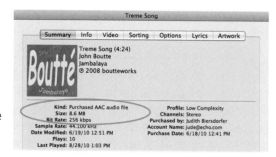

Ways to Browse Your Collection

INSTEAD OF JUST PRESENTING you with boring lists, iTunes gives you multiple ways to browse your media collection, some more visual than others. Just click the appropriate button at the top of the iTunes window. In all the views, an unadorned cloud or a ☁ icon next to a title means you bought the item on another device and can download it here from iCloud (page 116).

- **List View.** The all-text display (shown top right) is favored by people who use screen-reader software or find comfort in the layout of Excel spreadsheets. Clicking the Songs button automatically puts you in List view, but you can make List an option for other media by pressing Ctrl+comma in Windows or ⌘-comma on a Mac. That opens the Preferences box. Click the General tab and turn on the checkbox next to "Show list views for all media."

- **Playlist View Options.** After you click the Playlists button, you may want to see your custom compilations displayed as a grid of album covers or sorted by artist. Click the View icon in the Playlist window (circled, middle right) and choose a new look for your list.

- **Artist View.** Click Artists in the iTunes window to see all the bands and singers in your collection listed alphabetically along the left (shown bottom above). Click a band's name, and then click the Songs button in the middle of the window (circled) to see all the tracks you own by that band. Click the Gallery button to see online photos of the band, and click the "In the Store" button to see other albums by that artist.

- **Album view.** To see your music collection displayed as a striking collection of interactive album covers...turn the page.

Album View in iTunes 11

IN PREVIOUS VERSIONS OF iTunes, the Album view was a fairly straightforward affair—you got to see your music collection displayed as rows of colorful jacket art. (Unless, of course, you ripped the tracks from your own CDs and didn't manually add your own artwork—you then see a gray music note, but the next chapter tells you how to fix that.)

iTunes 11 takes the traditional Album view and makes it much more useful. To see for yourself, click the Albums button at the top of the iTunes window. Now, click an album cover.

As shown here, the middle of the iTunes window opens up to reveal all the tracks on that album. You also see the ratings you gave them (Chapter 11) and the running time for each song. If you want more from a particular artist, click "In the Store" on the right side of the screen, and Apple shows you everything else by that singer or band. And it will gladly sell you their wares.

The open Album view also gives you a play button (▶), a shuffle button (✕), and the ➋ menu icon. Click the latter to get menu options for adding the album to your Up Next list, creating a Genius playlist, or adding the album to a playlist (you'll find all these options explained in Chapter 12).

Search iTunes

AS YOUR ITUNES MEDIA library grows, you may have trouble remembering just what songs, movies, and so on you have, or what album a song came from. In times like these, take to the trusty search box in the right-hand corner of the iTunes window.

As with search boxes on Web browsers, operating systems, and every place else they tend to appear, you just have to start typing in a keyword (the artist's name, a song title, and so on). With each letter you type, iTunes shortens the list it displays, showing you only titles that match what you type.

For example, typing *train* brings up a list of everything in your collection that has the word "train" somewhere in the song's information—maybe in the song's title ("Mystery Train"), the band name (Wire Train), or the album name (*Train A Comin'*). The search function in iTunes 11 doesn't limit itself to just one type of media, either. As shown below, you get results from across your media empire. Click a result in the list to jump to that item.

Another way to search for specific items is to use Songs/List view and the Column Browser mentioned earlier in this chapter. (If you can't see the column browser, press Ctrl+B [⌘-B].)

Depending on how you configured the browser in View→Column Browser, it reveals your music collection grouped by genre, artist, album, composer, or grouping—all in a nice vertical list. Hit the same keys again (Ctrl+B [⌘-B]) to close the browser.

Shuffle Your Music in Many Ways

WITH ITS ABILITY TO randomly pluck and play songs, iTunes' Shuffle feature has a huge number of fans, especially those who don't want to think about what to listen to as they noodle around the Internet. To start shuffling, click ✕ at the top of the iTunes window; the icon turns blue when the player is set to shuffle. As you may remember from a couple of pages ago, you see this same icon in Album view when you have an album selected.

You're not stuck with a single shuffling method, either. Some days you may feel like mixing up your music song by song, and other days you may be in the mood to change things up by album.

To control just what iTunes shuffles, choose Controls→Shuffle and select Songs, Albums, or Groupings from the submenu. ("Grouping" is a way to keep certain tracks together in your iTunes library, like separate movements in a piece of classical music that are part of a larger work.)

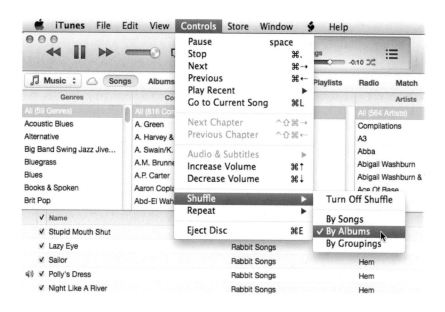

Animate Your Songs: iTunes Visualizer

VISUALIZER IS THE ITUNES term for an on-screen laser-light show that pulses, beats, and dances in perfect sync to your music. The effect is hypnotic and wild, especially when summoned midway through a sluggish day at the office.

You need to pick a set of animations first. Choose View→Visualizer to select from the iTunes Visualizer (lots of Disco in Space moments) or the iTunes Classic Visualizer (trippy psychedelic patterns-a-go-go, as shown below).

1. To summon the scenery, choose View→Show Visualizer. The show begins immediately. To see a tiny menu of even more controls for either Visualizer, press the / key and then the letter of the desired command listed on-screen. It's a great way to fiddle.

> **TIP** The keyboard shortcut for turning the Visualizer on and off is Ctrl+T (⌘-T).

2. If you find the iTunes window too constraining for all this eye candy, play it full-screen by going to View→Full Screen (View→Enter Full Screen). The keyboard shortcut for this coast-to-coast visual goodness is Ctrl+F (Ctrl-⌘-F) .

True, you won't get a lot of work done, but when it comes to stress relief, visuals are a lot cheaper than a hot tub.

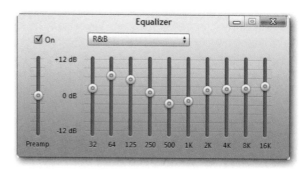

You'll learn to:

- Rate songs and albums

- Stream Internet radio

- Swap songs, music, and TV shows with family members

- Re-download previous Store purchases

- Keep copies of all your songs online

- Add album art and lyrics

iTunes Power Moves

NOW THAT YOU'VE SEEN how easy iTunes makes it to convert your favorite CD tracks into small, great-sounding files, it's time to do some serious tune-tweaking. Apple's music-management program lets you do things like rate albums and individual songs, tap into Internet radio, share music and videos with other folks on your network, and even download your past and present purchases to your iPod or other iOS devices right in the iTunes 11 window.

You can also use iTunes as an editor: It gives you the tools you need to change song formats, edit on-stage banter from live recordings, and apply preset or customized equalizer settings to tracks. Once you get everything to your liking, you'll learn how to add, delete, and manually manage the music on your 'Pod.

Finally, you'll learn how iTunes can help with a vital—but often ignored—part of music management: backing up your catalog for safekeeping in case your hard drive croaks and takes all your songs and videos with it.

You're the Critic: Rate Your Music

ALTHOUGH THERE'S NO WAY to give a song two thumbs up in iTunes, you *can* assign an album—or each song in your collection—a rating of from one to five stars. Then you can use the ratings to produce playlists of nothing but the greatest hits on your hard drive.

First, a couple of notes: If you assign an *album* a rating, then *all* the songs on the album get the same number of stars. If you rate just a few tracks on an album, the album's rating reflects the average of the *rated* songs—so an album with two five-star songs and a bunch of unrated tracks gets five stars.

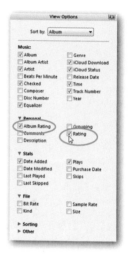

1. Click the Songs button at the top of the iTunes window. To add ratings, first make sure you turn on the Album Rating and/or Rating columns in iTunes' View Options box (Ctrl+J [⌘-J]).

2. Highlight the song you want to rate by clicking it. iTunes displays five dots in the Rating column (in the Songs view of iTunes main window). When you click a dot, it turns into a star. Now either drag your mouse across the column to create one to five stars, or click one of the dots itself to apply a rating (click the third dot, and iTunes gives the song three stars). You can also rate a song as it's playing by clicking the ❯ icon next to its title at the top of the iTunes window and swiping dots into stars.

3. Once you assign ratings, you can sort your song list by star rating (click the Album Rating or Rating column title), create a Smart Playlist of only your personal favorites (File→New Smart Playlist; choose Album Rating or Rating from the first drop-down menu), and so on.

You can even rate songs from within your iPod, and iTunes records the ratings the next time you sync up. To rate a song on your iPod Classic, start playing it and tap the Select button until you see dots on-screen. Use the scroll wheel to transform those dots into stars. Your star ratings show up on the iPod's Now Playing screen. To rate songs on the Touch, swipe the dots on the Now Playing screen (page 135). On the Nano, tap the Now Playing art, tap ☰, and then swipe the dots to convert them to stars.

TIP You can add stars from the iTunes menu, too. With a track or album selected, choose File→Rating, slide to the submenu, and then rate the music. This is also the place to go if you change your mind: Choose None to return a song to its unrated condition.

Listen to Internet Radio

NOT SATISFIED WITH BEING a mere virtual jukebox, iTunes also serves as an international radio—without the shortwave static. You can tune in everything from mystical Celtic melodies to Zambian hip-hop. Computers with high-speed Internet connections have a smoother streaming experience, but the vast and eclectic mix of music is well worth checking out—even with a dial-up modem. Click the Radio button at the top of the iTunes window to see a list of stations.

Stations are roughly organized by genre, like Blues, Classical, and Country. Click a genre to see its list of stations. Beyond these broad groupings are specialized categories, like College/University, Sports Radio, and Golden Oldies.

Once you listen to all the stations listed in iTunes, hit the Internet. You can find more radio stations at *www.shoutcast.com*. Windows 7 and Mac OS X users can play them through iTunes by clicking the yellow Tune In button. (If this is your first time at Shoutcast, a prompt asks how you want to hear the stream—click the button for iTunes.) XP users, save the offered *.pls* file to your desktop and then drag and drop it on Playlists. Click the resulting "tunein-station" playlist.

If you find a station you like on the Web, you can add it to iTunes by copying its server address—usually listed on the station's Web page, something like *http://78.129.189.128:8012*. Next, choose File→Open Stream and paste the URL into the box. The added streams don't show up in the Radio list but appear in the Playlists section of iTunes—where you can tune them in just by clicking.

Share Your iTunes Music and Videos

NOW THAT YOU'VE BUILT a fabulous media collection, you may feel like sharing it. You can, under one condition: Your fellow sharers need to be on the same network. For instance, family members on your home network: kosher. Cousin Ferdinand, living in another state: not kosher.

The power to share music—that is, stream it between computers—has been with iTunes for years. But iTunes' Home Sharing feature, introduced way back in iTunes 9, lets you do more than just stream songs; you can actually *copy* music and videos from one computer to another.

Sounds great, doesn't it? Home Sharing does have its limits, though. For starters, you can share content among only five computers. Each also needs the following:

- A connection to the same (wired or wireless) network.

- A copy of iTunes 9 or later installed.

- The name and password of a single Apple ID (see Chapter 13 if you still need to sign up for one).

Once you have all these things in hand, it's time to share:

1. Choose File→Home Sharing→Turn On Home Sharing. If you get told to authorize the computer for that Apple ID, choose Store→Authorize This Computer. Type in your Apple ID and password.

2. Repeat these steps for every computer you want to share with on your network (up to four others).

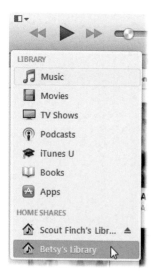

Once you set up all the computers with the two steps above, each computer's iTunes library in appears in the Library pop-up menu under Home Shares.

Select one of these shared libraries to explore its contents. For example, you can click a shared Music icon and then double-click a song title in your iTunes window to hear it. The music streams over your home network, letting you sample the musical tastes of others.

In addition to streaming audio files, you can stream videos, but their large size can make them skippy. This is where the power to *copy* files from one shared machine to another comes in handy.

Copy Files with Home Sharing

You can copy files between shared iTunes libraries two ways: *manually* or *automatically*. The manual method works well when you want to occasionally raid someone's media collection for random albums or videos. But if everyone listens to the same audiobook or just has to have every new album that comes into the house, the automatic method saves time and effort.

- **The manual method.** In the shared library, select the title (or Ctrl-click [⌘-click] to select multiple titles) of the audio or video files you want to copy to your Windows PC or Mac. Click the Import button in iTunes' bottom-right corner and wait as your selections pour into your own library. If, in the shared library, you want to see only the items that you *don't* have, jump down to the Show pop-up menu at the bottom-left of the iTunes window and choose "Items not in my library."

- **The automatic method.** With the shared library on-screen, click the Settings button at the bottom-right of the iTunes window. Turn on the checkboxes next to the types of content, like music, that you want to automatically Hoover onto your own machine. Click OK.

But what if you don't want to share *everything* in your library? Or if you want to password-protect your stuff from siblings or other annoyances? That's where the Sharing preferences box comes to the rescue.

Call up the iTunes Preferences box (Ctrl+comma [⌘-comma]) and then click the Sharing tab. Turn on "Share my library on my local network." You can choose to share your entire collection or selected playlists. (You can also tell your computer to look for other people's music here.)

To secure your library, turn on the checkbox for "Require password" and give your cypher to trusted network buddies. If *they* lock up *their* media, you'll need their passwords, too. Finally, click the General tab in this same preferences box. The name you type in the Library Name box will show up in your friends' iTunes Source lists.

Use iTunes In the Cloud

IT'S EASY TO BUY digital goods from the iTunes Store, but how do you easily get the stuff you buy on one gadget onto all your other computers and iOS devices if you're not home to use Home Sharing (explained on the previous page)? That's where Apple's iTunes In the Cloud service comes in. It acts as an online record-keeper for all the apps, music, and books you buy (and TV Shows, if you're downloading to a Windows PC or Mac). Once you buy something from the Store, iTunes in the Cloud *knows* it and can download copies to 10 computers and devices (or fewer) that use the same Apple ID. As with many things in the Appleverse (as well as automobiles), you have two ways to copy files across devices: automatic and manual. Here's how to do either:

- **Automatically download purchases.** To have iTunes on your computer automatically download to your iPod Touch a copy of the music, apps, and books you buy on other devices, choose Edit [iTunes]→Preferences→Store. Under Automatic Downloads, turn on the checkboxes next to Music, Apps, and/or Books; you need to manually download TV shows, which is described next. Click OK.

  To make your Touch reach out and grab stuff you bought through iTunes on your computer, go to the iPod's Home screen and tap Settings→iTunes & App Stores. Sign into your account and tap the On button next to Music, Apps, and/or Books to snag each type of file.

- **Manually download purchases.** If you just want certain of your Store purchases, you can download what you want when you want it. On your computer, click the iTunes Store button in the iTunes window and log into your account. In the Quick Links panel, click the Purchased link. On the next screen, you can see the music, TV shows, apps, and books you bought; click All to see everything, or "Not in My Library" to see items your computer lacks. Click an item's title, and then click the Cloud icon (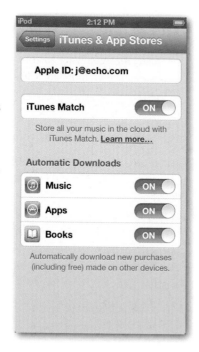) to download it.

To get selective on the Touch, tap iTunes open from the Home screen, and then tap the More icon at the bottom of the Store screen. On the next screen, tap Purchased. On the Purchased screen, tap the categories (Music, Movies, TV Shows, etc.) to see all your previous acquisitions. Tap All to see everything you've ever bought or "Not on this iPod" to see a list of the things missing from your player. Tap ⊕ to download an item to the Touch; enter your Apple ID and password if asked.

iCloud in iTunes 11

If you've been using iTunes for a few years and upgraded to iTunes 11, you may notice little cloud icons (☁) on or next to some of the items within your library —or even next to your Library pop-up menu. This is not a meteorological commentary on your taste in music and video. This is iCloud keeping track of the items you previously bought with your Apple ID. It lets you know that, hey, just because you bought and downloaded that Eric Clapton album on your work computer, you don't have to go all the way to the iTunes Store to click on the Purchased link to manually download it to *this* iTunes library.

To download the item to your current computer, click the cloud, which goes from ☁ to ⊕ as the download begins.

If you purposefully keep your iTunes purchases on separate machines and don't want to see clouds on virtual library items everywhere you look, turn off the fluffy icons and ignore those purchases by choosing View→Hide Music in the Cloud. That way, you'll see only the songs residing on your current computer.

Journeyman
Eric Clapton

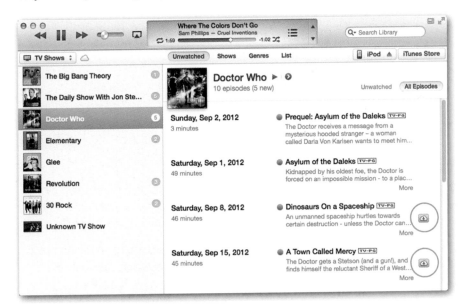

Use iTunes Match

YOU MAY BE SAYING to yourself, "Well, this iTunes In the Cloud thing is great in case my hard drive dies, but I didn't buy everything in my library from the iTunes Store. What about all the tracks I ripped from my CD collection?"

You have two options here. First, you can back up your computer (and iTunes library with it) to an external drive or set of discs with free software, like Windows' Backup utility or Apple's Time Machine for Mac OS X (page 213). Second, for $25 a year, you can use Apple's iTunes Match subscription service. iTunes Match safely stores any song in your music library on Apple's iCloud servers. You can download a copy to any of your iOS devices and computers (up to 10 total, and five of them can be authorized with the same Apple ID) so your library is always with you.

For home-ripped tracks that the iTunes Store also sells (it has 26 million songs), iTunes Match adds new Store copies to your iCloud account. For more obscure tracks, ones that the Store doesn't sell, Match uploads a copy of each rare gem from your computer to iCloud (and yes, that means Apple is wading around in your personal music files).

To use iTunes Match, you need an Apple ID (page 240), an Internet connection, and an iPod Touch, iPad, or iPhone running iOS 5 or later. Then there's the money part—you also need a credit card to pay $24.99 a year for an iTunes Match subscription, which covers up to 25,000 songs. And finally, you need some time while iTunes Match uploads your rare tracks to iCloud.

To sign up for iTunes Match, open iTunes on the computer, choose Store→Turn On iTunes Match, and then click the Subscribe button. After you sign up, Match adds your music and playlists, including any tracks iTunes had to upload, to your giant iCloud library.

Now you need to get your iPod into the mix. Tap Settings→Music. Flip on iTunes Match; it nags you if you haven't signed up for a subscription. (You can also turn on iTunes Match at Settings→iTunes & App Stores.) And while turning on Match  initially removes all the songs from your Touch, you can grab them again by tapping ⛅ and downloading at will. To see the tracks you've already downloaded, along with tracks you *can* download, tap Settings→Music→Show All Music→On.

The iTunes Match deal isn't without drawbacks. For one, you're on the hook for $25 a year to rent your online music locker. But hey, you've got all your music— right up there in the Cloud, whenever you need it.

Change a Song's File Format

SOMETIMES YOU'VE GOT A song in iTunes whose format you want to change—you might need to convert a byte-hogging AIFF file before loading it onto your Shuffle, for example. First, head over to Edit→Preferences (iTunes→Preferences), click the General tab, and then click the Import Settings button. From the Import Using pop-up menu, pick the format you want to convert *to* and then click OK.

Now, in your iTunes library, select the song you want to convert and choose File→Create New Version→Create MP3 Version (or AIFF, or whatever format you chose in the step above).

If you have a whole folder or disk full of potential converts, hold down the Shift (Option) key as you choose Advanced→Convert to AAC (or your chosen encoding format). A window pops up, which you can use to navigate to the folder or disk holding the files you want to convert. The only files that don't get converted are protected ones: Audible.com tracks and older tracks from the iTunes Store that still have copy-protection built in. If you bought a song after January 2009, though, odds are you have a high-quality iTunes Plus track (see page 255) that's delightfully free of such restrictions.

Now your library includes the song or songs in both their original format and their freshly converted format.

TIP If you collect music—in different formats and from all sorts of places besides the iTunes Store—you may find song volumes varying from track to track. You can try to even things out with iTunes' Sound Check feature. Open the Preferences box (Ctrl+comma [⌘-comma]), click the Playback icon or tab, and then turn on the box for Sound Check. You also need to turn on Sound Check on your iPod. On the Classic, choose Settings→Sound Check. On the Touch or Nano, choose Settings→Music, and then tap Sound Check to On. The next time you connect iPod to computer, iTunes makes the necessary audio adjustments.

Improve Your Tunes with the Graphic Equalizer

TO IMPROVE THE WAY your songs sound, you can use iTunes' graphic equalizer (EQ) to adjust various frequencies when you play certain types of music. You might want to boost the bass tones in dance tracks to emphasize the booming rhythm, for example.

To get the equalizer front and center, choose View (Window)→Equalizer to unleash some of your new EQ powers.

① Drag the sliders (bass on the left, treble on the right) to accommodate your listening tastes (or the strengths and weaknesses of your speakers or headphones). You can drag the Preamp slider up or down to compensate for songs that sound too loud or too soft. To create your own presets, click the pop-up menu and select Make Preset.

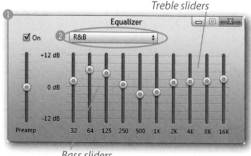

Treble sliders

Bass sliders

② Use the pop-up menu to choose one of the canned presets for different types of music (Classical, Dance, Jazz, and so on).

You can apply equalizer settings to an entire album or to individual songs.

③ To apply settings to a whole album, select the album's name (either in Grid view or in the iTunes browser pane). Then press Ctrl+I (⌘-I) and click Yes

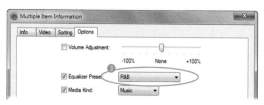

if iTunes asks whether you're sure you want to edit multiple items. In the box that pops up, click the Options tab and choose your preferred setting from the Equalizer Preset pull-down menu.

NOTE *Equalization* is the art of adjusting the frequency response of an audio signal. An equalizer emphasizes, or boosts, some of the signal's frequencies while lowering others. In the range of audible sound, *bass* frequency is the low rumbly noise; *treble* is at the opposite end of the sound spectrum, with high, even shrill, notes; and *midrange* is, of course, in the middle, and it's the most audible to human ears.

---

❹ You can apply equalizer presets to individual songs as well. Instead of selecting the album name in the iTunes window, click the song name, and then press Ctrl+I (⌘+I). Click the Options tab and choose a setting from the Equalizer Preset menu.

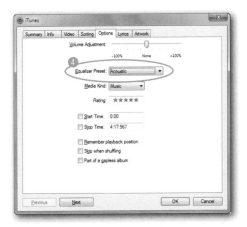

❺ Finally, you can change the EQ settings right from your Songs list view by adding an Equalizer column. Choose View→View Options and turn on the Equalizer checkbox. A new column appears in your track list, where you can select EQ settings.

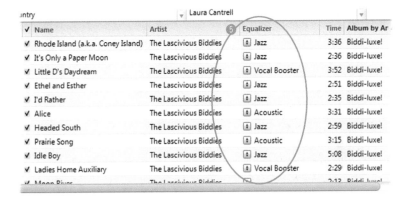

TIP The iPod itself has more than 20 equalizer presets you can use on the go. To set your iPod Touch's equalizer, choose Settings→Music→EQ. Flick down the list of presets until you find one that matches your music style, and then tap it. Your iPod now lists the preset's name next to EQ on the Settings menu. The process works pretty much the same way on the other iPods. You can tap your way into the Nano's EQ controls by going to the Home screen and choosing Settings→Music→EQ. The iPod Classic's EQ menu is at iPod→Settings→EQ.

Change a Song's Start and Stop Times

GOT A SONG FROM a live album with a bunch of onstage chit-chat before it starts or after the music ends? Fortunately, you can change a song's start and stop times to skip the boring parts and hear only the juicy middle.

To change a track's stop time, play the song and observe the status window at the top of iTunes. Watch for the point in the timeline where you get bored. Then:

1. Click the track you want to adjust.

2. Choose File→Get Info (Ctrl+I [⌘-I]) to call up the song's information box.

3. Click the Options tab and take a look at the Stop Time box, which shows the full duration of the song.

4. Enter the new stopping point for the song, the one you noted earlier.

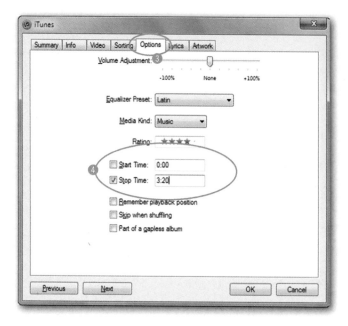

You can perform the same trick at the beginning of a song by adjusting the number in the Start Time box. The shortened version plays in iTunes and on your iPod, but the additional recorded material isn't really lost.

If you ever change your mind, go back to the song's Options box and turn off the Start Time or Stop Time checkbox to return the song to its original length.

Edit Song Information

TIRED OF SONG-NAME TYPOS from an online database marring your lovely library? You can change track titles in iTunes a couple of ways.

When you see a song title in any of the views (Songs, Albums, Artists, Genres, or Playlists), click the text you want to change, wait a moment, and then click again. The title now appears highlighted, and you can edit the text—just as you do when you change a file name on a desktop computer.

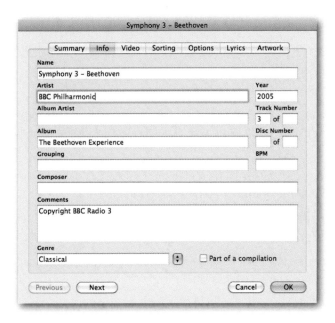

Another way to change a song's title, artist name, or other information is to click the song title in the iTunes window and press Ctrl+I (⌘-I) to summon the Get Info box. (Choose File→Get Info if you forget the keyboard shortcut.) Click the Info tab and then type in the new track information.

If you still have the CD, insert it into the computer, select it from the Library pop-up menu and click Options→Get CD Track Names to see if the Internet has any updated listings. If the track is something deeply obscure or homemade, the Gracenote database that iTunes uses may not know the name, either.

TIP   Once you've got a song's Get Info box on-screen, use the Previous and Next buttons to navigate to other tracks grouped with it in the iTunes song list. That way, you can rapidly edit all the track information in the same playlist, on the same album, and so on, without closing and opening boxes the whole time.

Edit Album Information

YOU DON'T HAVE TO adjust your track information on a song-by-song basis. You can edit an entire album's worth of tracks simultaneously by clicking the album name in the iTunes column browser (or by clicking its cover in Album view) and pressing Ctrl+I (⌘-I) to bring up the Get Info box.

Ever careful, iTunes flashes an alert box asking if you really want to change the info for a bunch of things at once. Click Yes.

You can make all sorts of changes to an album in the four-tabbed box that pops up. Here are a few examples:

① Fix a typo or mistake in the Album or Artist name boxes.

② Manually add an album cover or photo of your choice to the whole album by dragging it into the Artwork box. (You can add an album rating below that).

③ Click the Options tab and change the equalizer preset for all the songs. Right below that, use the Media Kind menu to change a mislabeled Music file to, say, Audiobook for proper sorting (see page 198).

④ Have iTunes skip the album when you shuffle music—great for keeping winter holiday music out of your summer barbecue album rotation.

⑤ Tell iTunes to play back the album without those two-second gaps between tracks by choosing "Gapless album" (perfect for opera and *Abbey Road*!).

Fetch Missing Album Covers

SONGS YOU DOWNLOAD FROM the iTunes Store often include artwork—usually a picture of the album cover. iTunes displays the picture in just about every view but the text-based Songs list. But even if you rip most of your music from your own CD collection, you're not stuck with artless tracks. You can ask iTunes to head to the Internet and find as many album covers as it can.

You need a (free) iTunes Store account to make this work, so if you haven't signed up yet, flip ahead to Chapter 13 to learn how. To make iTunes go fetch, choose File→Library→Get Album Artwork. Since Apple has to root around in your library to figure out which covers you need, you get an alert box warning you that the company will be getting (and then dumping) personal information from you (but it's not laughing at your Bay City Rollers tracks).

If you have a huge library, this may take a little while. When iTunes finishes, you should have a healthy dose of album art filling up the iTunes window.

If iTunes can't find certain album covers on its own, it displays a list of the missing artwork. You can use this helpful accounting to hunt for and place the art yourself. So, you ask, where do you handpick this artwork? In short: the Web.

Sites like Amazon are a great source of album covers. Here's what to do:

1. Locate the cover you want on the Web and save a copy of it by dragging it off the web page and onto your desktop, or by right-clicking (Ctrl-clicking) it and choosing the "Save Image" option in your web browser.

2. Add artwork by clicking a song title, typing Ctrl+I (⌘-I) to open the Get Info box, and then clicking the Artwork tab.

3. Click the Add button to call up a box that lets you choose an image from your hard drive—like the one you just snagged. If you don't like the album's art, you can add a JPEG photo of your own. Just select that picture when you click the Add button and use the slider to adjust its size. The opposite page shows how to art up a whole album with the same image at once.

Add Lyrics to Your Song Files

YOU CAN SAVE LYRICS with a song file just as you do album art. To add lyrics, select a song in iTunes and press Ctrl+I (⌘-I) to call up the Get Info box. Then click the Lyrics tab.

Here, you can either meticulously type in a song's verses or look them up on one of the hundreds of websites devoted to cataloging them. Once you find your words, getting them into iTunes is a mere cut 'n' paste job away.

If you want to add lyrics to all the songs on an album or to several songs on the same playlist, click the Next button (circled). That advances you to the next song, thereby saving you repeated keystrokes invoking the Get Info command. (These buttons also work on the Artwork window, described on the previous page.)

View Lyrics on the iPod

When you're out strolling with your iPod Classic and have a song playing, press the center button to cycle through all the information about the song. After four or five taps, the lyrics appear on the iPod's screen, making it a handheld karaoke machine you can sing along with as you go down the street.

Got an iPod Touch? Just tap the album cover on the Now Playing Screen (shown here) to see the lyrics fill the screen.

On the Nano, open the Music app and tap a song. On the Now Playing screen, tap the album art to make the song controls—and lyrics—appear.

TIP Some types of files that iTunes can play don't support the lyrics function. AAC and MP3 files are perfectly happy with lyrics, but QuickTime and WAV files can't handle them. So you need to convert that WAV recording of "Jumping Jack Flash" if you want to have a gas, gas, gas with lyrics.

What iTunes Can Tell You About Your iPod

ITUNES NOT ONLY LETS you decide which songs and videos end up on your iPod, it also helps keep your iPod's internal software up to date, see how much space you have left on your player, and change your music, video, and podcast syncing options.

Connect your iPod to your computer, and click the iPod button at the top of the iTunes window. Each tab at the top of the next screen lets you control a different kind of content, like music or photos.

On the Summary screen (first tab), iTunes tells you:

❶ The size of your iPod, its serial number, and whether it's formatted for Windows or the Mac.

❷ Whether your iPod has the latest software (and if you're having problems, you get the chance to reinstall it).

❸ Whether iTunes automatically synchronizes your iPod or whether you need to update its contents manually. (Automatic means everything in iTunes ends up on your iPod—space permitting, of course; manual means you get to pick and choose.) If you have a Touch, Nano, or Shuffle, you can turn on VoiceOver prompts to hear your iPod identify things like song titles, menu names, and so on. If you have an iPod Touch, a Backup section for iCloud or iTunes is in the Options area of the Summary screen.

❹ The bar at the bottom of the window uses color to identify the different media types filling up your iPod. Click it to see the information displayed in number of items, the amount of drive space used, or the number of days' worth of a particular type of media.

❺ Click the On This iPod button on the far right to see its contents, like your music, audiobooks, and any playlists you've made. (Keep in mind this button likes to hide if your iTunes window isn't open to a comfortable width.)

Adjust Your iPod's Syncing Preferences with iTunes

ONCE YOUR IPOD IS connected and showing up in iTunes, you can modify all the settings that control what goes onto (and comes off of) your media player. Thanks to iTunes' long, scrollable screen full of checkboxes and lists in most categories, it's easier than ever to get precisely what you want on your iPod.

So where do you start? See those tabs all in a row toward the top of iTunes? Click each one to see the preferences for that type of media. (The tabs vary slightly depending on the type of iPod you have; the Touch even has a Tones tab for your Skype phone calls.) Here's what you'll find there:

1. **Summary**. You'll find key iPod hardware info here: drive capacity, serial number, and software version (and a button to update the software when Apple releases a new version). The Options area lets you choose syncing preferences and whether you want to turn your iPod into a portable data drive for carrying around big files.

2. **Apps**. Here's where you sync all those wonderful little programs you downloaded from the App Store to your computer and then to your iPod Touch.

3. **Music**. Click this tab to synchronize all your songs and playlists—or just the ones you like best. Keep scrolling down—you can sync by artist and genre as well.

4. **Movies**. Full-length movies can take up to a gigabyte or more of precious iPod space, so iTunes gives you the option to load all, selected, or even just unwatched films.

5. **TV Shows**. As with movies, you can selectively choose which TV shows (or episodes thereof) you bring along on your iPod.

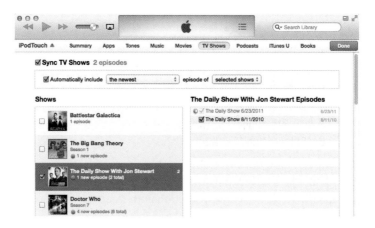

iPodTouch ⏏ | Summary | Apps | Tones | Music | Movies | TV Shows | Podcasts | iTunes U | Books | Photos | Info | On This iPod | Done

6. **Podcasts**. Your pal iTunes can automatically download the podcasts you've *subscribed* to through the iTunes Store (see Chapter 13); here, you can decide which ones you want to listen to on the go.

7. **iTunes U**. You don't need to be a registered student at any of the major universities to take advantage of the free audio lectures and video presentations in the iTunes U section of the Store. You download the content here, and then sync up your iPod.

8. **Books**. This literary tab lets you selectively sync up your audiobooks and your Touch's electronic iBooks files.

9. **Photos**. The Touch, Nano, and Classic can all display little copies of your digital photos. Click this tab to select where you want iTunes to look for them (like in an iPhoto or Photoshop Elements library) and which photo albums you want to bring with you.

10. **Info**. It's not just an all-purpose media player! The iPod Classic and Touch are happy to carry copies of all the addresses and phone numbers listed in your computer's address book (from Microsoft Outlook, the Mac OS X Address Book, and other programs). Scroll down the screen until you find an option to grab Outlook or iCal calendars. On the Touch, you can sync up web browser bookmarks and email account settings from your computer, too. If you have a free iCloud account (page 116), you can add the Touch to your collection of über-synced computers and iPhones to keep your info current across all your Internet-connected hardware.

11. **Nike + iPod**. If you're using the Nano's pedometer or the Nike + iPod app on your Nano or Touch, you can set the device to upload your workout results to the Nike website so you can track your progress online.

12. **On This iPod.** Click here to see the stuff currently *on* your iPod.

> **NOTE** The iPod Touch, Nano, Shuffle, and iTunes have features for the visually impaired to navigate audio content by verbal cues instead of on-screen menus. On the Touch's Summary screen in iTunes, click the Configure Universal Access button, and then turn on the VoiceOver radio button. On the Touch itself, you can turn the feature on or off at Settings→General→Accessibility. On the Nano, tap Settings→General→Accessibility, choose your speech options, and then tap VoiceOver to On. For the Shuffle, connect it to iTunes and turn on the checkbox next to Enable VoiceOver on the Summary screen. Using VoiceOver does change the way you control the iPod (especially the Touch), so be sure to read up on the feature at *www.apple.com/accessibility/*.

Load Songs onto an iPod from More Than One Computer

ITUNES' AUTOSYNC FEATURE MAKES keeping your iPod up to date a breeze, but there's a big catch: You can sync your iPod with only *one* computer. Lots of people have music scattered around multiple machines: a couple of different family Macs, an office PC and a home PC, and so on. If you want to load up your music from each of these sources, you have to change your iPod settings to *manual management*; you'll find specfic instructions for each iPod model in dedicated chapters of this book, but in a nutshell: connect your iPod to iTunes, click the iPod button, and then click the Summary tab in iTunes. Then:

- **Scroll down to the Options area and turn on the checkbox next to "Manually manage music and videos."** Click the Apply button in the bottom-right corner of iTunes to cement the change.

- **Don't forget to manually eject your iPod from iTunes when you want to safely remove it from your computer.** (Manual updates give you total control, but as Uncle Ben said in *Spider-Man*, "With great power comes great responsibility.") Eject the iPod by either clicking the Eject button (⏏) next to the iPod's name in the iTunes button row or by pressing Ctrl+E (⌘-E).

> **TIP** Your iPod's Summary screen (in iTunes) shows whether your iPod is formatted for Windows or a Mac. If you have a new iPod and want to use it with both a PC and a Mac, connect it to the PC first and have iTunes format it for Windows. A Mac can read the Windows format just fine, but Windows won't recognize the Mac format without special software. The iPod Touch, however, will talk to either type of computer, no matter which one you use it with first.

Manually Delete Music and Videos from Your iPod

PEOPLE WHO CHOOSE TO autosync their iPods don't have to worry about taking stuff off of their players. They can choose which playlists and media to automatically copy over to their iPods—or they can just delete unwanted items out of iTunes and resync their 'Pods to wipe the same files off the player.

But if you're a manual manager, you have to delete unwanted files yourself. (You can, however, have iTunes automatically update your podcast subscriptions; see Chapter 13 for more about podcasts.)

① To delete files from your iPod, connect it to your computer and click the iPod button in the horizontal row across the top of the iTunes window.

② On the iPod's screen click the On This iPod button on the far left. (If you don't see it, make sure your iTunes window is open to its full width.)

③ In the list that appears on the right side of iTunes, select the library, and then click the unwanted title. If you have a bunch of items you want to clear off your iPod in one fell swoop, Ctrl-click (⌘-click) to select multiple tracks. With the items selected, press the Delete key on the keyboard, and then confirm your choice in the iTunes alert box that appears. This removes the files from your iPod but doesn't whack them out of the iTunes library, where you can always reload them if you find you miss those old things after all.

Copy Your Music from iPod to iTunes

TO PREVENT RAMPANT PIRACY across the seven seas of Musicdom, Apple originally designed the data transfer between iTunes and the iPod as a one-way trip—you could copy music *to* a connected iPod, but not *from* an iPod to your computer. This is still pretty much Apple's way, although you can now copy iTunes Store purchases from your iPod to iTunes in a couple of ways:

- **Download them from iCloud.** As explained earlier in this chapter, if you bought something on another computer and synced it to your iPod, you can copy that item to the computer you're currently using, so long as you're using the same Apple ID on both machines. Just click the little cloud icon (⌒) next to the item in your iTunes library. (This obviously doesn't work for someone's home-ripped tracks you copied from another computer.)

- **Transfer Purchases.** If you bought stuff from iTunes and copied it to your iPod on another Windows PC or Mac—but don't care for any of that iCloud copying—you can move it to your current computer with an iTunes menu option. As shown below, choose File→Devices→Transfer Purchases from [Name of iPod]. This menu is also handy if you bought the new content directly on your iPod Touch over its WiFi connection to the iTunes or App Store and want to get it back to the mother ship for safekeeping.

But what if you *didn't* buy the content you want to transfer from iTunes? (Yes, people do shop elsewhere....)

There are times when perfectly honest people need to get their songs off of their iPods—like when your computer dies and takes your iTunes library with it.

The Web is full of tips and tricks for harvesting content off of an iPod and getting it back into iTunes, often by fiddling with system settings in Windows or Mac OS X. These methods can vary based on which iPod and which version of an operating system you have. Thankfully, there's also The Shareware Option. Several helpful folks have developed free or inexpensive programs to copy content from your iPod to your computer:

- **TouchCopy.** The program costs $35, but it works with Windows PCs and Mac OS X—and on all iPods (*www.wideanglesoftware.com/touchcopy*).

- **YamiPod.** A free program that runs off of the iPod itself and exports music back to Windows, Mac, and Linux systems (*www.yamipod.com*).

- **SharePod.** This freeware program for Windows (below) copies music and videos back to your PC, and lets you edit playlists, artwork, and song tags (labels) (*www.getsharepod.com*).

- **Senuti.** The name makes sense when you realize it's iTunes spelled backward. Senuti is a $19 shareware program for the Mac that lets you copy all (or just some) of the music on your iPod back to your iTunes library (*www.fadingred.org/senuti*).

Move Your iTunes Media Folder to an External Drive

MEDIA LIBRARIES GROW LARGE, and hard drives can seem to shrink as you add thousands of songs and hundreds of videos to iTunes. You may, in fact, think about using a big external drive for iTunes storage. That's just dandy, but you need to make sure that iTunes knows what you're up to.

If you rudely drag your iTunes Media (or Music) folder to a different place without telling iTunes, it thinks the songs and videos in your collection are gone. The next time you start the program, you'll find a newly created, empty Media/Music folder. (While iTunes remains empty but calm, *you* may be having heart palpitations as you picture your media collection vanishing in a puff of bytes.)

To move the Media/Music folder to a new drive, give iTunes a heads-up. Before you start, make sure iTunes has been putting all your songs and videos in the iTunes Media/Music folder by opening the Preferences box (Ctrl+comma [⌘-comma]) and confirming the folder location. Then:

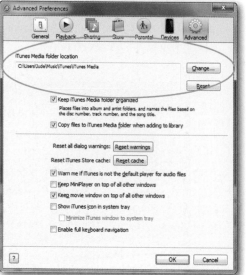

1. Click the Advanced tab, and then turn on the checkbox next to "Keep iTunes Media folder organized."

2. Click the Change button next to the phrase "iTunes Media folder location," and then navigate to your external hard drive.

3. Click the New Folder button in the dialog box, type in a name for the iTunes library, and then click Create.

4. Back in the Change Media Folder Location box, click the Open button.

5. Click OK to close the iTunes Preferences box.

6. Choose File→Library→Organize Library and then check "Consolidate files."

Ignore the ominous warning (*"This cannot be undone"*) and let iTunes heave a complete copy of your iTunes folder to the external drive. Once you confirm that everything is in the new library, trash your old iTunes Media folder and empty the Recycle Bin or Trash to get all those gigs of hard drive space back.

Where iTunes Stores Your Files

BEHIND ITS SLEEK WINDOW, iTunes has a very precise system for storing music, movies, and everything else you add to it. Inside its own iTunes folder on your hard drive (which, unless you moved it, is in Music→iTunes [Home→Music→iTunes]), the program keeps all your files and song information. (If you're running Windows Vista, your iTunes folder is at User→[User Name]→Music→iTunes, and Windows XP users can find it at My Documents→My Music→iTunes.)

Your iTunes Library file, *iTunes Library.itl* (*iTunes Library* on Macs with old versions of iTunes), is a record of the names of all the songs, playlists, videos, and other content you added to iTunes. It sits inside the iTunes folder. Be very careful not to move or delete this file if you happen to be poking around in the iTunes folder. If iTunes can't find it, it gives a little sigh and creates a new library—one that doesn't have a record of all your songs and other media goodies.

But even if you *do* accidentally delete the Library file, your music is still on your computer—even if iTunes doesn't know it. That's because all the song files are actually stored in the iTunes *Media* folder (or *Music* folder; see the Tip below), which is also inside the main iTunes folder. You may lose your custom playlists if your Library file goes missing, but you can always add your music files back (File→Add to Library) to recreate your library.

TIP Depending on whether you updated an older version of iTunes, your iTunes Media folder may actually be an iTunes *Music* folder. If you have a Media folder, iTunes neatly groups things like games, music, TV shows, movies, and other content in their own subfolders, making it much easier to find your downloaded episodes of *Mad Men* among all the song files. If you want to reorganize, media-style, choose File→Library→Organize Library and choose "Reorganize files in the folder iTunes Music."

Set Up Multiple iTunes Libraries

THERE'S HOME SHARING AND then there's home, sharing. Many families have just one computer. If everyone uses the same copy of iTunes, you soon hear the Wiggles bumping up against the Wu-Tang Clan if you shuffle your music tracks or when you autosync multiple iPods. Wouldn't it be great if everyone had a *personal* iTunes library to have and to hold, to sync and to shuffle—separately? Absolutely.

To use multiple iTunes libraries, follow these steps:

1. Quit iTunes.

2. Hold down the Shift (Option) key on your Windows PC or Mac keyboard and launch iTunes. In the box that pops up, click Create Library. Give it a name, like "Tiffany's Music" or "Songs My Wife Hates."

3. iTunes opens up, but with an empty library. If you have a bunch of music or videos in your main library that you want to copy over to this one, choose File→Add to Library.

4. Navigate to the files you want and add them. If the songs are in your original library, they're probably in Music→iTunes→iTunes Media→Music (Home→Music→iTunes→iTunes Media→Music), in folders sorted by artist name; videos are in TV Shows or Movies. Choose the files you want to add.

To switch among libraries, hold down the Shift (Option) key when you start iTunes, and you'll get a box that lets you pick the library you want. (If you don't choose a library, iTunes opens the last one used.) Tracks you copy go into whatever library you have currently open. Now that you have those files in your new library, you can switch back to the old one and get rid of them there.

Back Up Your iTunes Files

IF YOUR HARD DRIVE dies and takes your whole iTunes folder with it, you could be in for a major media migraine, depending on your backup situation. You can easily recover music, apps, TV shows, and books you purchased from the iTunes Store now, thanks to iTunes In the Cloud (page 192), but your hand-ripped tracks from your personal CD collection and music purchased from other online stores (page 259) are gone unless you're an iTunes Match subscriber (page 194). But iTunes Match doesn't upload copies of your video clips and personal home movies, so those may have just disappeared into the ether as well.

That's why it's important to back up the iTunes library—if not your whole computer—unless you *like* starting over from scratch. Here's how:

1. If you just want to back up your iTunes collection to a set of CDs or DVDs, fire up your disc-making program and burn a copy of your iTunes folder to the recordable platters. (The previous page explains how to find your iTunes folder and files.)

2. To back up your computer's contents to an external hard drive or recordable discs, use a dedicated pro-gram. There are plenty of third-party options out there (many offered as part of system security suites or included with new USB external hard drives), but your computer itself may have built-in tools. For example, Mac OS X 10.5 and later includes Apple's Time Machine utility  (shown here), which works with most external hard drives and makes frequent snapshots of your computer's contents throughout the day. Find it at Home→ Applications→Time Machine; bring your own dedicated external hard drive.

Windows Vista, Windows 7, and Windows 8 also include a backup program. Go to Start→Control Panel→System and Maintenance→Backup and Restore to find it and set it up. (If you use Windows XP, you may first have to install the backup program from your system discs, depending on which version of the operating system you have; Microsoft has details at *http://support. microsoft.com/kb/308422.*)

Online backup services like Mozy (*www.mozy.com*), iDrive (*www.idrive.com*), and Carbonite (*www.carbonite.com*) are alternatives to using USB drives. You typically get 2 gigabytes of free storage and then pay as little as $5 a month.

You'll learn to:

- Create and edit playlists in iTunes or on your iPod

- Make Genius playlists

- Let iTunes auto-create all kinds of playlists for you

- Beam your tunes to speakers with AirPlay

- Burn custom music mixes to CD

CHAPTER 12

The Power of Playlists

A *PLAYLIST* IS A group of songs that you think go well together. You create a playlist by dragging songs from your iTunes library into the list. You can include pretty much any set of tunes arranged in any order. For example, if you're having a party, you can make playlists out of dance tracks. If you're in a 1960s Brit-girl pop mood, you can whip together the hits of Dusty Springfield, Lulu, and Petula Clark. Some people may question your taste if you, say, mix tracks from *La Bohème* with Queen's *A Night at the Opera*, but hey—it's *your* playlist.

Creating playlists has become something of an art form since the iPod arrived in 2001. You can find books filled with sample playlists. Academics around the world write papers about group dynamics and cultural identity after studying how people create playlists—and which ones they choose to share with others. Some nightclubs even invite people to hook up their iPods so they can share their playlists with the dance-floor audience.

If you don't have time to make your own playlists, Apple lends you an expert hand. Its Genius feature lets you create one-click mixes of songs that sound as though they were actually meant to go together.

So get cracking and create a playlist (or 42) of your own.

Make a New Playlist in iTunes

TO CREATE A PLAYLIST, press Ctrl+N (⌘-N) in iTunes. You can also choose File→New→Playlist or click the **✚** button at the bottom-left corner of the iTunes window.

All freshly minted playlists start out with the rather impersonal name "playlist." Fortunately, iTunes highlights this generic moniker so you can change it—just type in a better name: "Cardio Workout," "Hits of the Highland Lute," or whatever you want to call it. As you add playlists, iTunes alphabetizes them in its Playlists area.

Once you create and name a spanking-new playlist, you're ready to add songs or videos. You can do so several ways, so choose the one you like best.

Playlist-Making Method #1

When you choose the New Playlist option, iTunes 11 pops open a panel on the right side of its window. This is your blank canvas to create a sonic masterpiece. At the top of the column, type the name you want to use for your new playlist if you haven't done so already. Make sure the pop-up menu on the left side of the iTunes window is set to Music. Now, click around the tabs at the top of the iTunes library window (Songs, Albums, Artists, and so on) and drag the songs or albums you like into the playlist column. Drag songs one at a time, or grab a bunch by selecting tracks one after the other; just Ctrl-click (⌘-click) each title Click the Done button when you finish.)

Playlist-Making Method #2

Want to add new songs to an existing playlist? No problem. Highlight the tracks you want to add in iTunes' main window (Ctrl-click [⌘-click] each song) and drag them over to the right side of the iTunes window—which conveniently pops open the new playlist panel so you can drop your songs on the playlist of your choice.

If your iPod happens to be connected to iTunes at the time, doing the click-and-drag-to-the-right move opens the iPod's playlist collections. Drop the selected songs on the desired iPod playlist.

Playlist-Making Method #3

1. You can also pick and choose songs in your library, and then create a playlist out of the highlighted songs. Select tracks by Ctrl-clicking (⌘-clicking) the titles.

2. Choose File→New→Playlist From Selection or press Ctrl-Shift-N (⌘-Shift-N). The songs you selected appear in a brand-new playlist. If all of them came from the same album, iTunes names the playlist after the album (but it also highlights the name so you can change it).

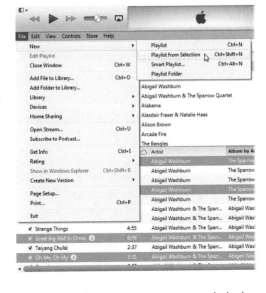

Don't worry about clogging up your hard drive. When you drag a song title onto a playlist, you don't *copy* the song, you just tell iTunes where to find the file. In essence, you're creating a shortcut to the track. That means you can have the same song on several playlists, but only one copy of it resides on your computer.

That nice iTunes even gives you some playlists of its own devising, like "Top 25 Most Played" and "Purchased" (a convenient place to find all your iTunes Store goodies listed in one place).

Change an Existing Playlist

IF YOU CHANGE YOUR mind about a playlist's tune order, drag the song titles up or down within the playlist window. Just make sure to sort the playlist by song order first (click the top of the first column, the one with the numbers listed in front of the song titles).

You can always drag more songs into a playlist, and you can delete titles if you find that your list needs pruning. Click the song in the playlist window, and then hit Backspace (Delete). When iTunes asks you to confirm your decision, click Yes. Remember, deleting a song from a playlist doesn't delete it from your music library—it just removes the title from that particular playlist. (You can get rid of a song for good only by pressing Backspace or Delete from within the *iTunes* library; select Music from the pop-up menu in the top-left corner of the iTunes 11 window to get there.)

You can quickly add a song to an existing playlist right from the main iTunes window, no matter which view you happen to be using: Select the song, right-click (Control-click) it, and then, in the pop-up menu, choose Add to Playlist. Scroll to the playlist you want to use and then click the mouse button to add the track to that list. (The previous page also has steps for adding to a playlist.)

If you want to see how many playlists contain a certain song, select the track, right-click (Control-click) it, and choose Show in Playlist in the pop-up menu.

In iTunes 11, you can quickly add tunes to an existing playlist another way. Click Playlists at the top of the window, click the playlist you want to change, and then click Add To at the top of the window. The playlist-editing pane opens, ready to accept changes. (You can also click the ⚙ icon at the bottom of the column and choose Edit Playlist for one more way to modify your work.)

Add a Playlist to Your iPod

ADDING THAT FABULOUS NEW playlist to your iPod doesn't take any heavy lifting on your part. In fact, if you set up your iPod to autosync with iTunes, the only thing you need to do is grab your USB cable and plug in your iPod. Once iTunes recognizes the iPod, it copies any new playlists over to it.

You can also tell iTunes to sync different playlists to different iPods—helpful if you're in a multiple-iPod-owning household and you all share the same computer and iTunes library. Just plug in your iPod, click its icon at the top of the iTunes window, and then click the Music tab. In the Sync Music area, click the button for "Selected playlists" and then turn on the appropriate checkboxes.

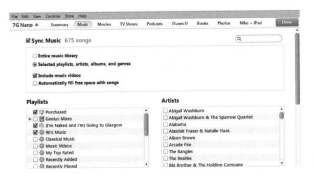

If you manually manage the syncing process, connect your iPod and click its icon at the top of the iTunes window, Next, click the On This iPod button in the row that appears at the top of the window. On this screen, click the Add To button on the right side. A panel showing your iPod's contents slides open on the right. Click the Playlists button at the top of the iTunes window, select the playlist you want to transfer (Ctrl-click [⌘-click] to snag more than one), and then drag it onto the iPod's open pane.

TIP If you find that your song-mix list is longer than the line for a One Direction concert, you can save some space by putting batches of song mixes, like "Dinner Party" inside *playlist folders*. Making a folder is easy: just choose File→New→Playlist Folder. Once the new folder appears in the Playlists area of the iTunes window, give it a name, and then drag a bunch of playlists onto the folder icon. To open the folder and crank up a playlist inside, click the flippy triangle next to the folder name to reveal the playlists. Click the triangle again to close the folder.

Delete a Playlist

ONCE THE PARTY'S OVER, you may want to get rid of a playlist or two. Start by clicking its name in the Playlists list, and then press the Backspace (Delete) key. iTunes presents you with a warning box, double-checking that you really want to vaporize the list. (Again, this maneuver just zaps the playlist itself, not the songs you had in it. Those remain available in the main iTunes window.)

If you have your iPod set to autosync, then any playlist you delete from iTunes will disappear from your iPod the next time you plug in and sync your player.

If you manually manage your iPod, connect the player, and click its name at the top of the iTunes window. Click "On This iPod" to see all its libraries and playlists. Click the playlist you want to dump and then hit Backspace (Delete).

Make and Edit Playlists on the iPod Touch and Nano

PLAYLIST INSPIRATION CAN STRIKE anywhere, and you may not be sitting in front of iTunes when it does. Thankfully, the Touch and Nano let you satisfy your whims wherever you may be. All you need are songs and a finger. Here's how:

- **Create a playlist.** On the Touch's Home screen, tap the Music icon. Tap Playlists. Near the top of the Playlists screen, tap Add Playlist and type in a name for it. A master list of all your songs appears. Each time you see one worth adding, tap its name (or the ● button). You can also tap one of the icons at the bottom of the screen, like Playlists, Artists, or Albums, to find the stuff you want. At the top of every list is an "Add All Songs" option that does just that—adds all the songs listed to your playlist-in-progress. When you finish, tap Done. Your playlist is ready for its debut.

On the Nano's Home screen, tap Music→Playlists. Tap the Playlists title bar at the top of the screen and then tap the Add button. Tap the name of the category—Songs, Albums, you know the drill—and then tap the ● next to the item you want to add. Swipe left to add stuff from several categories, so you can, for example, stick in a podcast for your post-jog cooldown walk. Tap Done when you finish. Your creation is called New Playlist 1, but you can change that after you sync the Nano with iTunes.

- **Delete or edit a playlist.** To whack a whole playlist on the Touch, tap Home→Music→Playlists→[Playlist Name]→Delete. On the Nano, tap Home→Music→Playlists. Tap the title bar on the next screen, press Edit, tap the Delete symbol (●), and then press Delete to remove the whole playlist. Tap the Clear button to keep the playlist name, but zap its songs.

To edit an existing playlist on the Touch or Nano, tap Home→Music→Playlists→[Playlist Name]→Edit; tap the title bar on the Nano to see the Edit button. Tap the Delete symbol (●) and then press Delete to remove a song, or tap **+** (or the Add button on the Nano) to browse for and add a new song. See that "grip strip" (≡) at the right edge of the screen? Press and hold it with a finger and drag the strip up or down to rearrange the song order. Tap Done when you finish.

Make a Playlist on an iPod Classic

THE IPOD CLASSIC MAY be older than the Touch and Nano, but it, too, lets you create playlists right there on the player. They sync back to iTunes the next time you connect. The iPod Classic calls its song collections "On-The-Go" playlists:

1. Scroll through your iPod's list of songs until you get to the title of the first one you want to add to a playlist.

2. Hold down the center button for a few seconds, until a new set of menus appears. Choose "Add to On-The-Go."

3. Scroll to the next song you want to add and repeat the process.

4. When you're done adding songs, press the iPod's menu button until you get to the Music menu; go to Playlists→On-The-Go. Under On-The-Go, you see the number of songs you just compiled. Press Select to see the song titles.

5. If you like what you see, scroll up to Save Playlist and click the center button. If you don't like the collection, choose Clear Playlist to dump the songs and start over. If you like some, but not all, of the songs, you can remove individual tunes by selecting one, holding down the center button, and choosing "Remove from On-The-Go."

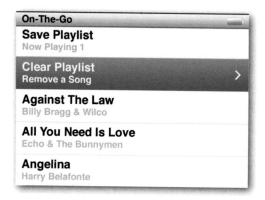

Your freshly inspired playlist now appears in your Playlists menu as On-The-Go 1. The next one you make and save will be On-The-Go 2, and so on. When you reconnect your iPod to iTunes, you can click these names and change them to something peppier—or more descriptive.

TIP You can also add a whole album to your On-The-Go inspiration. Just select the LP title in your Albums list, hold down the center button, and choose Add to On-The-Go.

Make a Genius Playlist in iTunes

PLAYLISTS ARE FUN TO make, but occasionally you just don't have the time or energy. If that's the case, call in an expert—the iTunes Genius. With the Genius feature, you click any song you're in the mood for and iTunes crafts a playlist of 25 to 100 songs that it thinks go well with the one you picked.

The first time you use it, Genius asks permission to go through your music collection and gather song information. Then it uploads that data anonymously to Apple. When your information has been analyzed (by software) and added to a giant database of everybody else's song info (to improve the Genius's suggestions), the Genius is ready for duty. Here's the procedure:

1. Click the Songs button atop the iTunes window, and then click a song title.

2. Click the ❯ icon at the end of the song's name in iTunes' song-list window and choose Create Genius Playlist; you can also click ❯ next to the name of the song currently playing in iTunes' display window to get the same menu.

3. iTunes presents you with your new playlist in a flash.

4. Use the Refresh button (↻) at the top of the Genius window to refresh it with new songs if you want a different mix. Click the triangle next to the number of songs to change it from the default 25 to 50, 75, or 100 songs.

iTunes saves your new Genius playlist with all your other playlists—click the Playlists button at the top of the iTunes window to see it. The Genius doesn't work if it doesn't have enough information about a song—or if there aren't enough similar songs for it to draw from. In that case, pick another tune. If you frequently add new music to your library and want to get it in the mix, inform the Genius at Store→Update Genius.

> **NOTE** If you declined iTunes' initial offer to activate the Genius, you can summon it again by choosing Store→Turn On Genius. And if you regret inviting the Genius into your iTunes home, kick it out by visiting the same menu and choosing Turn Off Genius.

Make a Genius Playlist on the iPod

YOU MAY GET SO hooked on making Genius playlists in iTunes that you never want to leave your computer. Before you end up on a neighborhood "Lost" flier, consider this: You can also make Genius playlists on the iPod itself. You just need to have a recent Touch, Nano, or Classic.

To use your portable pocket Genius, though, you first have to upload your information from iTunes to Apple, as described on the previous page. But you've probably done that by now, so here's how to make the Genius do your bidding when you're away from your computer.

1. On the Touch, tap Music→Playlists→ Genius Playlist, and then tap the song you want the Genius to use as a starting point. If you're currently *listening* to that song, tap the screen to summon the playback controls (Chapter 3), and then tap the ❄ icon.

   On the Nano, tap the song you want to start with and tap the album cover on the Now Playing screen. Tap the screen again to show the hidden controls, and then tap the ❄ icon. You can also tap Music→Playlists→Genius, and then tap the name of the song you want to use as the basis for the playlist.

   On a Classic, select a song and hold down the iPod's center button for a few seconds, until a menu appears; choose Start Genius. If you're already playing the song you want to use, press the center button until you see the Genius option appear, and then flick the click wheel over to Start.

2. If you don't like the resulting mix, select or tap the Refresh option atop the screen to get new tunes.

3. If you love the work of the Genius, select or tap Save at the top of the screen.

As with iTunes, the Genius titles its playlists after the name of the song you chose as the foundation for your mix. When you sync your iPod with iTunes, the traveling Genius playlists get copied back to iTunes, where you can edit the title.

Genius Mixes in iTunes

YES, THE ITUNES GENIUS feature takes almost all the effort out of making playlists—all you do is click the Genius button. But if even a one-button click seems like too much effort, iTunes makes playlist creation even *easier*. Welcome to Genius Mixes.

The Genius Mix feature works like this: iTunes takes it upon itself to search your music library and then automatically compose (depending on the size of your library) up to 12 different types of song collections. Unlike a Genius playlist of songs calculated to go well together, a Genius Mix is more like a radio station or cable-TV music channel, with the music based on *genre*. Depending on what's in your iTunes library, the Genius could present you with a hip-hop mix, a country mix, a classical mix, and so on. In addition, the Genius Mix creates up to 12 playlists at once, all saved and ready to play, unlike the Genius's single mix that you have to save to preserve.

If you don't already see a square purple Genius Mix icon (::) in your iTunes Source list, choose Store→Update Genius. Once activated, the Genius quietly stirs up its sonic concoctions from your music library.

To play a Genius Mix, click the Playlists button at the top of the iTunes window, and then click the Genius Mixes icon in the list on the left. iTunes displays the different mixes it's created. It represents each by a quartet of album covers from tracks in the mix. Pass your mouse over the album squares to see the name of the mix, or click the squares to start playing the songs.

Like more traditional radio stations, you don't get to see a playlist of what's actually *in* a particular Genius Mix—unless you know where to look. (If you want to, jump to page 227, which explains the Up Next feature.) If you don't care for a song at the moment, playback controls on the Genius Mix album covers let you jump forward or backward in the mix.

Genius Mixes can be another great way to effortlessly toss on some background music at a party, and you may even hear songs you haven't played in forever. Want to take the Genius Mix with you? Turn the page.

Genius Mixes on the iPod

AS WITH MOST PLAYLISTS (except for those mobile, made-on-the-iPod kind), you need to copy Genius Mixes over to the iPod by way of iTunes. But there's one other little requirement: You have to copy the Genius Mixes over by *syncing* them through iTunes.

People who autosync their entire libraries don't have to do anything to get the Genius Mixes onboard their iPods. People who manually manage music by dragging tracks from the iTunes library onto the iPod can't physically drag a Genius Mix onto the player—for now, anyway. For those who selectively sync, copying a Genius Mix takes a few steps:

1. Connect your iPod to your computer and click its icon at the top of the iTunes window.

2. On the horizontal list of things you can sync to your iPod (lined up along the top of the iTunes window), click the Music tab.

3. If you haven't done so, turn on the checkbox for Sync Music and click the button for "Selected playlists, artists, and genres," as shown at the top right. (If you selectively sync anyway, you've already done this.)

4. Turn on the checkboxes next to the Genius Mixes you want to copy to your iPod. Click the Apply and/or Sync button to transfer them to the player.

5. To play a mix on your iPod Touch, tap Home→Music→Genius, as shown bottom-right. Swipe your finger across the screen until you get to the mix you want, and then tap the Play triangle to fire it up. (The dots at the bottom of the screen tell you how many mixes you have.)

On a Nano, tap the Genius icon and swipe the screen to browse the mixes.

On a Classic, choose iPod→Music→Genius Mixes. Use the click wheel's Next or Previous buttons to get to the right mix. Press the center button or Play/Pause to listen it.

Manage Your Expectations With Up Next

EVER HAVE ITUNES BLASTING out a playlist, a Genius Mix, or your whole library on shuffle—and find yourself curious about the next song in the rotation? Maybe it's a track you're not in the mood for, so you want to skip it. You can sneak a peak at the upcoming song (and several others after it) with the new Up Next feature built into iTunes 11.

To use Up Next while iTunes is playing, click the ⦂☰ icon in the display area of the iTunes window, as shown below. The Up Next list pops up to reveal, well, what's up next in your music queue.

Up Next can do a lot for your impromptu music-management whims:

- You can drag and drop albums, playlists, and songs onto the Up Next button to add them to the list of upcoming tracks.

- Want to move a song up in the current play order? Select the track in the Up Next list, click ❯ and choose Play Next.

- To delete one song from the Up Next list, move the mouse cursor over the title and click ✕ next to the name; to whack all the tracks in the Up Next list, click the Clear button in the menu.

- To see the songs iTunes has already played, click the clock icon. Click the icon again to go back to the Up Next list.

Don't worry if you've spent the last 15 minutes rearranging your Up Next list and now have to go to work. iTunes remembers what you did and preserves the Up Next list the way you left it when you open the program again.

Smart Playlists: Another Way for iTunes to Assemble Song Sets

AS COOL AS THE Genius is, sometimes you want a little more control over what goes into your automatically generated mixes. That's where iTunes' Smart Playlists rise to the occasion.

Once you give it some guidelines, a *Smart Playlist* can go sniffing through your music library and come up with its own music mix. A Smart Playlist even keeps tabs on the music that comes and goes to and from your library and adjusts itself based on that.

You might tell one Smart Playlist to assemble 45 minutes' worth of songs that you rated higher than four stars but rarely listen to, and another to play your most-often-played songs from the 1980s. The Smart Playlists you create are limited only by your imagination.

1. **To start a Smart Playlist, press Ctrl+Alt+N (Option-⌘-N) or choose File→New→Smart Playlist in iTunes**. A Smart Playlist box opens: It sports a ✿ icon next to its name in the Source list (a regular playlist has a music-staff icon with a music note on it).

2. **Give iTunes detailed instructions about what you want to hear**. You can select a few artists you like and have iTunes leave off the ones you're not in the mood for, pluck songs that fall within a certain genre or year, and so on. To add multiple, cumulative criteria, click the plus (**+**) button on each line.

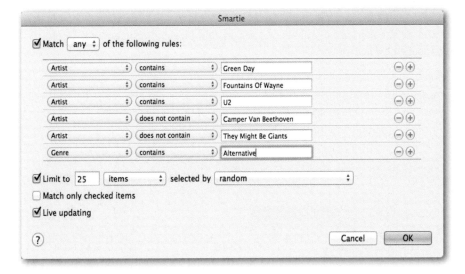

3. **Turn on the "Live updating" checkbox**. This tells iTunes to keep the playlist updated as your collection, ratings, and play count change. (The play count tells iTunes how often you play a track, a good indicator of how much you like a song.)

4. **To edit an existing Smart Playlist, right-click (Control-click) the playlist's name**. Then choose Edit Smart Playlist. This reopens the box pictured above, where you can go back to tinkering with your magic formula until you get just the right mix.

A Smart Playlist is a dialogue between you and iTunes: You tell it what you want in as much detail as you want, and the program whips up a playlist according to your instructions.

You can even instruct a Smart Playlist to pull tracks from your current Genius playlist. Click the + button to add a preference, choose Playlist as another criteria, and select Genius from the list of available playlists.

TIP You can skip the trip up to the iTunes menu bar and start a new Smart Playlist by clicking the **+** button at the bottom of the iTunes window. This gives you a drop-down menu with a New Smart Playlist option.

Beam Playlists with AirPlay

SOME PLAYLISTS ARE SO great, they deserve to be blasted through bigger speakers than those on your computer. That's where Apple's AirPlay technology comes in handy. Chapter 16 has more on using AirPlay for streaming music and video to Apple TV-connected television sets or AirPort Express-connected external speakers, so if you haven't set up your streaming system yet, flip to page 294 for instructions.

If you already have all that set up and just want to know how to beam your music from iTunes on the computer to something bigger and louder, click the ⌷ icon next to the playback controls at the top of the iTunes window. Select your Apple TV or speakers from the menu, as shown below.

If you have different speakers set up in different rooms, click the Multiple button and select the speakers you want to use. A green checkmark indicates which speakers are currently blasting the music. While you're in this menu, you can adjust the volume of your speakers (right from iTunes!). Use the Master Volume slider to change the overall sound output, or the individual sliders to lower or raise the volume on a specific set of speakers or Apple TV.

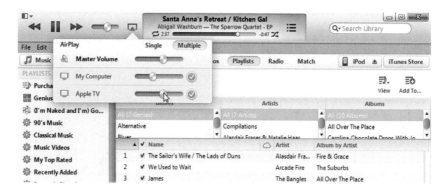

Three Kinds of Discs You Can Create with iTunes

IF YOU WANT TO record a certain playlist on a CD for posterity—or for the Mr. Shower CD player in the bathroom—iTunes gives you power to burn. In fact, it can create three kinds of disc:

- **Standard audio CDs.** This is the best option. If your computer has a CD burner, it can serve as your own private record label. iTunes can record selected sets of songs, no matter what their original source (except for non-iTunes Store tunes that are copy-protected). When

it's all over, you can play the burned CD on any standard CD player, just like the albums you get from Best Buy—but this time, you hear only the songs you like, in the order you like. Turn the page for playlist-burning instructions.

- **MP3 CDs.** A standard audio CD contains high-quality, enormous song files in the AIFF format. An *MP3* compact disc, however, is a data CD that contains music files in the MP3 format. Because MP3 songs are much smaller than AIFF files, many more of them fit in the standard 650 or 700 MB of space on a recordable CD. The bottom line? Instead of 74 or 80 minutes of music, a CD full of MP3 files can store *10 to 12 hours* of tunes. The downside? Older CD players may not be able to play these discs.

- **Backup CDs or DVDs.** If your computer can play and record CDs and/or DVDs, you have another option: iTunes can back up all the songs in a playlist by copying them to a CD or DVD. (The disc won't play in any kind of player; it's just a glorified backup disk for restoration when something goes wrong with your hard drive.) You can back up all the songs in your library by selecting them all and choosing File→New Playlist From Selection—and then burning *that* monster playlist to a set of data discs.

To see if your disc drive is compatible with iTunes, select a playlist and click the Burn Disc button in the iTunes window to get the Burn Settings box. If your drive is listed next to "CD Burner," iTunes recognizes it.

> **NOTE** Even if you've got a DVD drive, you still see it listed next to the label "CD Burner."

Burn a Playlist to a CD

MAKING A CD OUT of your favorite playlist takes just a few steps with iTunes, so get your blank disc ready and click along.

1. **Select the playlist you want to burn**. Check to make sure your songs are in the order you want them; drag any tune up or down to reorder.

2. **When you're ready to roll, choose File→Burn Playlist to Disc or right-click (Control-click) the playlist in the Source list and then choose Burn Playlist to Disc**. When the Burn Settings box pops up, pick the type of disc you want to create (see the previous page for your choices).

3. **Insert a blank disc into your drive when prompted**. If your computer has a CD platter that slides out, push it back in. Then sit back as iTunes handles the transfer.

iTunes prepares to record the disc, which may take a few minutes. In addition, iTunes has to convert the files (if you're burning an audio CD) to the industry-standard format for CDs.

Once iTunes has taken care of business, it lets you know that it's burning the disc. Again, depending on the speed of your computer and disc burner, as well as the size of your playlist, the recording process could take several minutes. When the disc is done, iTunes pipes up with a musical flourish. Eject the disc and off you go. But if you want to make a nice-looking CD cover...

Print Playlists and Snazzy CD Covers

YOU USED TO HAVE to do a lot of gymnastics just to print a nice-looking song list that would fit into a CD case. But with iTunes, all you need to do is choose File→Print, select a preformatted option, and then click Print.

The Print dialog box is *full* of choices.

- **CD jewel case insert.** You can print out a perfectly sized insert for a CD jewel case, complete with a song list on the left and a miniature mosaic of all your album artwork on the right—or just a plain list of songs on a solid-color background. Your resulting printout even comes with handy crop marks to guide your scissors when you trim it down to size.

- **Song listing.** If you want something simpler, you can opt for a straightforward list of all the songs on the playlist. This option is also great for printing out a list of all the podcasts you currently have in your iTunes library—just click the Podcasts icon in the Source list, click the "Song listing" option, and print away.

- **Album listing.** You can print a list of all the albums that contributed to your playlist, complete with the album title, artist name, and the songs' titles and play times for each track culled from that album.

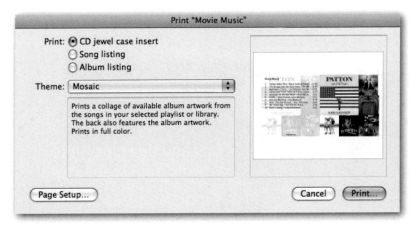

Want to use one of your own photos for the cover of your CD case? Start by adding the artwork of your choice to a track (Chapter 11). When you're ready to print, select that track on the playlist and then choose File→Print→CD jewel case insert→Theme: Single Cover to place your photo front and center. This also works great if you want to create jewel-case inserts that look just like the ones that come with commercial CDs.

You'll learn to:

- Navigate the iTunes store
- Buy and download music, videos, books, and more
- Set up an Apple account
- Subscribe to podcasts
- Share your tastes on Facebook and Twitter
- Give iTunes gifts

CHAPTER 13

Shop the iTunes Store

MUSIC FANS HAVE BEEN downloading songs from the Internet since the 1990s, from sites that were legal and others that were, well, not so much. People loved the convenience, but record companies saw potential profits slipping down millions of modem lines. They fought back by suing file-sharing services and other software companies for aiding and abetting copyright infringement.

The need for a legal music-download site was obvious, but most early efforts resulted in skimpy song catalogs and confusing usage rights. Things changed dramatically in April 2003, when Apple opened its online iTunes Music Store, selling legal, iPod-ready digital versions of popular songs for 99 cents a pop. In January 2009, Apple did away with the restrictive copy protections built into most Store songs. This liberating act gave consumers unfettered use of their songs and even the ability to play them on (gasp!) non-Apple players.

Now simply called the iTunes Store, the media emporium's virtual shelves stock millions of songs, plus full-length movies, TV shows, iPod Touch programs, audio books, ebooks, podcasts, music videos, and more. It's all custom-tailored for the iPod, and best of all, once you buy a title, it's yours to keep (rentals, of course, come with a time limit). This chapter shows you how to find and use the media you're looking for, and how to get the most out of the iTunes Store.

Get to the iTunes Store

COMPARED WITH BUYING GAS, fighting traffic, and finding a parking spot at the mall, getting to the iTunes Store is easy. All you need is an Internet connection and a copy of iTunes running on your computer. Then you can either:

1. Click the iTunes Store button (circled) in the top-right corner of the iTunes window. You land squarely on the Store's home page, where you can start clicking on what looks good.

2. If you like to get places by way of menus or keyboard shortcuts, iTunes lets you live the dream. In Windows, press Crtl+B to show the iTunes menu bar (if it's not visible already) and choose Store→Home. The keyboard shortcut is Ctrl+Shift+H. On the Mac version of iTunes, choose Store→Home, or press ⌘-Shift-H on the keyboard.

Once you land in the iTunes Store, you can preview suggested songs by clicking the ▶ icon that appears in front of a track's title when you pass your cursor over the song. The Buy button is always nearby waiting for your impulse purchase, making it extremely easy to run up your credit card tab.

If you have an iPod Touch and are in range of a wireless network, you can get to the Store a third way: over the airwaves, as explained on the next page.

TIP Longtime iTunes Store customers—especially those still stuck on dial-up modems— may be deeply dismayed to see the loss of the Shopping Cart feature from earlier versions of iTunes. The Shopping Cart, which let you pile up songs and then download them all at the end of your shopping session, has been loosely replaced with the Wish List feature, described on page 251.

Shop the iTunes Store via WiFi

OWNERS OF THE IPOD Touch don't even *need* a computer to shop the iTunes Store—those lucky souls can tap their way right into the Store over a wireless Internet connection. Many WiFi-enabled Starbucks coffee shops also let you hook into the iTunes Store for free to browse and buy music, including whatever track is playing *at* Starbucks.

To buy stuff when you're out and about—and in the mood to shop:

1. Tap the purple iTunes icon on the Touch's Home screen. Make sure you have a WiFi connection; see Chapter 5 for guidance on making that happen.

2. The Store appears on-screen. Tap your way through categories like "New Albums" until you find an album or song that interests you. (Tap an album to see all its songs.)

3. Tap a song title for a 90-second preview.

4. Tap the Music, Videos, or Search buttons at the bottom of the window for targeted shopping, or type in search terms from the Touch keyboard.

5. To buy and download music or videos, tap the price button, and then tap Buy.

6. Type in your Apple ID and let the download begin. You can check the status of your purchase-in-progress by tapping the Touch's Downloads button, which also lets you pause a download if you need to. If you don't have an Apple ID (which Apple sometimes colloquially refers to as "an iTunes Store account"), tap the Create New Account button on the Sign In screen and follow the steps. You sign in and out of your account with a link at the bottom of the media listings. Tap the Purchased icon to see all the things you've ever bought from iTunes on any computer or iOS device—and download them again here.

When iTunes finishes downloading your purchases, you have some brand-new media ready to play on your Touch—the new acquisitions land on your media app's Purchased page. To get those freshly harvested songs or videos back into the iTunes library on your computer, sync up the Touch. The tracks pop up in the iTunes playlist creatively titled "Purchased."

The iTunes Store Layout

THE ITUNES STORE IS jam-packed with digital merchandise, all neatly filed by category in links across the top of the main window: Music, Movies, TV Shows, and so on. The clean design of iTunes 11 makes the Store even more browse-worthy than before. Click a link to go to a Store "aisle." You can also hover your mouse over a link and click the triangle that appears; a pop-up menu lets you jump to a subcategory within that category (Blues or Pop in Music, for example).

The main part of the iTunes Store window—that big piece of real estate smack in the center of your browser—highlights iTunes' latest audio and video releases and specials. It's usually stuffed full of digital goodies, so scroll down the page to see featured movies, TV shows, and apps. Free song downloads and other offers appear down below, too.

To find a specific item, use the search box in the upper-right corner; enter titles, artist names, and other searchable info.

The Quick Links box on the right side of the window has shortcuts to iTunes gift certificates (see page 250), iTunes Match (page 194), Genius suggestions, an advanced search feature, your account settings, tech support, and more.

As you scroll, you also see Top Ten lists along the right side of the screen, showing you the hottest-selling items in the Store at that very moment.

Navigate the Aisles of the iTunes Store

YOU NAVIGATE THE ITUNES Store just as you navigate a website—by using links on the Store's page. Most artist and album names, for example, are links—click on a performer's name or an album cover to see a list of associated tracks.

Click the button with the small house on it (circled below) to jump to the Store's home page, or click iTunes' Back button in the upper-left corner (to the far left of the house) to return to a previous page.

When you find the name of an album or performer you're interested in, click it to jump to a detail page. You'll see a list of all the tracks on an album. Click the Ratings and Reviews button to see opinions from other iTunes users. Click Related to see a list of similar albums you can buy. Double-click a track title to hear a 90-second snippet. If you're shopping for videos or audiobooks, you can preview them, too.

If you get excited by something you find and want to share it with friends—or want to drop a not-so-subtle hint for birthday gifts—click the black triangle next to any Buy button to get a pop-up menu that lets you email a link to the item to a pal or post your discovery on your Facebook or Twitter page.

Set Up an Apple Account

BEFORE YOU CAN BUY any of the cool stuff in the iTunes Store, you need to set up an account with Apple, also known as an Apple ID. To do so, click the Sign In button on the upper-right corner of the iTunes window. In iTunes 11, you can also choose Store→Create Apple ID from the main menu bar.

If you've ever bought or registered an Apple product on the company's website, signed up for an AppleCare tech-support plan (page 311), ordered prints, books, or calendars from iPhoto, or used another Apple service, you probably already have the requisite Apple login info. All you have to do is remember your Apple ID (usually your email address) and password.

If you've never had an Apple ID, click Create Apple ID. That launches the iTunes Store Welcome screen, where you follow three steps:

1. Agree to the terms for using the Store and buying music.

2. Select a user name and password.

3. Supply a credit card or PayPal account number and billing address.

As your first step in creating an Apple ID, you must read and agree to the long, scrolling legal agreement on the first screen. The multipage statement informs you of your rights and responsibilities as an iTunes Store and App Store customer. It boils down to this: *Thou shalt not download an album, burn it to CD, and then sell bootleg copies of it at your local convenience store* and *Third-party crashware apps are not our fault.*

Click the Agree button to move on to step 2. Here you create an Apple user name, password, and secret questions and answers. If you later have to click the "Forgot Password?" button in the Store sign-in box, this is the question you'll have to answer to prove that you're you. Apple also requests that you type in your birthday to help verify your identity—and to make sure you're old enough to use the service (iTunes account holders have to be 13 or older).

On the third and final screen, tell Apple how you want to pay for purchases: provide a valid credit card number and a billing address, or type in your PayPal account info.

Click Done. You've got yourself an Apple ID. From now on, you can log into the iTunes Store by clicking the Sign In button in the upper-left corner of the Store's horizontal toolbar.

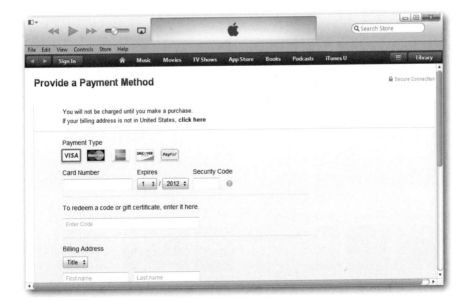

Browse and Buy Media From the Store

Over the past decade, the iTunes Store has grown from a rare source of legal music-files downloads with just 200,000 tracks to a sprawling mall of 26 million songs. And that's just music: The iTunes Store also has 45,000 movies, 190,000 TV episodes, 700,000 apps, and all kinds of other digital goodies like podcasts, ebooks, and free educational content from iTunes U.

So, you've got your Apple ID and you've just clicked the iTunes Store button on the iTunes 11 toolbar. Now what? Basically, you browse, you buy, and you download.

For many people, the browsing is the fun part—clicking around through the different categories of digital merchandise, listening to samples, watching previews, and getting acquainted with the stuff in the Store. The row of buttons across the top of the window take you to each type of content.

You can jump into shopping here two ways. The first is to click the button for the kind of media you want—Movies, TV Shows, and so on. To browse songs and albums, for example, click the Music button. You'll see *all* the styles of music the Store has to offer. To narrow your choices, click the All Categories drop-down menu on the right side of the page. It, too, lists the genres of music the Store carries; click one to see the selection.

If you know what kind of media you want right off the bat—say a little Latin pop to pep you up—use the second option: jump to subcategories for each type of content by sliding your cursor over the category name and clicking the arrow that appears next to the name. For example, clicking the arrow next to Music gives you a world of music styles to choose from (below).

Speaking of media categories, here's what you'll find in the iTunes Store just by clicking the buttons lined up in a row at the top of the window:

- **Music.** Millions of tracks await you here, all as high-quality 256 kilobits-per-second AAC files that play on iPods, iPhones, Apple TVs, and even hardware Apple doesn't sell. Prices for single tracks start at 69 cents, move up to 99 cents, and generally top out at $1.29. Entire albums can cost anywhere from about $8 to $15, but many come with digital versions of the old-school CD booklet. You also get album artwork on each track, which makes your collection look amazing in the new Album view of iTunes 11 (Chapter 10).

- **Movies.** Hollywood has an aisle in iTunes, with the latest home video releases arriving in the Store every week. You often have a choice of picture quality: standard definition or high-definition, depending on what your device can handle. If you don't want to buy, you can often rent a film to watch within 24 hours—but you have 30 days to start that 24-hour period. Some movies include iTunes Extras, DVD-like bonus features you can watch on your Windows PC or Mac. Movie rentals start at $2 for a standard-def short, and the latest HD release with all the Extras will run you about $20.

- **TV Shows.** Like movies, you can buy many TV show episodes in standard definition or high-definition format, for a respective $2 or $3 a pop. Since TV shows tend to come out regularly, you can buy a Season Pass (usually $25 and up) or a Multi-Pass (typically about $10 for the next 15 installments of a half-hour daily talk show or similar program) and have iTunes download them automatically, as you'll see later in this chapter.

- **App Store.** iPod Touch owners can browse away for new games and programs to run on their devices here from the comfort of the big iTunes window. Some apps are free, lightweight bits of code, but there's nothing "mini" about many Touch programs these days—a 250-megabyte word-processing program for $10 and $7 games with fancy graphics that take up more than a gigabyte of Touch-space are among the thousands of offerings.

- **Books.** No matter whether you like to read books yourself or have them read to you, you'll find ebooks that work with the Touch's iBooks app here, as well as audiobooks that work on *all* iPods. Prices start at free and go up to about $15 for a current best seller in ebook form, or $30 in audiobook form. The Books department of the Store sells textbooks, children's books, books in Spanish, and digital comics as well.

- **Podcasts.** Like those free audio and video shows? Click the Podcasts button to find them (and turn the page to read more about them).

- **iTunes U.** Apple's free-and-massive collection of educational materials from major universities can be found here, ready for you download and absorb.

Download and Subscribe to Podcasts

PODCASTS ARE ONE OF the iTunes Store's hidden gems. You'll find thousands upon thousands of these free audio (and video!) programs put out by everyone from big television networks to a guy in his basement with a microphone.

To see what podcasts are available, click the Podcasts link at the top of the Store's main page. You'll see three buttons atop the page that opens: All, Audio, and Video. Click one of the latter two to jump to just audio or video podcasts, or click the triangle beside the Podcasts button for a list of podcast topics. On the main Podcasts page, you can browse shows by category, search for podcast names by keyword (use the Store's search box), or click around until you find something that sounds good.

Many podcasters produce regular installments of their shows, releasing new episodes as they're ready. You can have iTunes keep a lookout for fresh editions and automatically download them; all you have to do is *subscribe* to the podcast. Click the podcast you want, and then click the Subscribe Now button underneath the artwork. If you want to try out a single podcast, click the Free link near its title to download just that one show.

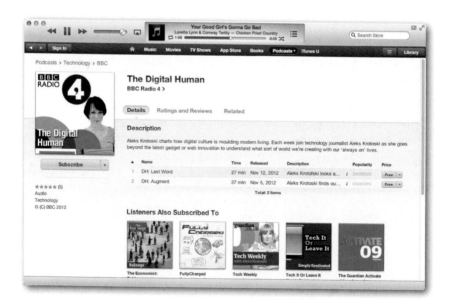

Although podcasts have a reputation as home-brewed projects—and there are many of those in the Store—you can also find hundreds of professional productions. Missed your favorite nightly network newscast? Check iTunes, where you might be able to grab it for free (NBC and PBS are among the companies that make many of their shows available as complimentary video downloads for a short time after the initial broadcast.) You can find many BBC and NPR radio shows available as podcasts as well, which lets you time-shift your listening.

Once you subscribe to a podcast, you can manage your episodes back in your iTunes library. Click on the Library drop-down menu in the top-left corner and choose Podcasts. The page displays all the shows you subscribe to and includes the number of episodes (both played and unplayed) waiting for you in iTunes.

As shown above, you can tell iTunes to automatically check for new episodes of each subscribed podcast more or less often (every hour to every week). Click the Settings icon (circled) on the library's Podcasts screen to set your options.

Tired of a podcast and want to stop the downloads? Select Podcasts from the Library's drop-down menu in the top-left corner of the iTunes window. Select the show in the list and then click the Unsubscribe button at the top of the window. To remove a podcast and all its episodes, click a title and hit the keyboard's Delete button.

TIP Podcasts, music, movies, books—there are so many things in the iTunes Store to look at, it's hard to remember it all. If you can't quite recall where you saw that cool thing you wanted to buy but didn't at the time, you can kickstart your memory with the History button (≡). Click it in the iTunes Store window to see a list of items you recently browsed. You need to be logged into your Apple ID to see the browsing trail, but it does provide a quick trip down memory lane.

Change the Information in Your Apple ID Account

YOU CAN CHANGE YOUR billing address, switch the credit card you have on file, and edit other information in your Apple account without calling Apple. Just launch iTunes and choose Store→View My Apple ID. In the box that appears (shown below) enter your Apple user name and password and click the View Account button. (If you're already signed in and shopping around when you want to change your account information, go to the left side of Store's toolbar and click the button that has your Apple user name on it to get to the box shown here.)

You land on your Account Information page. To change your billing address or payment information, click Edit next to the item you want to change. You can also deauthorize all the computers that can play songs purchased with this account (more on why and when you'd want to do that on page 257).

You can change other account settings here, too, like the nickname that appears when you post a customer review in the Store. You can also see how many of your iOS devices and computers you have looped into the automatic downloads feature of iTunes in the Cloud (page 192), review your Purchase History (a list of everything you've ever bought from the iTunes Store, as you'll find out later in this chapter), and control the alerts the iTunes Store sends you when it thinks you should spend more money inside its electronic walls.

When you finish making your changes, click Done at the bottom of the screen.

> **NOTE** By the way, any changes you make to your Apple user name through iTunes affect other programs or services you use with your account, like ordering pictures with iPhoto (Mac owners only).

Resuming Interrupted Store Downloads

IT'S BOUND TO HAPPEN sometime: You're breathlessly downloading a hot new album or movie from iTunes, and your computer freezes or your Internet connection goes on the fritz. Or you and your iPod Touch were in the middle of snagging an album when the rest of the gang decided it was time to leave the coffee shop.

If that happens, don't worry. Even if your computer crashes or you get knocked offline while you're downloading purchases, iTunes is designed to pick up where it left off. Just restart the program and reconnect to the Internet.

If, for some reason, iTunes doesn't go back to whatever it was downloading, choose Store→Check for Available Downloads to resume the download.

You can use this same command to check for available purchases any time you think you might have something waiting, like a new episode from a TV show Season Pass. You'll also find any digital booklets that come with albums you bought here—those don't download to your Touch from the WiFi Store because they're PDF files meant to be viewed on your computer.

TIP If you need help from a human at Apple, you can either call them at (800) 275-2273 or drop them an email. To email them, click the Support link on the iTunes Store's main page. You'll see the main iTunes service and support page; click any link in the Customer Service area and then, at the bottom of the page that appears, fill out the Email Support form. Live online chat is also available for some issues.

---

iTunes and Social Media

IF YOU SPEND ANY amount of time online these days, there's no escaping Facebook and Twitter as sources of breaking news, information, and sharing. Social media is here to stay.

Ping, Apple's two-year attempt at a music-themed social network, regally cannonballed into the Pool of Public Indifference and shut down in September 2012. But even in the absence of Ping, you can use the power of Facebook and Twitter to share your taste in music, movies, books, apps, and podcasts with your friends and followers—right from the iTunes Store.

On just about any product page in the Store, the Buy button offers a menu (shown below) with four ways to share your idea of a cool purchase: Tell a Friend (by email), Copy Link (for pasting into a blog or other online page), Share on Facebook, and Share on Twitter. Once you make your selection, iTunes creates a link to the item; your recipients and readers see your endorsement and can click on the link to go right to that item in the Store.

Yes, using these links gives Apple free publicity by having you flog its wares. But sharing links from the Store can also help promote a small indie band, a new podcast, or a TV show you think your friends should be watching—so you can all talk about it online.

You can also tout your taste in Music on the iPod Touch versions of Apple's iStores. In the top-left corner of any product page, tap the ⤴ icon to open up a menu of sharing options: Mail, Messages, Twitter, Facebook, or the good old Copy option.

To use the Facebook and Twitter options, you need to have your accounts linked to the iPod's Facebook or Twitter apps (Chapter 4) in iOS 6; Messages is also covered there. If you haven't set up Mail yet, take a stroll through Chapter 5.

Get iTunes News on Twitter

Apple maintains a number of official Twitter feeds. To keep up with the latest news from iTunes World, follow these self-explanatory accounts:

- **@iTunesMusic**
- **@AppStore**
- **@iTunesTV**
- **@iTunesMovies**
- **@iTunesU**
- **@iBookstore**
- **@iTunesPodcasts**

To follow any Twitter account, open the Touch's Twitter app (page 76), tap the Q icon, and then type in the name of the account. On the search results screen, tap the People tab at the top of the window, find the account (say, @iTunesU) in the list, and then tap Follow to add the account to your Twitter feed.

Give the Gift of iTunes

IF YOU'RE STUMPED TRYING to find something for The Person Who Has Everything, consider a gift of iTunes Store credit or music. Apple conveniently gives you several ways to send the gift that keeps on giving—or at least the gift that keeps on rocking out.

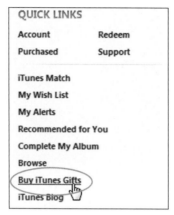

- **Gift certificates.** To buy an iTunes gift certificate, click Buy iTunes Gifts in the Quick Links box on the Store's main page, and then select a gift denomination ($10 to $50). You can email the certificate to the recipient, or you can print it out and deliver it yourself. The rest of the process is like buying anything else on the Web: fill in your address, add a message, and so on. You need an Apple ID to send and use gift certificates.

  To redeem an electronic gift certificate, go to the iTunes Store and click the Redeem link in the main window. Copy the Redeem Code from your email and paste it into the box provided. (If you got a printed certificate, type in the gift code.) Click Redeem, and then start shopping.

- **Gift cards.** The brightly colored prepaid iTunes Music Card is a fun spin on the gift certificate concept. Available in dollar amounts from $15 to $100, givers can find cards at places like Amazon.com, Target, and Apple's own stores. You can also buy them in the iTunes Store (and have them mailed out by the Postal Service) by clicking the Buy iTunes Gifts link. Recipients can spend it all in one place—the iTunes Store—by clicking the Redeem link on the Store's main page.

- **Gift content.** In a daring feat of bending a noun into a verb, the iTunes Store also lets you "gift" selections of music, videos, or apps. Your recipient can download your thoughtful picks right from the Store onto their own computers. You can send iTunes goodies to any pal with an email address. Click the triangle next to an item's Buy button and choose "Gift This..." from the menu.

Plan Ahead: Wish Lists

WITH NO PAPER MONEY flying about to remind you of reality, it's easy to rack up hefty credit card charges at the iTunes Store. Consider, then, making an iTunes *Wish List* to keep track of songs you want to buy...when your budget allows.

For iTunes customers still using dial-up Internet connections, the Wish List replaces the old Shopping Cart feature as a place to park your stuff before you're ready to download all your purchases at the end of your shopping session. (The 1-Click instant download iTunes offers can overwhelm a poor dial-up modem if you aren't done shopping.)

Adding items to your Wish List is easy: When you see something you want, click the triangle next to the Buy button and choose Add to Wish List from the pop-up menu.

To see all the items piled up in your list, visit the Quick Links box on the Store's home page (shown on the opposite page) and click My Wish List. If your wishes have changed since you added an item to the list, select the item and click the circled **x** that appears next to it to remove it. When you're ready to buy something on your Wish List, click the item's Buy button. The file begins downloading to your computer.

If you've been using the Wish List as a substitute Shopping Cart to hold your songs until you're ready to download them all, there's a special button just for you. It's the Buy All button up in the top-right corner of the Wish List. Click it and let your dial-up modem have a few hours to itself to download your purchases.

> **NOTE** The iTunes Store sends out invoices by email, but they don't arrive right after you buy a song. You usually get an invoice that groups together all the songs you purchased within a 12-hour period, or for every $20 worth of media you buy.

iTunes Allowance Accounts

ALLOWANCE ACCOUNTS ARE A lot like iTunes gift certificates. You, the parent (or other financial authority), decide how many dollars' worth of Store goods you want to give a family member or friend (from $10 to $50). Unlike gift certificates, however, allowance accounts automatically replenish themselves on the first day of each month—an excellent way to keep music-loving kids out of your wallet while teaching them to budget their money.

Both you and the recipient need to have Apple IDs, but you can create one for the recipient during the set-up process. To set up an allowance, from the iTunes Store's main page, click Buy iTunes Gifts, scroll down to the Allowances section, and then click "Set up an allowance now." Fill out the form. After you select the amount you want to deposit each month, fill in your recipient's Apple ID.

Once the giftee logs into the designated Apple account, she can begin spending—no credit card required. When she exhausts her allowance, she can't buy anything else until the following month. (Of course, if the recipient has a credit card on file, she can always put the difference on her card.) If you need to cancel an allowance account, click the Account link on the Store's main page to take care of the matter.

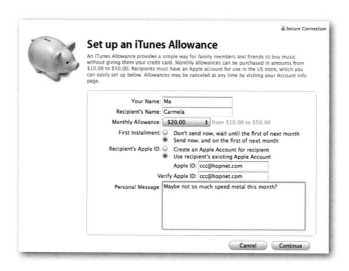

TIP Here's one education students don't have to pay for: iTunes U content. The iTunes U link on the main Store page leads to audio and video content from hundreds of schools around the country. Presentations, video tours, lectures, and more are available at iTunes U—yay, rah, Fightin' Downloaders!

Set Up Parental Controls for the Store

IF YOU HAVE CHILDREN with their own allowance accounts, you may not want them wandering around the iTunes Store buying just *anything*. With the Parental Controls feature, you can give your children the freedom to spend and discover, but restrict the types of things they can buy—without having to helicopter over them every time they click a Store link.

1. In the iTunes Preferences box (Ctrl+comma [⌘-comma]), click the Parental Control tab.

2. A box unfurls with all the media you can limit. For Store material, you can block songs and other items tagged with the Explicit label, restrict movie purchases to a maximum rating (G, PG, PG-13, or R), and choose one of the TV show content ratings geared to kids (TV-Y, TV-Y7, TV-G, TV-PG, TV-14, or TV-MA). You can also limit app purchases, including games, to age restrictions of 4+, 9+, 12+, and 17 years and older—and block explicit books.

3. Click the lock to password-protect the settings so the kids can't change them themselves.

You can also block certain icons from appearing in the iTunes Source list, including those for podcasts, Internet radio, shared libraries, and even the entire iTunes Store itself. You can, however, make an exception for iTunes U content—you want to keep the kids learning, after all.

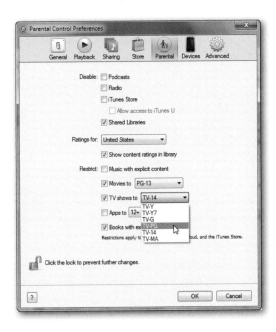

Adjust Your Store Preferences

THE ITUNES STORE AIMS to be a one-stop-shopping hub for all your digital entertainment: music, movies, TV shows, audio lectures on universal themes in the *Harry Potter* novels, and so on. In fact, some people have even canceled their cable TV subscriptions, preferring instead to go à la carte with iTunes.

If you use iTunes' Season Pass feature, which lets you buy a whole season of a TV show in advance, or if you preorder an album before it's released, you may never know when iTunes will decide to jump up and start downloading your pre-purchased content. This could be a little inconvenient if, say, your weekly Season Pass episode of *Raising Hope* starts downloading on your big computer monitor while you're trying to play an online game.

To control how iTunes behaves around your Internet connection, visit the Store tab of the iTunes Preferences box (Ctrl+comma [⌘-comma]). Here, you can decide whether iTunes should automatically download the music, apps, and books you buy on iOS devices (like an iPhone or iPad) to your iTunes library via Apple's iTunes in the Cloud service (see page 192 for details). The lower part of the Store preferences has your options to make iTunes check for downloads and to download pre-purchased content.

NOTE Music, videos, and other content you download from the iTunes Store lands in its respective Source list library—songs in the Music library, *The Good Wife* episodes in TV Shows, and so on. Those paid-for music and videos also live on the Purchased list in the Source list, a one-click trip to see where all your spare cash went.

Usage Rights: What You Can Do with Your Purchases

THE STUFF YOU BUY at the iTunes Store is yours to keep (unless you rented it). Apple doesn't charge you a monthly fee, and your digitally protected downloads don't go *poof!* after a certain amount of time.

You do have to cope with restrictions on some iTunes purchases, namely anything that's copy-protected. Copy-protected media include movies, TV shows, music videos, and songs you bought before April 2009, when Apple still copy-protected its music files (it no longer does; see below). For those types of files, you're bound by the iTunes Store usage agreement:

- You can play protected songs on up to five different iTunes-equipped Windows PCs or Macs (in any combination) and on as many iPods as you like, and you can burn playlists that include protected songs to CD up to seven times.

- You can watch movies, videos, and TV shows on any five computers, on as many iPods, iPads, and iPhones as you own, or piped over to your TV with an AV cable or via an Apple TV box (page 295).

- You can download music to a single iPod from up to five iTunes accounts, but the 'Pod won't accept files from a sixth account—a restriction designed to prevent someone from filling up their player with copyrighted content from the accounts of, say, their entire sophomore class.

You can burn backup CDs and DVDs of your purchases, but you can't burn an iTunes movie or TV show to disc and watch it on your DVD player. (On the flip side, some newer DVDs come with an "iTunes Digital Copy" that you can add to your iTunes library; instructions are in the package.)

So how does Apple keep track of how many devices you play protected media on? Easy: You have to authorize your computer or iPod through Apple, which maintains a giant tote board of registered devices. Turn the page to learn how.

Now, about those unprotected (post-April 2009) music files. The good news is, you can play them on *any* player (registered with Apple or not) that supports the AAC song format, and you can burn copies to CD for personal use and play them in commercial CD players. The bad news? To do most anything else with these copy-free songs, like playing or copying them via Home Sharing and re-downloading them if you accidentally erase them, the devices involved have to be authorized with Apple.

Authorize Your Computer to Play iTunes Purchases

WHEN YOU BUY A song, movie, TV show, or other media from the iTunes Store, Apple automatically authorizes the computer you used to make the purchase. To authorize a second computer (say, a desktop machine you use when you don't feel like hunching over the laptop), open iTunes on that machine and choose Store→Authorize This Computer. Type in your Apple user name and password on the computer. Repeat for up to three more computers.

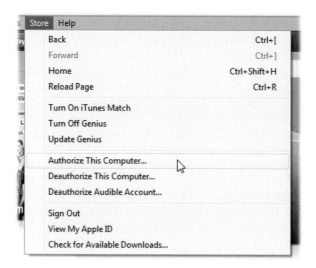

Each computer you authorize must have an Internet connection to relay information back to Store headquarters. (You don't have to authorize each and every purchase you make in the Store, you just authorize the computers themselves.)

Deauthorize Your Computer

IF YOU HAVE PROTECTED music, movies, TV shows, books, or other purchased content and you try to play them on a sixth computer, Apple's authorization system will see five other computers already on its "authorized" list and deny your request. That's a drag, but a user agreement is a user agreement.

To play protected files on computer #6, you have to deauthorize another computer. From the computer about to get the boot, choose Store→ Deauthorize This Computer, and then type in your Apple ID. The updated information zips back to Apple.

Are you thinking of putting that old computer up for sale? Before erasing the drive and selling it off, be sure to deauthorize it, so your new machine will be able to play copy-protected files. Erasing a hard drive, by itself, doesn't deauthorize a computer.

If you forget to deauthorize a machine before getting rid of it, you can still knock it off your List of Five, but you have to reauthorize every machine in your iTunes arsenal all over again. To make it so, in the iTunes Store, click the Account link. On the Account Information page, click Deauthorize All.

TIP Have a ton of tracks from the early days of the iTunes Store (before 2009) and would prefer the hassle-free life of a copy-protection-free iTunes Plus library? Go to the iTunes Store and click the iTunes Plus link on the main page. You can upgrade your older tracks to iTunes Plus versions for 30 cents a pop—instead of having to buy them all over again at full price. And the cherry on top: iTunes Plus tracks have higher audio quality (a bit rate of 256 kilobits per second, if you want to get technical) than old regular iTunes songs, which used the much lower (and lower fidelity) 128 kbps setting.

See Your iTunes Purchase History and Get iTunes Store Help

THE ITUNES STORE KEEPS track of what you buy and when you buy it. If you think your credit card was wrongly charged, or if you suspect that one of the kids knows your password and is sneaking in forbidden downloads, you can contact the Store or check your account's purchase history page to see what's been downloaded in your name.

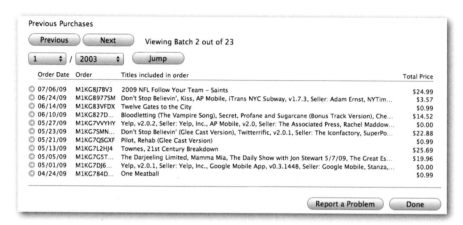

To do the latter, choose Store→View My Apple ID and log into your account. On your Account Information page, scroll down to Purchase History and click See All. Your latest purchase appears at the top of the page; scroll down to see a list of previous acquisitions. You'll see everything billed to your account over the months and years, including gift-certificate purchases. If you see something wrong, click the "Report a Problem" link and say something.

If you have other issues with your account or you want to submit a specific query or comment, the online help center awaits. From the iTunes Store's main page, click the Support link. Your browser presents you with the main iTunes service and support page; click the link that best describes what you want to learn or complain about. For billing or credit card issues, check out the iTunes Account and Billing Support link on that same page.

NOTE Want to get way more bang for slightly more buck on your album purchase? Visit the main Music page and click the iTunes LP link. Certain albums, available as iTunes LPs, offer more than just songs—they give you extra features like bonus tracks, digital liner notes booklets, artist interviews, video documentaries, and more. An iTunes LP averages $13 to $15—not that much more for all the extra perks that can take you behind the scenes of that new album.

Buy Songs from Other Music Stores

THERE ARE MANY ONLINE music services out there, and every one of 'em wants to sell you a song. But due to copy protection, some of these merchants' songs won't work on your iPod. Still, some of them do. Thanks to recent moves by many stores to strip out the digital rights management (DRM) protection on song files, their music has been liberated into the friendly MP3 play-anywhere format. Vive la musique!

Buying songs from somewhere other than the iTunes Store is as easy as supplying a credit card number and downloading the file using a web browser. Once you have the file on your computer, use iTunes' File→Add to Library command to add it to your collection. Here are some of the online music services that now work with the iPod:

- **eMusic.** Geared toward indie bands, eMusic offers several subscription plans based on quantity: For 16 bucks a month, for example, you can download 34 songs of your choice. (*www.emusic.com*)

- **The Internet Archive.** Thousands of live concert recordings, old-time radio shows, historic gems rescued from wax cylinders and old 78 rpm records, and much more await you here. And it's all free. (*www.archive.org*)

- **Amazon MP3 Store.** From Amazon's main page, click Amazon MP3 Store. The MP3 pages have a link to a free piece of software called the Amazon Cloud Player for iOS (as well as for Windows PCs and Macs). Once you install it, you can use it to download or stream your MP3 purchases from the Amazon Cloud (a big server in the sky) to your iPod Touch and computer. (*www.amazon.com*)

You'll learn to:
- Add videos to iTunes
- Play videos in iTunes
- Sync videos to your 'Pod
- Play movies, TV shows, and music videos on your iPod
- Play videos on a big-screen TV

CHAPTER 14

It's Showtime: Video on the iPod

VIDEO-PLAYING IPODS HAVE BEEN around since October 2005, when Apple introduced that year's player with a video chip on the inside and a video screen on the outside. Among the 2012 iPods, the Touch, the Nano, and the faithful old Classic all play moving pictures.

The iPod Touch, with its high-resolution, 3.5-inch screen, has become the premier video iPod on all levels. After two years of tiny, video-free Nano models, Apple restored video playback to the 2012 Nano and its 2.5-inch screen.

Touch, Nano, or Classic—no matter which iPod you use, you're not stuck watching just 2- or 3-minute music videos. As explained in the previous chapter, the iTunes Store has all kinds of cinematic goodies you can buy: full-length Hollywood movies and entire seasons or single episodes of TV shows. Some videos even come in super-sharp, high-definition format, which looks great on both your TV and your computer screen. And yes, if you want music videos, like the kind MTV used to play back when it, uh, played music, you can choose from thousands of them.

This chapter shows you how to get videos from computer to iPod—and how to enjoy them on your own shirt-pocket cinema.

Add Your Own Videos to iTunes

THE ITUNES STORE IS full of videos you can buy or rent (Chapter 13 shows you how), but sometimes you want to add your own flicks to your iTunes library. No problem; you can do that in four ways. One is to drag the files from your desktop and drop them anywhere in iTunes' main window. The second is to choose File→Add to Library, and then locate and import your files.

Additionally, you can add videos (and songs, for that matter) by dragging them into the folder labeled Automatically Add to iTunes. New since iTunes 9, this folder checks a file's extension and, based on that, shelves it in the right media library for you.

You find the auto-folder not through iTunes itself, but by navigating your hard drive. In Windows, it's usually at C:/Music→iTunes→iTunes Media→Automatically Add to iTunes; for Macs, it's at Home→Music→iTunes→iTunes Media→ Automatically Add to iTunes. If iTunes doesn't recognize a file extension, it dumps the file into a Not Added subfolder.

If you copy over a lot of videos from your camcorder, make it easy to get to the auto-folder by creating a desktop shortcut

for it. That way, you can drag files directly to the shortcut without having to root around your hard drive.

Once you add videos to your iTunes library, you can play them right there in iTunes (see opposite page), copy them to your iPod for on-the-go viewing (page 264), or watch them on a big TV screen (page 270).

If you bought a TV show from the iTunes Store on another iOS device, like an iPad or iPhone, and never synced the file back to iTunes, you can re-download that show and then sync it to your iPod. Page 264 explains how.

Play Videos in iTunes

CRANKING UP YOUR ITUNES movie theater is a lot like playing a song: Double-click a video's title in your library, and iTunes starts playing it.

You can play the video in iTunes' main window; in a separate, floating window as shown below; in iTunes' artwork window (the small pane that also displays album art at the bottom of the Source list); or full-screen on your computer. Slide your mouse cursor over the screen to get to the video playback controls.

To pick your preferred window size for the video you have on-screen, choose View→Video Playback. In the submenu that appears (shown below), you can pick the window that suits your needs at the moment. For example, while the Full Screen view is very nice for turning your computer into a movie theater, it may not be the best choice if, say, you're at work and trying to catch up on your favorite video podcast. In situations like those, dragging the corner of the iTunes window to make it smaller might be a wise idea.

Transfer Videos to Your iPod

AS YOU MAY HAVE read earlier, you can sync all kinds of files between iTunes and your trusty iPod. If you don't feel like flipping back to Chapter 11, here's a quick summary:

- **Synchronization.** Connect your iPod to your computer and click its icon in the iTunes window. Click the Movies tab and turn on the Sync Movies check-box. You can choose to sync only certain movies to save space on your iPod. If you have TV programs in your iTunes library, click the TV Shows tab and adjust your syncing preferences there.

- **Manual management.** Select the appropriate library in the Library pop-up menu (Movies, TV Shows, Podcasts, and so on), and then drag the files you want from the main iTunes window onto your connected iPod's icon.

If you made any video playlists in iTunes, you can copy those over to your iPod, just as you would a music playlist. If you haven't tried making a video playlist, it's just like making a music playlist; see page 216 for details.

Video Formats That Work on the iPod

AS DESCRIBED IN CHAPTER 13, the iTunes Store sells movies (which you can also rent), TV shows, and music videos. You can also import your own home movies, downloaded movie trailers, and other videos into iTunes, as long as the files have one of these extensions at the end of their names: *.mov, .m4v*, or *.mp4*. Once you can sync these files to your iPod, you can play them on the go.

Other common video formats, like *.avi* and Windows Media video (*.wmv*), won't play in iTunes (or on your iPod), but you can convert them with Apple's $30 QuickTime Pro software or any of the dozens of video-conversion programs floating around the Web. (If you find you have an incompatible file type, first try dragging the file into iTunes' main window, and then choosing Advanced→Create iPod or iPhone Version. That converts some, but not all, files, and Apple doesn't specify which ones.)

Here are a few popular video-conversion tools:

- **PQ DVD to iPod Video Converter Suite.** This $40 program for Windows converts TiVo recordings, DVD video, DivX movies, Windows Media Video, RealMedia files, and AVI files to the iPod's video format (*www.pqdvd.com*).

- **Videora iPod Converter.** With this free software, you can gather up all those *.avi* and *.mpg* video clips stashed away on your PC and turn them into iPod clips. Find it at *www.videora.com*.

- **HandBrake.** Available for Windows and Mac OS X, this freeware converts DVD video and other files for your iPod. It's at *http://handbrake.fr*.

- **Magic DVD Ripper.** This $40 program for Windows, converts DVD video into iTunes-friendly .mp4 versions (*http://www.magicdvdripper.com*).

- **Mac DVDRipper Pro.** Mac users have their own DVD conversion program, which has a free try-before-you-buy edition, along with the full $25 program (*http://www.macdvdripperpro.com*).

Play Videos on the iPod Touch and Nano

WATCHING VIDEO ON THE Touch or the Nano is a breeze. Just tap open the Videos icon on the Home screen, flick to the movie, TV show, or video podcast you want to watch, and then tap the title to start the show.

Want to fast-forward, jump back, pause, and perform other video-playback moves? Just tap the screen to call up the touch-based controls. Want to dismiss the control panel? Tap the screen again so you can watch your show without the clutter. Apple has crammed a lot of buttons into a small space, and here's what each one does:

- **Stop (Done).** When you finish watching a video, tap this button (in the top-left corner) to stop the show and return to the Videos menu.

- **Scroll slider.** The bar at the top of the screen shows you how much time has elapsed in your current video—and how much more you have to go. Stuck in a boring part or want to see something again? Drag the white dot forward or backward to move through the clip.

- **Zoom/Unzoom.** Want full-screen or widescreen playback on the Touch? Tap the ◾ or ◼ icons in the top-right corner of the screen to zoom in or out of the picture. The next page explains a bit more about zoom levels.

- **Captions. (💬)** Some videos have alternate audio tracks for other languages or subtitles. Tap here to see your options.

- **Chapters. (☰)** Tap here to jump around DVD-style chapters and scenes.

- **Play/Pause (▶/II).** These buttons start the show—and pause it when you need to take a break.

- **Previous, Next (I◀◀, ▶▶I).** Press down to zip through the video in the chosen direction; the longer you hold down the button, the faster you rewind or fast-forward.

  You can jump around between major scenes in iTunes Store–bought movies (and in any other videos with DVD-like chapter markers in them) by quickly tapping the I◀◀ or ▶▶I buttons.

- **AirPlay (▱).** On the iPod Touch, you can stream the video to a television screen with a second- or third-generation Apple TV and a WiFi network. Just tap the ▱ icon and choose Apple TV from the menu. Page 294 has more on AirPlay.

- **Volume.** If you don't feel like using the volume buttons on the side of the Touch, tap the screen and drag the white dot in the volume slider at the bottom of the screen forward or backward to raise or lower the sound level.

Zoom/Unzoom on the iPod Touch

The 2012 Touch has a bright, razor-sharp screen—Apple's high-resolution Retina display packs 1136×640 pixels into the 4-inch screen. That's 326 pixels per inch, four times as many as the earliest Touch models.

The screen, however, is still rectangular, in the 16:9 widescreen ratio. That means that older TV shows in the squarish standard-definition format (also known as the 4:3 aspect ratio) don't fill the screen from side to side, so the Touch fills in the gap with black letterbox bars. On older Touch models with smaller screens, TV shows and movies in the high-def widescreen standard are a bit *too* wide, which means you get black letterbox bars on the top and bottom of the screen.

Some movie lovers are used to this and ignore the letterboxing, because they want to see the film as the director originally envisioned it. But other people want their video to fill the screen in all directions, even if it means cutting off the edges. The Touch tries to satisfy both groups. With the playback controls on-screen, tap ▣ to expand the video full-screen, or ▣ to shrink it to its original size—if the video's original format is smaller than 16:9.

If you don't want to hunt around for the buttons, there's an even quicker way to zoom in and out: double-tap the video while it's playing. If you decide you hate the way the picture looks, double-tap again to reverse course.

TIP Want your video to remember where you paused or stopped it? Easy. In iTunes, select the video and then press Ctrl+I (⌘-I). Click the Options tab and turn on the checkbox next to "Remember playback position."

Play Videos on the iPod Classic

VIDEOS YOU BUY OR rent from the iTunes Store (and other iTunes-friendly videos) appear in your iPod's Videos menu after you copy them onto your Classic. To watch a movie, TV show, or music video, scroll through the various Video submenus (Movies, TV Shows, and so on) until you find what you want.

Say you want to watch a TV show. Select TV Shows from the main Videos menu. The next screen lists all your iPod's TV shows by title. Scroll to the show you want and click the center button. The resulting menu lists all the *episodes* you have for that series. Scroll to the one you want and press the Play/Pause button to start the show.

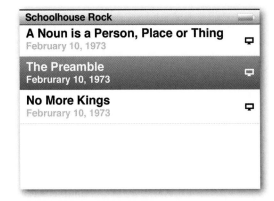

Here's a quick tour of the iPod Classic's main video playback controls:

- **Press the Play/Pause button to pause the program.** Pausing the iPod works just like pausing a DVD player or TiVo so you can get more Doritos—just press the Play/Pause button. Tap it again to pick up where you left off.

- **To increase or decrease a video's volume, run your finger along the scroll wheel.** Adjusting the volume of a video on the Classic works the same way as controlling the volume of a song.

- **To fast-forward or rewind through part of a video, tap the Select button twice.** A time-code bar appears along the bottom of the screen. Use the scroll wheel to advance or retreat through a big chunk of the video. For moving forward and backward in smaller increments, hold down the Fast-Forward and Rewind buttons on the click wheel (see page 147).

When your video ends, the iPod flips you back to the menu you were on before you started watching the show. If you want to bail out before the movie is over, press the Menu button.

Some videos come in letterbox format, which leaves a strip of black above and below your video window. If you're not into widescreen HamsterVision, visit the Settings area of the Videos menu and turn on the "Fit to Screen" option.

TIP Both iTunes and the iPod Touch and Classic can play videos that have closed-captioned text on-screen for the hearing impaired. To turn it on in iTunes, open the Preferences box (Ctrl+comma [⌘-comma]), click the Playback tab, and then put a checkmark in the box next to "Show closed captioning when available." On the iPod Touch, tap your way to Home→Settings→Video to get to the controls. On the Classic, choose iPod→Videos→Settings→Captions.

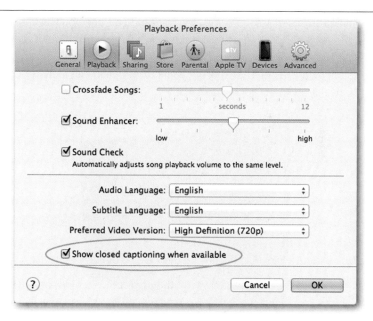

Play iTunes and iPod Videos on Your TV

MOVIES ON THE IPOD and computer screen are great, but watching them on a bigger screen is often more gratifying. In case you were wondering, you *can* watch all those videos on your TV—you just need to connect your computer or iPod to your television. *What* you connect them with depends on what you start with. (And in case you've maybe upgraded to a new iPod and want to use your old model as a pocket TiVo for the secondary TV, this page covers AV connections for many past iPod models as well.)

If you're connecting your computer to the TV, here are your best options:

- Connect computers that have S-video connections with an S-video cable— that pipes high-quality video to your TV. For the audio side of things, a $10 Y-shaped cable with a stereo mini-plug on one end and the standard red and white RCA plugs on the other provide the sound.

- If you have a computer-friendly television (the kind that doubles as a computer monitor thanks to VGA or DVI ports), you can plug your laptop right into the TV using one of the cables described below.

Now then, to mate your iPod with your TV, here are your options:

- **Early video iPods (the ones that came out before Apple dubbed the model the "Classic").** You can connect these iPods to your TV with a special cable, like the Apple iPod AV Cable. This cord, available from third-party resellers online for $20 or less) has a stereo mini-plug on one end (for the iPod's headphones jack) and red, white, and yellow RCA plugs on the other end that link to the audio and video ports on your TV. Some similar camcorder cables may work, as do third-party cables from Belkin and Monster Cable, and special iPod video docks from Apple and others.

- **The iPod Touch or Classic (or older video-friendly Nanos with the Dock Connector jack).** You need a different cable—one that unlocks the chip that controls the iPod's ability to pipe video to your TV. (Older iPod cables and many third-party offerings won't work with these models, unless you use them with one of Apple's Universal Docks for iPods.)

  The easiest place to find these cables is the Apple Store (*www.apple.com/ ipodstore*). Here, you can get the Apple Composite AV Cable for TVs with older video inputs. You can also find the Apple Component AV Cable, made for high-end TVs and widescreen sets that can handle higher-quality video and audio connections. Each cable costs about $50, but that includes an integrated AC adapter to make sure your 'Pod is powered for a whole-weekend movie marathon.

- **The 2012 iPod Touch with Lightning connector.** You can play the videos on your Touch screen on an HDTV with the help of Apple's $49 Lightning Digital AV Adapter. Plug the Lightning end of the adapter into the iPod, then use an HDMI cable (not included) to connect the TV to the corresponding jack on the adapter. (Although it plays videos just fine on its own screen, the new Nano does not support video output to the TV.)

Once you connect your iPod to your TV, set it up so the video appears on the big screen. The iPod Touch automatically senses the connection in most cases and is ready to play. On the Classic and older Nanos, choose iPod→Videos→Settings and turn TV Out to On. While you're in the settings area of the older iPods, you can choose the TV signal (pick NTSC if you live in the U.S.) and whether you want video to play back in widescreen format. You can also turn on closed captioning for videos that support the on-screen titles.

Once you get the iPod or computer hooked up to play movies, be sure to select the alternate video source or display input on your TV set, just as you would to play a DVD or game.

If you have an iPod Touch, a home wireless network, and a second-generation Apple TV (the little black box) connected to your television set, you can stream videos to the big screen *wirelessly* with Apple's AirPlay feature. Page 294 has the details on watching big video without wires.

TIP Not sure which iPod you have? Apple has an illustrated chart of almost every pre-2011 'Pod that ever scrolled the Earth at *http://support.apple.com/kb/HT1353*. And if you're not sure which ones support TV Out, see *http://support.apple.com/kb/HT1454*.

You'll learn to:

- Copy photos from computer to iPod

- View pics on your 'Pod

- Play slideshows

- Display photos and slideshows on your TV

- Share photos using iCloud's Photo Stream

CHAPTER 15

Picture Your Photos
On the iPod

WHO WANTS TO SHARE treasured photos with friends when they're in a cracked plastic picture sleeve? If you have an iPod Touch, Nano, or Classic, you can transfer your prized shots from your computer to your 'Pod and display them on a glossy color screen wherever you happen to be.

And if you have an iPod Touch running Apple's iOS 6 software, you can share photos in more ways than ever: You can tweet them to your Twitter followers, post them on your Facebook page, zip them to other iOS users as instant messages, add them to your iCloud photo stream, or go retro and send them as good old-fashioned v attachments.

The picture-perfect fun doesn't stop there, either. This trio of 'Pods can create slideshows of your images right there in the palm of your hand. And as with many previous iPod models, you can plug the Touch or the Classic into a TV set and enjoy your stills on a big living-room screen. This chapter shows you how to do everything but microwave the popcorn.

Set Up: Get Ready to Put Photos on Your iPod

TO MOVE PICTURES TO your 'Pod, you need a computer loaded with iTunes and an iPod outfitted with a screen—sorry, Shuffle owners, the photos thing is just not happening for you, but you probably knew that already.

Even with a photos-compatible iPod in tow, you need a couple of other things to make your pictures portable:

- **Compatible photo software for your Windows PC or Mac, or a folder of photos on your hard drive.** iPods can sync pics with several popular photo-management programs that you may already use. Windows mavens can grab pictures from Adobe Photoshop Elements 3.0 or later. On the Mac, there's Aperture or iPhoto 6 or later. You can also transfer pictures from a folder on your computer, like the Pictures (or My Pictures) folder on a Windows system, the Mac's iPhoto Library folder (for those who haven't upgraded past iPhoto 6), and even the Mac OS X Pictures folder.

- **Digital photographs in the proper format.** iTunes plays well with the photo formats used by most digital cameras, web pages, and email programs, as well as a few other file types. Windows users can display JPEG, GIF, TIF, BMP, PSD, SGI, and PNG pics on your 'Pod. On the Mac, JPEG and GIF files, along with images in the PICT, TIFF, BMP, PNG, JPEG 2000, SGI, and PSD formats work just fine. (If you have iPhoto 5 or later, you can also sync MPEG-4 videos over to your iPod Touch.)

There are a couple of other things to remember when you add images to your iPod. For one, you can't import pictures from one of those photo CDs from the drugstore or from a backup disc you made yourself. Photos you store on DVDs or CDs won't cut it, either. iTunes needs to pull photos directly from your hard drive. The solution in both cases? Transfer your pics from the disc to your computer so they're ready for your iPod.

When it comes to photos, the iPod allies itself with just a single computer. That means that, unlike manual music management, where you can grab songs from several different computers, you can only synchronize pictures between one

iPod and one computer. If you ignore the warning box (above) and try to load photos from a different computer, iTunes replaces all your iPod's existing photos with the pictures from that new machine. Ouch.

You also can't dump photos directly into the iPod from your digital camera—you need to go through iTunes. (There used to be a handy gadget called the iPod Camera Connector that siphoned photos from your camera's memory card to the iPod's hard drive, but it doesn't work on modern iPods, nor does Apple's *iPad* Camera Connection Kit. One can only hope that a variation of this device comes out for the iPod Touch/iPhone one of these days....)

Get Pictures onto Your iPod

OKAY, SO YOU'VE GOT your screen-outfitted iPod and a bunch of pictures in an iTunes-friendly format on your hard drive. How do you get those photos from your drive to your iPod? The same way you transfer music—through iTunes. First, you need to set your preferences in iTunes and on the iPod so they sync just the photos you want to carry around, like so:

1. Connect your iPod to your Windows PC or Mac with the iPod's USB cable (or use iTunes Wi-Fi Sync on the iPod Touch, as page 19 explains).

2. Once your iPod shows up in the iTunes window, click its icon to select it.

3. In the iTunes tabs for your iPod, click Photos.

4. Turn on the checkbox next to "Sync photos from" and then choose your photo-management program or photo-storage folder; that lets iTunes know where to find your pics. You can copy over every image or just the *albums* (sets of pictures) you select.

5. Click Sync (or Apply, if this is your first time syncing photos).

TIP If you own a Touch and use the Places feature in iPhoto '09 or later to embed GPS location data into your photos (also known as *geotagging*), you can see your pictures represented by pins on a map by tapping Photos→Places; tap a pin to see the photos taken and tagged in that location.

If you don't use a photo-management program and just want to copy a folder of photos from your hard drive to your iPod, select "Choose folder" from the menu and navigate to the desired folder. Then decide whether you want to sync just the free-floating photos in that folder, or the free-floating photos and any photos tucked away in folders *inside* the folder.

If you use a photo-management program, select it, and then select the "All photos and albums" option to have iTunes haul every single image in your photo program's library over to your iPod. If you don't want to copy over those bachelorette-party snaps, opt for "Selected albums" and choose only the folders you want from your photo program. (Of course, you need to make sure those party pics aren't *in* any of those folders.)

If you use a Mac with iPhoto '09 or later and take advantage of the program's face-recognition feature, you can also sync photos according to who's in the pictures. Scroll down the photo-sync preferences page to the Faces area and turn on the checkboxes next to the names of your favorite people. You can sync iPhoto *Events* (typically, photos taken on the same day) here as well.

Whenever you connect your iPod to your computer,

iTunes syncs the photo groups you designate, copying any new pictures you added to the groups since you last connected. During the process, iTunes displays an "Analyzing..." message in its status window, like the one shown here.

Don't let the term "analyzing" scare you: iTunes hasn't taken it upon itself to judge your photographic efforts. The program simply creates versions of your pictures that look good on anything from your tiny iPod screen to your big TV screen (in case you want to connect your iPod to it).

Want to get certain albums or photos *off* of your iPod? Reconnect it to iTunes, go back to the Photos tab, deselect the albums you no longer want, and then sync up. If you want to banish individual pictures, remove them from your desktop album and sync. On the iPod Touch, you can delete photos in the Camera Roll album by tapping 🖉, selecting the images to go, and then tapping Delete.

> **TIP** Want to take a snap of some cool thing you see on your Touch's screen? Hold down the Home button, and then press the Sleep/Wake button as though it were a camera shutter. The resulting screenshot lands in Photos→Camera Roll. If your computer has a photo-organizing program that senses a connected digital camera, it will likely leap up and offer to pull in the connected Touch's screen shots, just as it would digicam photos.

View Photos on the iPod Touch

WITH ITS BIG COLOR screen, the iPod Touch shows off your photos better than other iPods—and lets you have more fun viewing them because it's literally a hands-on experience.

To see the pictures synced from your computer, tap the Photos icon on the Home screen. Tap the buttons in the bottom row to see photos grouped by Albums, Photo Stream, Faces, or Places. Tap an album title, name, or place to see thumbnails of those photos. To get back to your library, tap the Albums (or whatever) button at the top-left of the screen.

To see a full-screen version of a picture, tap its thumbnail image. The Touch displays photo controls for a few seconds; tap the photo to make them go away (tap it again to make them reappear). Double-tap a photo to magnify it. You can also rotate the Touch so that horizontal photos fill the width of the screen instead of getting letterboxed. (In Edit mode, you can also make basic fixes to your pictures, like cropping out unwanted parts or taming red-eye in your subjects. Page 41 has details.)

Here are some other things you can do with your photos on the Touch:

❶ Tap the triangle icon at the bottom of a full-frame photo to start a slideshow. You can pick a transition style and music track here, and tap Start Slideshow to begin. Page 282 has more on the settings.

❷ To set a photo as the wallpaper for your Touch (you know, that background picture you see when you wake the Touch from a nap), tap 📨 in the lower-left corner, and then tap Use As Wallpaper. The 📨 icon also calls up buttons that let you email photos or send them as instant messages over the Touch's WiFi connection, share pictures with your Twitter followers or Facebook friends, add them to your iCloud Photo Stream, and assign a photo to someone in your Touch contacts list. And, if you have a printer that works with Apple's AirPrint technology, you can even make a color print of the photo. See Chapter 4 for info on printing and sharing pics.

③ Spread and pinch your fingers on-screen (one of those fancy Touch moves described in Chapter 2) to zoom in and out of a photo. Drag your finger around the screen to pan across a zoomed-in photo.

④ Flick your finger horizontally across the screen in either direction to scroll through your pictures at whizzy speeds. You can show off your vacation photos *really* fast this way (your friends will thank you).

As mentioned earlier, tapping ➦ with a single photo on-screen attaches that image to an email message; tapping the Edit button on the *thumbnails* screen lets you attach *multiple* photos to a message. Tap the thumbnails of all the pics you want to send, tap Share→Mail, type in an address, add a note, and then tap Send.

TIP To make a new photo album on the Touch, tap the Albums icon at the bottom of the screen, open an album, and tap Edit in the top-right corner. Tap the photos you want to use, then tap the Add To button. Tap the Add to New Album button, name it, and tap Save.

View Photos on the Nano or Classic

ONCE YOU GET YOUR photos freed from the confines of your computer and onto your Nano or Classic, you probably want to show them off to friends and relatives—or admire them yourself when you're stuck on a train or traveling far from home. Here's how to get a palm-sized picture show:

iPod Nano

Tap the Photos icon on the Nano's Home screen to call up a list of your photo albums, along with an "All Photos" option. Select an album and flick up or down to see all the thumbnails in it. Tap a thumbnail to see a picture full-screen. Flick your finger on the screen from right to left to glide through the images.

Double-tap a picture to zoom in and out of it. To see more of a photo while you're zoomed in, drag your finger on the screen to pull a different part of the picture to the center. You can also use the "pinch and zoom" moves (described in Chapter 7) to zoom in on a particular part of a photo if double-tapping doesn't get you there.

You can tap the screen once to call up the navigation controls, which give you a ▶ button that starts an automatic slideshow (page 282), and ← and → arrows so you can advance through an album at your own pace.

The control bar also has a small square grid icon in the top-left corner; tap it to go back to all the thumbnail photos in that particular album. To get back to your list of Nano photo albums, swipe the screen from left to right.

iPod Classic

Choose Photos→All Photos (or select an album) from your Classic's main menu to see a screen of thumbnail images. Use the scroll wheel to maneuver the little yellow highlight box, and then zoom along the rows until you get to the pic you want. If you have hundreds of pee-wee pics, tap the Previous and Next buttons to advance or retreat through the thumbnails by the screenful. Highlight a photo and press the center button to call up a large version of it. Press the Previous and Next buttons—or scroll the click wheel—to move through pics one by one. Press Menu to return to the full album.

Store High-Quality Photos on Your iPod

WHEN ITUNES OPTIMIZES YOUR photos for iPodification, it streamlines the images a bit instead of transferring the big, full-resolution files. But if you want the high-res photos, you can copy them over to your Nano or Classic—good news if you're an avid photographer and want to haul a big, print-ready photo collection from one machine to another. (Sorry Touch owners, you can't enable your iPods to work as external hard drives without third-party software.)

Nano and Classic users can follow these steps:

1. Connect your iPod and select it in the iTunes window. Set up your iPod as a portable hard drive by clicking the Summary tab and then turning on the "Enable disk use" option.

2. Click the Photos tab in the iTunes window.

3. Turn on the "Include full-resolution photos" checkbox.

After you sync, full-resolution copies of your photos land in the Photos folder on your iPod's drive. (The Photos folder also includes a subfolder called Thumbs that's full of iPod-optimized images in special *.ithmb* format; you can safely ignore these.) Now connect your iPod to another computer, open its Photos folder, and copy the full-res photos over to the second computer.

Play Slideshows on Your iPod

A PHOTO SLIDESHOW TAKES all the click-and-tap work out of showcasing your images, freeing you up to admire your pictures without distraction. To run a slideshow on an iPod, you need to make some decisions, like how long each photo appears on-screen and what music accompanies your trip to Disneyland.

Slideshow Settings on an iPod Touch or Nano

To customize the way photos slide by on your Touch or Nano, press the Home button and then tap Settings→Photos. Now set some options:

- **How long each picture stays on-screen.** Tap the time shown to get a menu of choices, which includes 2, 3, 5, 10, or 20 seconds per shot.

- **The transition between photos.** As mentioned on page 278, the Touch keeps Hollywood-style dissolves, wipes, and ripples ready to select when you tap the ▶ button on a selected photo in the album. (The Nano doesn't offer any slideshow transitions.)

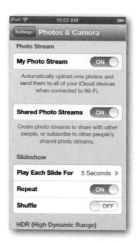

You can also choose to have the iPod shuffle your photos in random order or repeat a slideshow when it ends, so that it loops until you manually stop it. The Touch's photo settings, shown above left, also hold a switch you can flip to turn on the Photo Stream feature of Apple's iCloud service; page 286 has more.

NOTE The iPod Nano doesn't include a slideshow music option in its Settings menu. To get a soundtrack going for Nano Theater, go to the Home screen, tap the Music icon, and then tap up a song or playlist. When the music starts, jump back to Photos and start your slideshow. It's a little clunky, but then again, you're watching a slideshow on a screen that's about the size of a postage-stamp book.

Slideshow Settings on the iPod Classic

YOU SET SLIDESHOW OPTIONS on the Classic by choosing Photos→Settings. You'll see a slew of options ready to shape your slideshow experience.

- **Use the Time Per Slide menu to set how much time (from 2 to 20 seconds) each photo stays on-screen.** During the show, you can also go to the next image with a tap of the click wheel.

- **Use the Music menu to pick a song from your iPod's playlists to serve as the soundtrack for your show (assuming you want one).** You may even want to create a playlist in iTunes for a particular slideshow.

- **As with music tracks, you can shuffle the order of your photos and repeat the slideshow.** You can also add fancy transitions by choosing Photos→Settings→Transitions. You get to pick from several dramatic photo-changing styles, including effects that let you zoom out and fade to black.

- **To make sure your slideshow plays on your iPod's screen, turn the TV Out setting to Off, which directs the video signal to your iPod.** Alternatively, you can select Ask, so that each time you start a slideshow, the iPod inquires whether you intend to display it on the big or small screen. (Turn the page if you want to project your slideshow on a TV.)

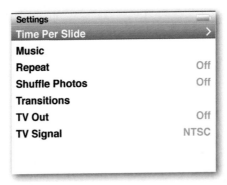

Once you get the settings the way you want them, select the album or photo you want to start the show with, and then press the Play/Pause button on the click wheel. Press Play/Pause again to temporarily stop the show, and press it again to continue.

The show's time per slide, music, and transitions should all match the settings you chose. All you have to do now is sit back, relax, and enjoy your handiwork.

Play Slideshows on Your TV

TO SEE YOUR DIGITAL goodies on the big screen, you first need to connect your TV and iPod (Touch or Classic only; sorry, Nano owners, your model can't do this). Flip back to the previous chapter if you need help connecting. Once you make the iPod-TV link, you need to adjust a few more settings on your iPod.

For the iPod Touch

1. **Connect your Touch to the TV.** If you have a fifth-generation iPod Touch with the Lightning port, you can use an HDMI cable and the Lightning Digital AV Adapter. If you have the older, fourth-generation Touch with the Dock Connector jack, you can use Apple's Composite AV Cable or Component AV Cable. When you connect your Touch, your slideshow automatically appears on your TV instead of on your iPod. Third-party AV cables may also work, but make sure they're approved for your particular Touch model. Touch owners who also have a second- or third-generation Apple TV can ditch the cable and connect with AirPlay (page 295).

2. **Turn on your TV and select your iPod as the video source**. You tell your TV to use the iPod as the video source the same way you tell it to display the signal from a DVD player or game console: Typically, you press the Input or Display button on your TV's remote to change from the live TV signal to a new video source.

3. **On the iPod, navigate to the album you want**. Tap the photo you want to start with, and then tap the Play triangle at the bottom of the screen to begin your show.

For the iPod Classic

1. **Choose Photos→Settings→TV Out→On**. The On option tells your Classic to send the slideshow *out* to a TV screen instead of playing it on its own screen. (You can change your iPod's Ask setting so that it always asks you which screen you want to use; see page 283.) If you have a Classic or older Nano and use one of Apple's AV cables, TV Out gets set to On automatically.

2. **Select your local television broadcast standard**. If you're in North America or Japan, choose Photos→Settings→TV Signal→NTSC. If you're in Europe or Australia, choose Photos→Settings→TV Signal→PAL. If you're in an area not listed above, check your television's manual to see what standard it uses or search the Web for "world television standards."

3. **Turn on your TV and select your iPod as the video source**. You select your iPod as the video source the same way you tell your TV to display video from a DVD player or game console: Typically, you press the Input or Display button on your TV's remote to change from a live TV signal to a new video source.

Now, cue up a slideshow on the Classic and press the Play/Pause button. Your glorious photographs—scored to the sounds of your selected music, if you wish—appear on your television screen. (Because television screens are horizontal displays, vertical shots end up with black bars along the sides.)

Your pre-selected slideshow settings control the show, though you can advance through it manually with your thumb on the click wheel. If you have the $59 Apple Universal Dock, you can also pop through shots with a click of its remote control. Although just one photo appears at a time on the TV, if you're driving the Classic, your *iPod* displays not only the current picture, but the one before and after it as well, letting you narrate your show with professional smoothness: "OK, this is Shalimar *before* we got her fur shaved off after the syrup incident...and here she is later."

NOTE As explained in the previous chapter, the type of iPod you have dictates the equipment you need to display photos and videos on your TV. To find out the requirements for your model iPod, visit *http://store.apple.com* and click the Cables & Docks link. The page for each product lists compatible iPod models. Third-party iPod accessory sites should also list the models each item works with—something you need to pay close attention to now that iPods can have either a Lightning port or the older Dock Connector.

Share and Stream Photos With iCloud

The iPod Touch can take photos, but so can iPhones, iPads, and, of course, digital cameras. But wouldn't it be great if you could somehow get all the photos taken on all those devices in *one* place? With iCloud's Photo Stream, you can.

With Photo Stream in action, iCloud stores the last 1,000 pictures you've taken for 30 days, which should give you plenty of time to sync your pics across all your devices and, most importantly, to your desktop computer, which serves as the archive for your gallery. So, while iCloud holds only your last thousand shots up in the sky, all your pictures are permanently stored on your Windows PC or Mac—which probably has a bit more storage space than your Touch.

To use Photo Stream, you have to activate it on your Touch, on your other iOS devices, and on your desktop computer. If you didn't turn on Photo Stream when you set up your Touch (page 16), go to the Home screen and tap Settings→iCloud→Photo Stream→On. Repeat this step on all the iOS 5 or iOS 6 devices that you want to paddle along in the Stream. (You can also turn on Photo Stream by tapping Settings→Photos & Camera→Photo Stream→On.)

Once your iOS devices are ready, you need to bring your computer into the Photo Stream mix so it can serve as the archive of all your full-quality photos.

Photo Stream for Windows

If you use a Windows PC, you first need to install the iCloud software for Windows; download it from Apple at *http://support.apple.com/kb/DL1455*. Once you get the iCloud software installed, choose Start→Control Panel→Network and Internet→iCloud. When the dialog box opens, type in your iCloud user name and password. Next, turn on the checkbox next to Photo Stream and click Options.

In the box that appears (shown right), you can turn on the Photo Stream feature, the option to share Photo Streams (see the next page), and select a folder for iCloud to use for moving all these photos around. By default, iCloud sets up a Photo Stream folder in your Windows Pictures library (specifically, in a subfolder called My Photo Stream). Click the Change button next to either folder to pick a different name. Click OK when you're done and ready to start streaming photos to your computer and iOS devices.

Photo Stream for Mac OS X

Apple makes things a bit easier for its own operating system and computers. You just need to use the most recent version (and update) of its iPhoto '11 or Aperture programs for organizing and editing pictures. To turn on Photo Stream in either Mac program, click the Photo Stream icon in the left panel, and then click the Turn On Photo Stream button that appears in the window.

To see Photo Stream preferences in iPhoto (and adjust them if needed), choose iPhoto→Preferences→Photo Stream. In the Preferences box, (like the one below), turn on the checkbox next to My Photo Stream. You can also turn on checkboxes next to Automatic Import (which lets iPhoto

include Photo Stream images in its Events, Photos, Faces, and Places albums) and Automatic Upload (which pushes the photos you import from your camera's memory card up to iCloud, where smaller versions are dispatched to your iOS devices). You can also turn on Shared Photo Streams, as described below.

Share Your Photo Stream

Tired of emailing your photos to friends and family? If they're all hooked into the iCloud Universe as well, you can share each other's Photo Streams, which is like having a personal, private subscription to pictures you actually might want to see. Here's how:

1. In your computer's iCloud settings (shown on these pages), turn on Shared Photo Streams.

2. On the Touch, choose Settings→iCloud→Photo Stream→Shared Photo Streams→On.

3. On the Touch, tap Home→Photos→Photo Stream. Tap the **+** button. Here, you invite other iOS 6 users to share your photos. Type a name for your shared album. (You can also turn on the Public Website option to display the photos on *icloud.com*).

4. Add one photo by tapping 🔀 and choosing Photo Stream; add several by tapping Edit on the album screen, selecting the pics, and then tapping Share→Photo Stream. Tap ❯ to edit your Stream's subscribers—or delete the shared stream entirely.

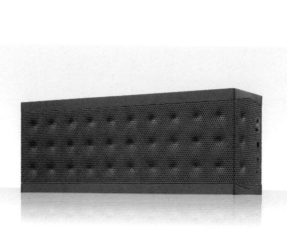

You'll learn to:

- Blast tunes through your home stereo system

- Integrate your 'Pod with your car's stereo system

- Add external speakers

- Stream audio and video using AirPlay

- Find iPod accessories

iPod and iTunes Out Loud

NOW THAT YOU'VE GOTTEN your iPod loaded with all kinds of cool entertainment, you can listen to your playlists, albums, audiobooks, and podcasts on the go. But that's not your only aural option. You can also crank your tunes on a booming stereo setup wherever you happen to be—your car, living room, bathroom, wherever. If you can load it onto your iPod, you can channel it through most any sound system—and at pretty reasonable cost, too. This chapter explains the simple steps you follow to play your 'Pod through the woofers and tweeters in your life.

Got an iPod Touch running at least iOS 5, a second-generation Apple TV, and a zippy WiFi network? You can stream videos, photos, and more between your iPod and big-screen TV without getting tangled up in cables and jacks. And if you have a different iPod, no Apple TV, or no WiFi, you can still watch video on the big screen; page 270 has details.

Wireless Bluetooth speakers also work with the Touch and latest Nano. But before you plunk down cold cash on any fancy audio gizmo, take note: Apple has made a lot of iPod models over the years, and not every accessory works with all iPods, especially the new Lightning port models. To be safe (particularly if you just bought your 'Pod), check the product's fine print to make sure your add-on and iPod will be happy together.

Take Your iPod on the Road

SINCE THE GLORIOUS DAYS of crackly AM radio, music and driving have gone hand in hand. These days, a stereo system with an AM/FM radio and a CD player is the minimum for most cars, and late-model vehicles now cruise around with all sorts of high-end equipment, from multi-disc CD players to satellite radio.

If having your playlists with you is your idea of paradise by the dashboard light, you can integrate your 'Pod with your car's stereo several ways. No matter which you choose, you have to consider two factors:

- **How you connect your iPod to your existing audio system.** You have your pick of a wired or wireless connection. (If you have a new iPod Touch or Nano with the smaller Lightning port, make sure your car's audio cable fits that port or get a 30-pin-to-Lightning-port adapter for $29 from Apple.)

- **How to power your iPod.** Of course, your iPod runs fine on its battery for everyday trips, but if you're retracing historic Route 66, you probably want to invest in an adapter that can power your 'Pod from your car's electrical system.

You can get your iPod's sounds piping through your car speakers five ways, some more satisfying (and expensive) than others. Here are the typical options. (In addition to the manufacturer's sites, you can get most of the gear discussed here from the iPod accessories superstores listed at the end of this chapter.)

❶ **Via an FM transmitter**. These inexpensive devices let you borrow an empty FM frequency from your car's radio and play the iPod's music over the airwaves—with no cables snaking across the dashboard (though some transmitters include iPod charger cords for the car's 12-volt cigarette lighter). Setup is easy: Scan your FM dial for an unused channel, connect the transmitter to your iPod, and push Play.

Advantages: Convenience; everybody's got an FM radio.
Disadvantages: Long road-trippers constantly have to search for new frequencies. It may be tough for urban dwellers to find unused channels.
Audio quality: Fair.

If it involves iPod playback in a car, odds are Griffin Technology has a product for it. From the left: $50 iTrip FM Transmitter for older Docker Connector iPods, the $15 DirectDeck wired cassette adapter, and the $10 auxiliary audio cable. You can find all these items at www.griffintechnology.com.

- **Using a wired adapter**. Another option—if your car still has a cassette player—is one of those cassette-shaped gadgets that slip into your tape deck and come with a 3.5 mm miniplug for the iPod's headphones port. Griffin Technology, Belkin, and Monster all make 'em.
  Advantages: Simplicity; insert cassette and you're good to go.
  Disadvantages: Not everyone has a cassette deck anymore.
  Audio quality: Fair.

- **Using the auxiliary jack**. If your car's stereo console has a 3.5 mm jack as an auxiliary input, you can use a simple male-to-male miniplug audio cable to connect your iPod to the stereo. Radio Shack, Griffin Technology, and Monster Cable can help you out for less than $10.
  Advantages: High-quality sound.
  Disadvantages: You still have to run your iPod using its controls.
  Audio quality: Great.

- **Using a special iPod aftermarket kit or custom installation**. If you *really* want fine sound and have the budget for it, several companies offer kits that add an iPod-friendly cable to your existing in-dash stereo system. Apple lists your options by car manufacturer at *www.apple.com/ipod/car-integration*. Equipment-wise, Alpine stereo fans may be able to use the $30 iPod Interface KCE-422i cable (*www.alpine-usa.com*), while Pioneer Electronics owners can find compatible iPod cables, adapter boxes, and accessories at *www.pioneerelectronics.com*.
  Advantages: Great sound, integrates controls into existing car audio system.
  Disadvantages: None, aside from price.
  Audio quality: Great.

- **Making sure your new car has an iPod jack**. Many automakers now integrate iPod playback capability in their cars. If you're in the market for new wheels anyway, why not ask about iPod compatibility?
  Advantages: Great sound, integrates controls into existing audio system.
  Disadvantages: None, though may add to cost of car.
  Audio quality: Great.

NOTE While the adapter that lets Apple's Lightning port on newer Touch and Nano models connect to gear made for the bigger, older 30-pin Dock Connector ports, not all features may work properly. To be safe, do some research on any product's fine print before you buy it.

You can connect your iPod to several Pioneer car stereo systems with the $79 Pioneer CD-IB100ii iPod Interface Adapter. On iPods still sporting the older 30-pin Dock Connector port, the dashboard display even shows the track titles and lets you shuffle songs. Check it out at http://www.pioneerelectronics.com/PUSA/Apple+Compatibility.

Connect Your iPod to a Home Entertainment System

CD PLAYERS THAT CAN play discs full of MP3 files cost less than $100. But if you have an iPod, you already have a state-of-the-art MP3 player that can connect to your existing home stereo system for under $20—or spend a little more and get the full iPod AV Club experience.

Connecting with an Audio Cable

To link your iPod to your stereo, you need the right kind of cable and a set of input jacks on the back of your receiver. Most audio systems come with at least one extra set of inputs (after accounting for the CD player, cassette deck, and other common components), so look for an empty jack labeled "AUX."

You need a Y-shaped cable with a 3.5 mm (1/8-inch) male stereo miniplug on one end and two bigger male RCA plugs on the other end (top right). The stereo miniplug is the standard jack for headphones, microphones, and some speakers; RCA plugs are the standard red-and-white audio connectors for stereo components.

Plug the miniplug into the iPod's headphone jack and the RCA plugs into the left and right AUX speaker jacks on the back of your stereo. Most online iPod superstores, like XtremeMac, Griffin Technology, DLO, and Belkin, sell their own versions of the Y-shaped cable. (See the list of sites at the end of this chapter.)

Connecting with an iPod Dock

Investing in an iPod dock is another way to link your player to your home-entertainment system. A typical dock provides a notch for your iPod to sit upright, with cable jacks on the back for tethering the dock to your stereo or receiver. As a bonus, you usually get a remote to control the iPod from across the room. Apple sells its $50 iPod docks and $50 AV cables at *www.apple.com/ipodstore*, and you can find even fancier gear from other manufacturers. Just remember to *check the specifications* on the dock you have in mind to make sure it fits your iPod's Dock Connector or Lightning port—or to make sure you can use an adapter.

iPod Speaker Systems

WHILE YOU CAN HOOK up your iPod to a home audio system to share your sounds, sometimes it's more convenient to get your iPod a set of speakers to call its own. Some speakers connect to the iPod's headphone jack with a stereo miniplug cable, while others connect via an iPod dock. So you may need Apple's Lightning-to-Dock Connector adapter (page 296) to get a newer iPod Touch or Nano to fit a dock designed for the older Dock Connector port.

The price and quality of iPod speakers can range from $15 cheap plastic things sold at the grocery store to $300 systems from high-end audio companies like Bose, Philips, Sony, Tivoli, and others. Wireless speaker systems range in price from about $200 to $700. Here are a few to sample:

- **Philips SoundShooter Wireless Bluetooth Speaker .** Available in four colors (and slightly resembling a grenade thanks to its carabiner clip), this tiny Bluetooth speaker can attach itself to bag strap and wirelessly stream tunes from the latest Touch or Nano. The three-watt speaker sells for $50 around the Web and at *www.usa.philips.com*.

- **Bose Sound Dock.** Bose is known for superior acoustics in its speakers and headphones, and continues the tradition for the iPod with two options: its Sound Dock (which uses a Dock Connector cradle) and its wireless SoundLink speakers (in both Bluetooth and AirPlay versions). Prices start at about $200, and you can see the models at *www.bose.com*.

- **Jawbone Jambox.** This stylish speaker can link up with an iPod by way of a wireless Bluetooth connection or a wired connection to the iPod's headphone port with the included 3.5 mm cable. Capable of a whopping 85-decibel output, the Jambox (below) makes *sure* that party gets started. The Jambox is available in six colors and sells for $200. It also has a larger sibling, known as the Big Jambox, that brings mega-bass and 3D sound to your gathering. The Big Jambox comes in three colors and sells for $300. You can find both Jamboxes at *www.jawbone.com*.

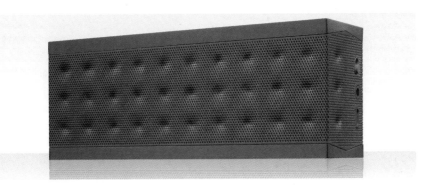

Stream Music and Video from iTunes

THERE ARE A COUPLE of ways to stream entertainment from your 'Pod to the portals around your house. AirPort Express (Apple's portable wireless base station) handles music, while Apple TV lets you stream sounds, video, and photos.

Make AirPort Express Sing

What do you get when you mix an existing home WiFi network with iTunes and AirPort Express? Music anywhere you want it, thanks to Apple's AirPlay feature. Just plug in one of these flat white boxes anywhere you've got a stereo or powered speakers. If you don't have an AirPort Express, you can buy one for $99 at *http://store.apple.com* and other places. Here's how to get started:

1. **Plug the AirPort Express into an electrical outlet near your stereo (or near a pair of powered speakers)**. Repeat this step in any other room where you want to beam music.

2. **Connect your stereo system or powered speakers to the AirPort Express**. After you plug the AirPort Express into the wall, buy a Y-shaped cable (the one with the two RCA plugs on one end and the miniplug on the other, mentioned on page 292) to connect the Express to your stereo system or to a pair of powered speakers. If your system has a digital TOSLINK port, you can use a digital fiber-optic cable to connect the two for better sound. (Speakers that use a USB connection don't work here.)

3. **Install the AirPort Utility software from the CD in the box**. The Utility program (Start→All Programs→AirPort [Applications→Utilities→AirPort]) walks you through the setup process, automatically picking up your WiFi settings and prompting you to name the AirPort Express. Naming it something like "Living Room Stereo" is helpful when it comes to using iTunes, as you'll see in the next step.

4. **Open iTunes and look for a pop-up menu that lists your AirPort Express**. Once you launch iTunes with the Express running, you'll see a pop-up menu on the top left of the iTunes window (circled). If you installed multiple Expresses, each one is listed. (If you don't see the pop-up menu icon, choose Edit [iTunes]→Preferences→Devices and make sure you have "Look for remote speakers with AirPlay" selected.)

5. **Press Play**. With everything connected and turned on, select the AirPort Express base station in the iTunes pop-up menu and click the Play button on your iPod to blast your playlists across your home. To play music through more than one set of speakers, choose Multiple Speakers, and then put a checkmark next to the name of each base station you want to use.

View Video and Photos with Apple TV

In addition to streaming music through connected speakers, you can stream iTunes music, video, and photos over a wireless network to an Apple TV. On the Apple TV (the little black model, second-generation or later), you stream using iTunes' Home Sharing feature (page 190). If you haven't turned it on, choose Advanced→Turn On Home Sharing and type in your iTunes account name and password so Apple TV can see your library and pull the stream into your TV.

You can also stream videos, photo slideshows, and music directly from your iPod Touch to your television with the AirPlay technology built into it and the Apple TV. On your iPod, call up the file you want to play, tap the AirPlay icon (⬓), and then tap the name of the screen you want to watch it on. It may take a minute or two to buffer up, but then your video or slideshow magically appears on the big TV. When you're done watching, tap the AirPlay icon and choose "iPod Touch" to return the picture to the small screen.

Using the iPod Touch as a Remote

If you have a Touch and don't want to be tied to your computer to manage your media, the iTunes App Store offers a cool program called Remote. It detects your WiFi network so you can control your media from anywhere in the house. Even better, it's free!

Install the Remote app from the iTunes Store (Chapter 13). Make sure you turn on Home Sharing (page 190) on your Touch, and make sure it's on the same WiFi network as your computer. Tap the Remote icon and turn on Home Sharing there, logging in with the same Apple ID you used in iTunes. Once the Remote app and iTunes meet up over your home network, you can tap into your iTunes library and control playback right from the Touch—so go ahead and play, pause, skip, and jump through your music library to your heart's content. If you have an Apple TV, you can use the Remote app on your Touch to control *it* as well.

Find a Power Source for Your iPod

WHETHER YOU'RE HOME OR on the road, your iPod needs power at some point. New iPods ship with only a USB cable for charging, so you need an AC adapter or charging dock to top up the battery when you're not around a computer. And with an automobile charger, your car's cigarette lighter can serve a far healthier role than its original purpose: It can breathe new life into a drained iPod. Here are a few options for powering up off and on the road:

- **Apple Lightning Cables and Adapters.** In the fall of 2012, Apple began to change the connection port on many of its iPod, iPhone, and iPad models from a wide, 30-pin Dock Connector port to a smaller 8-pin Lightning port. A new port means new cables with the right plugs on the ends. In the beginning, Apple was the only place

  selling Lightning cables and adapters that let you use older Dock Connector accessories with new iPods. Other manufacturers will eventually catch up, but in the meantime, if you need an official Lightning cable, Lightning-to-Dock Connector adapter, or AC power cube, visit a nearby Apple Store, or go online to the big one at *www.apple.com/ipodstore.*

- **PowerDuo.** This $40 set of chargers from Griffin Technology powers 'Pods on the road and at home. It includes the PowerJolt 12-volt car charger for mobile juicing and the PowerBlock AC charger (with a folding set of prongs) for wall outlets. The kit includes a Dock Connector-to-USB cable for the iPod Classic and older iPods, but you need to pick up a $19 Lightning-to-USB cable from Apple to connect the new Touch and Nano; you can find the PowerDuo at *www.griffintechnology.com.*

- **Belkin MixIt Home Charger.** Hate having to worry about getting back to the computer to recharge your iPod? Skip the stress and get Belkin's tiny green-and-white MIXIT charger. It's a simple set of AC prongs sticking out of the front of a tiny cube with a USB jack on the back to connect your Lightning cable—and then iPod. It's $20 at *www.belkin.com.*

Where to Find Cool iPod Stuff

SINCE THE IPOD'S ARRIVAL in 2001, its accessories market has been growing by leaps and bounds. Several online iPod superstores have a huge selection of merchandise, from stylish cases to cleaning kits to travel speakers. If you want to see what's out there without having to leave your desk, the bigger 'Pod-focused web shops include these:

- **The Apple Store** (*www.apple.com/ipodstore*). Apple has pages and pages of products for all its iPod offspring. You can shop the store based on the model of iPod you have—which should help ease any compatibility worries.

- **The iStore** (*www.theistore.com*). Jam-packed with a collection of cases, docks, car chargers, earphones, speakers, and more for iPods, this site also sells quite a bit of iPad and iPhone gear. The iStore features products from several manufacturers, so along with Apple's iPod store, it's a good place to see a wide selection of goods.

- **Belkin** (*www.belkin.com*). With fashionable cases, chargers, and a Y-shaped adapter that connects two sets of headphones to one iPod, Belkin sells a variety of fun—and functional—iPod extras. There's even WiFi-enabled WeMo Baby gadget that turns your iPod Touch into a baby monitor so you can eavesdrop on your offspring no matter where in the house you are.

- **XtremeMac** (*www.xtrememac.com*). XtremeMac has a good amount of iPod merchandise. It's notable for offering colorful cases for active iPod lovers, creative charging solutions, and portable travel speakers so you can blast your music wherever you happen to be.

- **Griffin Technology** (*www.griffintechnology.com*). With its iTrip line of FM transmitters and its DirectDeck, Griffin's forte is products that get your iPod thumping through car and home stereo speakers. The company also sells a handful of cases and items like iFM, which is designed to add FM broadcast radio to the iPod Touch.

Other companies, like Kensington (*www.kensington.com*) and Monster Cable (*www.monstercable.com*), have healthy iPod accessory sections on their sites, especially if you're looking for cables, docks, FM transmitters, and similar after-market products. Just check the specifications and to make sure the product works with your particular model iPod.

Computer and electronics stores like Fry's and Best Buy usually have a section devoted to iPod cases and speakers, too. And, in a sign of just how mainstream iPods have become, even all-purpose suburban bazaars like Kmart and Target include a rack or two of iPod stuff.

You'll learn to:

- Reset your iPod
- Restore an iPod
- Reinstall iTunes
- Update the iPod software
- Replace the battery
- Find an iPod repair shop

CHAPTER 17

What to Do When Your iPod Isn't Working Right

IT'S BOUND TO HAPPEN sometime: Your iPod locks up, freaks out, or just isn't its usual cheerful self. Luckily, you can solve many iPod problems with a button-tap here or a battery charge there. Then your portable 'Pod is back to normal.

But your iPod is a mini-computer in its own right, and getting it back in working order might involve more than a tap or two—and maybe even the attention of a technical expert. This chapter explains what to do if your iPod starts acting up—and where to go if you can't fix it yourself.

iPod triage isn't all about magnifying glasses and tiny screwdrivers. Yes, the iPod is a nice piece of hardware, but where there's hardware, there's software. In this chapter, you'll also learn how to keep your iPod up to date with the most recent software from Apple so you have the latest bug fixes and new features right in your pocket.

The Five "Rs" of iPod Repair

YOU NEVER KNOW WHEN disaster (or annoyance) will strike, but when you encounter trouble with a Nano, Shuffle, or Classic, Apple suggests its easy-to-remember "Five Rs" approach to troubleshooting:

- **Reset** your iPod, as explained on the next page.

- **Retry** your iPod connection by plugging it into a different USB port on your computer.

- **Restart** your computer and check for iPod software updates (page 304).

- **Reinstall** your iPod and iTunes software (download iTunes at *www.apple.com/itunes*).

- **Restore** your iPod's software (page 306).

If you have an iPod Touch, try this set of "Rs:"

- **Recharge.** Make sure your Touch has gas in its battery tank.

- **Restart.** Press the Sleep/Wake button until the red Off/On slider appears. Slide the Touch off, and then press Sleep/Wake to turn it on again. If that doesn't do much, try resetting the Touch as described on the next page.

- **Remove.** Synced content may be sinking your Touch. Connect your iPod to iTunes, remove any recently added stuff (since they may have triggered the problem), and resync.

- **Reset Settings.** Tap Settings→General→Reset→Reset All Settings. The option to erase all your content and settings may also solve your Touch's problem, but it's a drastic move. (If you're just having trouble connecting to the Internet, try the Reset Network Settings button first.)

- **Restore.** Connect your Touch to iTunes and click Restore to reformat it.

The next few pages cover these steps and more, so you can avoid that sixth, painful "R": *Ramming* your head into the wall when your iPod won't work.

> **NOTE** No matter which iPod you have, when you're having trouble and don't know where to start to fix a problem, take a browser ride to Apple's iPod troubleshooting guides (pictured above) at *www.apple.com/support/ipod/five_rs*.

Reset Your iPod

IF YOUR IPOD SEEMS frozen, confused, or otherwise unresponsive, you can *reset* it without losing your music and data files. You might not be able to save some settings, like bookmarks in long audiobooks or unsynced playlists, but you can get things running again with this quick, easy fix—after you check to make sure the issue isn't simply an out-of-juice battery.

Here's the reset sequence for all four 2012 iPod models:

- **iPod Touch.** If restarting the Touch (see the previous page) does nothing for you, go for the Reset. Simultaneously hold down the Sleep/Wake and Home buttons. Let go when you see the shimmering Apple logo. This handy reset move works on the earlier models of the iPod Touch as well.

- **iPod Nano.** Hold down the Sleep/Wake buttons (on the top) and its Home button (on the front) for about 6 seconds, and let go when you see the Apple logo pop up on-screen.

- **iPod Shuffle.** The tiniest iPod may also need a good, firm reset from time to time, but like the Shuffle itself, resetting it is a bit simpler than wrestling with the other iPods: Turn the On/Off switch to the Off position, wait 10 seconds, and then flip it back to the On position.

- **iPod Classic.** Slide the Hold switch on and off. Press and hold down the Menu and center Select buttons simultaneously until you see the Apple logo on-screen. This could take up to 10 seconds, and you may have to do it twice, but keep at it until you see the logo.

If the technology gods are smiling at you, your iPod will go through its start-up sequence and return you to the main menu. If you suspect your battery might be a bit low to begin with, plug the iPod into a power source before you perform the reset maneuver to make sure it has the power to boot itself back up.

Download and Reinstall iTunes and iTunes Updates

IF ITUNES IS ACTING up, you may need to download and install a fresh version of the program. The latest version is always waiting at *www.apple.com/itunes/ download*. Your iTunes program itself may alert you to a new version—or you can make sure it does so in the future:

- If you installed iTunes on a Windows PC and installed the Apple Software Update utility at the same time, iTunes displays an alert box when an update is ready; it also offers to install the new version. If you skipped installing the utility, choose Edit→Preferences→General and turn on "Check for updates automatically." If you prefer to check manually, choose Help→Check for Updates. In either case, your iPod prompts you to snag any available updates.

- The Mac's Software Update program is designed to alert you, via a pop-up dialog box, about new iTunes updates. If you turned Software Update off (in System Preferences), you can run it manually by choosing ⌘→Software Update.

As with any update, once you download the software, click the Install button or double-click the installer file's icon and follow along as the program takes you through the upgrade excitement. If the iTunes version you're installing is newer than the one you've got, you get Upgrade as a button option when you run the installer—and an upgrade usually takes less time than a full reinstallation.

If you're installing the same version of the program, the iTunes installer may politely ask if you want to either *Repair* or even *Remove* the software.

Choosing Repair can often fix damaged files or data that iTunes needs to run properly. It can also be a quicker fix than fully removing and reinstalling the program.

Use the Diagnostics Tools in iTunes for Windows

WITH DIFFERENT WINDOWS PC manufacturers out there and multiple versions of Windows in the mix, the PC side of the iTunes/iPod fence can be a little unpredictable. To help sort things out, iTunes for Windows includes a feature called Diagnostics, which helps troubleshoot four categories of iPod woes. They are:

- **Network Connectivity.** These tests check your computer's Internet connection and its ability to access the iTunes Store.

- **DVD/CD Drive.** If you're having trouble importing music to iTunes from a CD—or if you can't burn your own discs—these tests inspect your PC's disc drive for problems and incompatibilities.

- **Device Connectivity.** These diagnostics don't actually test the iPod's hardware or software, they examine the way your PC connects to your iPod.

- **Device Sync.** These programs actually *do* test the Touch's hardware and software to make sure it can transport the data you're trying to sync.

To run this battery of tests, choose Help→Run Diagnostics, select a category, and then follow the on-screen directions. Each program runs tests and then displays a red, yellow, or green light. Click the Help button next to a red or yellow light to get troubleshooting help from Apple's website. (Green means groovy.)

Once you finish the tests, you can copy the results to the Clipboard and save them to a text file so you can share them with support techies. If the Diagnostics tests don't resolve the problem or point you in the right direction for fixing it, check out Apple's discussion forums just for Windows users. It's at *https://discussions.apple.com/community/itunes/itunes_for_windows*.

Update the iPod's Software

UPDATING THE IPOD'S INTERNAL software—which Apple does occasionally to fix bugs and add features—is much easier than it used to be, thanks to iTunes. No matter which iPod model you have, iTunes 10 and later handles all software update chores for you.

If you formatted your iPod Nano or Classic for Windows, then update it on a Windows PC; update a Mac-formatted iPod on a Macintosh. You can tell which system you formatted your iPod for by choosing Settings→General→About on the Nano; flick down to Version to get to the format info. On the Classic, choose Settings→About and press the Select button twice.

You can update a Touch from either a Windows PC or Mac. (If you have an iPod set to autosync with a particular computer, update it on that computer to avoid erasing your iPod.) In fact, if you have at least iOS 5 installed on your WiFi-connected Touch, you don't even need a computer. Just tap Home→Settings→General→Software Update to check for new software. And with iOS 5 and later, the updates go much faster because you're just getting the new code, not the whole iPod operating system again.

To make sure you have the latest version of iPod software, follow these steps:

1. Connect your iPod to your computer, and then select it in the Devices list.

2. On the Summary tab, click Check for Update in the Version area. If your iPod is up to date, iTunes tells you so.

3. If iTunes finds new iPod software, it prompts you to download it (shown below). Click the Downloading icon in the Source pane to monitor your progress. Sometimes iTunes will have already downloaded the software; if that's the case, just click the Update button in iTunes' main window.

4. Follow the on-screen instructions. As it works, your 'Pod displays info about the update, like the version number of the software you're installing and other support information.

If you update via iTunes, your iPod displays an alert box like the one on the opposite page. The Touch displays a similar note on its update screen if you update its software over the air.

Older iPod models may require an AC adapter for the update, but newer iPods mainly just sit there quietly with a progress bar and an Apple logo on-screen. Once all that goes away, your iPod screen returns to normal and iTunes displays a message letting you know it finished the update.

If you're updating an iPod Shuffle, play close attention to the progress bar on the iTunes screen and follow any instructions given. Since the Shuffle has no screen, iTunes is where you monitor the update. You'll know when iTunes is done because it returns the Shuffle's icon to the Devices list.

NOTE In addition to the "5 Rs" page mentioned on the opposite page, Apple's iPod support section (*www.apple.com/support/ipod*) has grown tremendously since the company introduced the first iPod in 2001. The site includes knowledge-based articles and user forums for troubleshooting just about every iPod model out there.

But if you need to dig deeper or want to attempt your own hardware repairs, check out the iPod forums and repair guides at the do-it-yourself site *www.ifixit.com/Browse/ iPod*. If it's an out-of-warranty hardware problem that's too daunting for your taste, try a specialized iPod repair shop like *www.iresq.com* or *www.techrestore.com/ipod*. And when it does come time to upgrade or replace your 'Pod, you can learn about Apple's recycling policy at *www.apple.com/recycling*.

Start Over: Restoring Your iPod's Software

JUST LIKE THE OPERATING system that runs your desktop computer, your iPod has its own system software to control everything it does. *Restoring* your iPod's software isn't the same thing as updating it. Restoring is a much more drastic procedure, like reformatting the hard drive on your computer. For one thing, restoring the software *erases everything on your iPod* (unless you're restoring your Touch from a previous backup; see the note below).

So restore with caution and do so only after you try all the other troubleshooting measures in this chapter. If you decide to take the plunge, first make sure you have the most recent version of iTunes (flip back a page for information on that), and then proceed as follows:

① Start iTunes and connect your iPod to your computer with its cable. (You can't wirelessly restore your Touch, so go find that USB cable.)

② When your iPod appears in iTunes' Devices list, click its icon to see the Summary information (in the main area of the iTunes window).

③ In the Summary area, click the Restore button.

NOTE As with any computer, it's a great idea to back up your data regularly, and the Touch is no exception. In fact, it's such a good idea that iTunes does it automatically as you sync your Touch. When disaster strikes and your Touch is a zombie—or worse, stolen—you can restore your contacts, calendars, notes, and settings without having to start from scratch. Just connect the Touch (old or new replacement) and right-click (Control-click) on its icon. Choose "Restore from Backup" and click Restore in the box that pops up. You can also restore the Touch from an iCloud backup when prompted during the iPod setup.

④ If you have an iPod Touch, iTunes gives you the chance to back up your settings—like your contacts and calendar syncing preferences. This means much less work getting your Touch all re-personalized if you have to reinstall its software. If you want to wipe every trace of your existence from the Touch, skip the backup.

⑤ Because restoring erases everything on your iPod, you get a warning message. If you're sure you want to continue, click Restore again. If you use a Mac, you then enter an administrator password. A progress bar appears on your iPod's screen to show you the update in action.

⑥ Leave the iPod connected to your computer to complete the restoration. You may also see an Apple logo appear on-screen.

After iTunes restores your iPod, its Setup Assistant window appears, asking you to name your iPod and choose your syncing preferences—just like when you connected your iPod for the first time. In fact, if you have everything that was originally on your iPod in your iTunes library, let iTunes autosync all the files and settings back to your 'Pod. Alternatively, you can manually add back your songs, photos, apps, and videos. Once you're done, see if the restore fixed your iPod's ailment.

TIP If you manually manage your music and you restore your iPod's software, you'll lose any songs not stored in your iTunes library (like music you copied from a PC, but didn't sync back to iTunes). If you manually update, you may want to get a program that lets you harvest songs off of your iPod (*www.ilounge.com* lists several, and so does Chapter 11) and back them up to iTunes regularly.

Understanding the iPod's Battery Messages

REMEMBER HOW YOU WERE taught that certain kinds of batteries (in laptops and camcorders, say) worked better if you occasionally fully drained and then recharged them? Forget it. You want to keep the iPod's lithium-ion battery *always* charged, or else you'll lose your clock, date, and other settings.

The color screens on the Touch, Nano, and Classic display a green battery that virtually runs out of juice as you use the player. When the battery turns red, it's time to recharge, because you have less than 20 percent of your iPod's power left. The screenless Shuffle communicates its battery needs through a small colored light: green for a good charge (between 100 and 50 percent), amber for 25 percent of the charge left, and red for a battery that needs juice pronto.

Some imperiled iPods display a dull gray charging icon and won't turn on. This means the poor thing doesn't even have enough energy to display its battery-charging icon in color. On other iPod models, you may see a yellow triangle next to a colorless battery graphic and the stern message, "Connect to Power."

Plug your iPod into your computer or an optional AC adapter, and give it about half an hour of power to get back to its regular screen. (When the battery gets this depleted, you may have to charge it up for a while before your iPod even shows up in iTunes.)

> **NOTE** If you leave your iPod plugged into your computer all night and it still barely shows a charge, it's probably because something went to sleep besides you: your computer. An iPod won't charge properly when your machine goes into Sleep, Hibernate, or Standby modes, so adjust your computer's power-saving settings to make sure it doesn't conk out before your iPod gets juiced up. An AC adapter, available at most iPod accessory shops (Chapter 16), lets you skip the whole computer-charging thing.

Apple's Tips for Longer iPod Battery Life

APPLE HAS POSTED VARIOUS recommendations on its website for how to treat an iPod battery to ensure a long life:

- Don't expose your iPod to extreme hot or cold temperatures. (In other words, don't leave it in a hot, parked car, and don't expect it to operate on Mount Everest.)

- Use your iPod regularly (not that you wouldn't). And be sure to charge it at least once a month to keep that battery chemistry peppy.

- Put the iPod to sleep to conserve battery power. (Press the Play/Pause button until the iPod display goes blank, settling into slumber; on the Touch, click the Sleep/Wake button on top.)

- Take the iPod out of any heat-trapping cases before you charge it up.

- On the Classic, use the Hold switch when you're not actively fiddling with the iPod's controls; that keeps you from turning it on accidentally.

- When you see the Low Battery icon or message, plug your iPod into a computer or an electrical outlet.

- iPod features like the backlight and the equalizer—or jumping around within your media library—can make the battery drain faster, as can using big, uncompressed song-file formats, like AIFF.

- That wireless chip inside the iPod Touch saps power even if you're not trawling the Web. Save energy by turning it off when you don't need it at Settings→WiFi. Lowering the frequency with which your Touch checks email or has data pushed to it from the Internet can save some energy as well—you can make those adjustments by choosing Settings→Mail, Contacts, Calendars.

- Background Touch apps (page 127) may be draining power. To quit these vampires, double-click the Home button to reveal the apps panel. Press an app's icon until the ⊖ appears, and tap those ⊖ icons to close those apps.

Replace Your iPod's Battery

THE IPOD USES A rechargeable lithium-ion battery. Unlike players that run on Duracells, you can't easily pop out an old battery and replace it when the cell wears out after repeated charge-and-use cycles.

But that doesn't mean you *can't* replace the iPod's battery; it just takes a little time and effort. If your battery is too pooped to power your 'Pod, here are some options:

- You get a full one-year warranty on your iPod battery (two years with the optional AppleCare Protection Plan; see the opposite page). But Apple itself offers an out-of-warranty battery replacement service for $49 to $79, depending on the iPod model, at *www.apple.com/support/ipod/service/battery*.

- Milliamp (*www.ipodjuice.com*) offers do-it-yourself iPod battery replacement kits for most iPod models, with prices starting at around $20.

- PDASmart.com will replace your iPod's ailing battery for $50 (parts and labor included). Learn more at *www.pdasmart.com/ipodpartscenter.htm*. The company also fixes broken screens and hard drives.

- Other World Computing sells high-capacity NewerTech iPod batteries for all models of iPod. The company has do-it-yourself instructional videos on its site, but will also replace the battery if you send in your iPod (*http://eshop.macsales.com/shop/ipod*).

AppleCare—What It Is and Whether You Need It

YOU PROBABLY HAVE AN insurance policy on your house and car, so why not get one for your iPod? That's the logic behind the AppleCare Protection Plan. The price for this peace of mind? For the iPod Classic and Touch, it's $59, while coverage for the Nano and Shuffle is $39.

When you buy a brand-new iPod, you automatically get free telephone support to fix one problem within your first 90 days of iPod ownership, plus a year-long warranty on the hardware. The latter means that if the iPod starts acting up or stops working altogether, Apple will fix it for free or send you a replacement.

If you buy the AppleCare Protection Plan (available in many places where you buy iPods or at *www.apple.com/support/products/ipod.html*), you get the following:

- Two full years of free telephone support from the date of your iPod purchase

- Two full years of hardware protection from the date of your iPod purchase

If you need an iPod repair or replacement, you're covered, and the plan covers your iPod's earphones, battery, and cables, too. Paying an extra $39 or $59 for the extended warranty may not appeal to everyone, but if you want a little peace of mind with your new iPod, it's a small price to pay.

Index

Have it your way.

Get even more for your money.

Join the O'Reilly Community, and register the O'Reilly books you own. It's free, and you'll get:

- $4.99 ebook upgrade offer
- 40% upgrade offer on O'Reilly print books
- Membership discounts on books and events
- Free lifetime updates to ebooks and videos
- Multiple ebook formats, DRM FREE
- Participation in the O'Reilly community
- Newsletters
- Account management
- 100% Satisfaction Guarantee

Signing up is easy:

1. **Go to: oreilly.com/go/register**
2. **Create an O'Reilly login.**
3. **Provide your address.**
4. **Register your books.**

Note: English-language books only

To order books online:

oreilly.com/store

For questions about products or an order:

orders@oreilly.com

To sign up to get topic-specific email announcements and/or news about upcoming books, conferences, special offers, and new technologies:

elists@oreilly.com

For technical questions about book content:

booktech@oreilly.com

To submit new book proposals to our editors:

proposals@oreilly.com

O'Reilly books are available in multiple DRM-free ebook formats. For more information:

oreilly.com/ebooks

O'REILLY®

Spreading the knowledge of innovators   oreilly.com

iPod

THE MISSING CD

There's no CD with this book; you just saved $5.00.

and
s

sing
ment
m.
we

ailable,
and
Manual